The Johns Hopkins Symposia in Comparative History

The Johns Hopkins Symposia in Comparative History are occasional volumes sponsored by the Department of History at the Johns Hopkins University and the Johns Hopkins University Press comprising original essays by leading scholars in the United States and other countries. Each volume considers, from a comparative perspective, an important topic of current historical interest. The present volume is the twenty-third. Its preparation has been assisted by the James S. Schouler Lecture Fund.

Port Cities and Intruders

The Swahili Coast, India, and Portugal in the Early Modern Era

Michael N. Pearson

The Johns Hopkins University Press

Baltimore and London

Published 1998
Printed in
the United States of America
on acid-free paper
9 8 7 6 5 4 3 2 1

The Johns Hopkins University Press
2715 North Charles Street
Baltimore, Maryland 21218-4363
The Johns Hopkins Press Ltd., London

Library of Congress Cataloging-in-Publication Data
will be found at the end of this book.
A catalog record for this book is available
from the British Library.

ISBN 0-8018-5692-2

For Denni

Contents

Acknowledgments

I have accumulated many debts as I have worked on this project. Research was supported in several ways while I was at the University of New South Wales. The library staff did wonders in finding obscure publications for me. Financial support was provided by a three-year Australian Research Council Small Grant, and by several grants from the Faculty of Arts, which has always supported my work as lavishly as funds permitted. These grants enabled me to travel twice to the Swahili coast, and also to England. My colleagues at Southern Cross University, where I am now located, provided a congenial place in which I could undertake the process of turning lectures into a longer text. I am grateful to Chris Meagher, who produced the maps and illustrations. I owe especial thanks to the then Deans of the Faculty of Arts at both universities, respectively John Milfull and Leon Cantrell.

In England, the staff at the library of the School of Oriental and African Studies of the University of London were always helpful, as were librarians at the British Library, including the India Office. I ran up a long list of obligations in East Africa. My thanks to Henry Mutoro in Nairobi; George and Lorna Abungu and Richard Wilding in Mombasa; John Sutton at the British Institute in Eastern Africa; numerous local authorities in Lamu and Zanzibar; and Gerhard Liesegang and Ricardo Teixeira Duarte in Maputo, all of whom helped a novice come to terms with a new place and a new scholarship.

This book is based on the James S. Schouler lectures, which I delivered at the Johns Hopkins University on 30 and 31 October and 2 November 1995. Three hours of lectures enabled me only to sketch several of the matters with which I was concerned. The present text is a major expansion of the themes touched on in the lectures, and also a substantial revision of parts of them as a result of comments both at the time of delivery and later.

My greatest debt is to John Russell-Wood, who initiated my giving the Schouler lectures. Quite fortuitously, when he first contacted me I was ready to try to write up the material I had collected on east Africa. The lectures required me to take a broad approach, and this book represents my attempt to do this. I owe many thanks to Russell-Wood and his colleagues in the Department of History at the Johns Hopkins University for making my stay in Baltimore so pleasant and so productive. Working with the Johns Hopkins University Press has been a pleasant and collaborative effort, and I must record my indebtedness to Henry Tom, the executive editor, for his advice and enthusiasm. Lesley Yorke improved the text immensely; it was a pleasure to work with such a thorough and courteous editor. I must also acknowledge the helpful comments of the Press's reader, which helped me to reformulate and restructure the whole manuscript.

Finally, and as always, I would have achieved little without the love and support of Denni and James.

Port Cities and Intruders

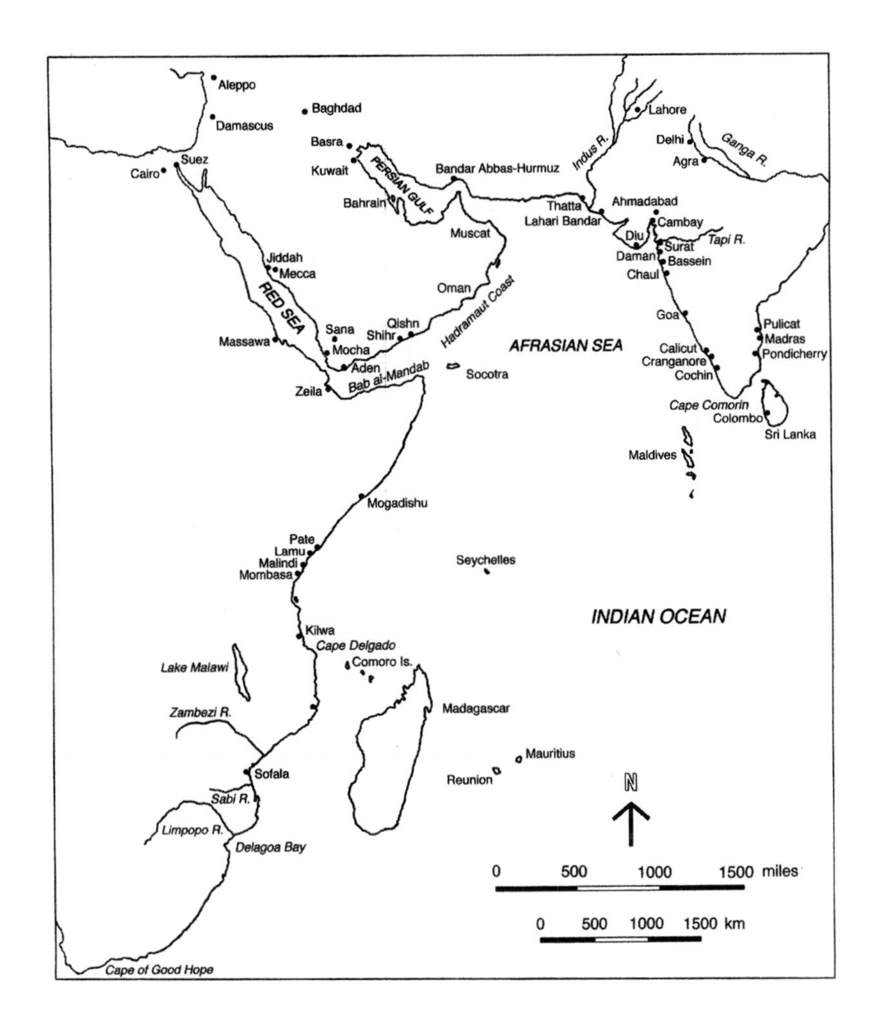

The Western Indian Ocean

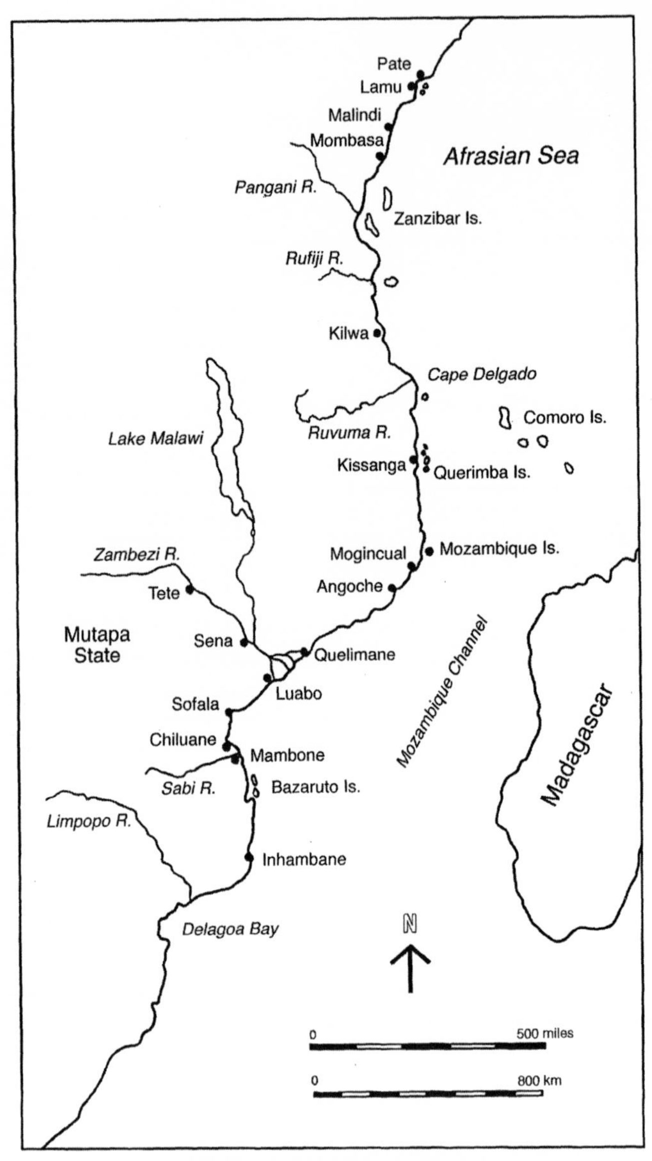

The Southeast African Coast

Chapter 1

Introduction

Locating Coastal East Africa

The modern notion of "world history" is a relatively new, and still largely misunderstood, concept. Yet it is very much on the scholarly agenda today both in the United States and elsewhere. Perhaps confusingly, world history is not global history. It does not aim to deal with everywhere on our globe. Nor is it the history of the world, just as world music is not the music of the whole world. Political economists, especially those associated with Immanuel Wallerstein's concept of world-systems, have long been explicitly writing "world history." More than twenty years ago, Wallerstein introduced the notion of the modern world-system, which did not incorporate the whole globe until late in the nineteenth century. Before this, he uses the terminology of "a 'world' system, not because it encompasses the whole world, but because it is larger than any juridically-defined political unit."[1] The less explicitly economist "world historians" and their mouthpiece, the *Journal of World History*, certainly agree. The editor, Jerry H. Bentley, is certain that world history does not have to include the whole world. Rather, it is "a historical perspective that transcends national frontiers." Scholars need "a regional, continental, or global scale" to look at many important forces in history. The key is to get away from national, state-based histories.[2] World history investigates themes, trends, and relationships that extend beyond the bounds of any particular "state."

There is, however, a difference between "world history" and "world-system" history. The latter, as promoted by Immanuel Wallerstein, is both more rigorous and more restrictive than the former. World history is rather diffuse and even unfocused. This has both positive and negative results. On the one hand, it means that world history is not shackled by a particular straitjacket of neo-Marxist theory, but, on the other hand, it does lack the attractive totalizing ambitions of world-system theory. Whether they are successful or not, Wallerstein and his followers aim to explain how we got to where we are, and even where we are going. The grandeur of this enterprise and vision are obviously not to everyone's taste. Chapter 4 of this book focuses precisely on the utility of world-system theory for one place and time.

At first glance, world history looks very much like what used to be called "comparative" history, where cognate phenomena from different areas or historical times were compared. Perhaps most of us have been writing world history without being aware of what we were doing. I would argue, instead, that comparative history too often ended up merely finding that in one area one had apples and in another, oranges, or that one had apples in several different places and times. As I see it, the important innovation of "world history" is that it is more theoretically self-conscious, that it goes beyond finding similarities and differences, because, at least implicitly, it is grounded in a model or "theory," and this gives it much greater analytical and explanatory power than crude empirical comparison.

If we look at a recent attempt at a definition of world history by an eminent practitioner, this matter becomes clearer. Philip D. Curtin claims that his recent book is to be considered comparative world history, "'comparative' because it abstracts particular phenomena . . . and looks for similarities and differences; 'world' because it tries to avoid a Western ethnocentric outlook, not because it will try to 'cover' what went on everywhere; 'history' because it is concerned with change over the very long run of time."[3] Looking for "similarities and differences" is not enough.

"World history" has another connotation, which is that it aims to write of the world without privileging Europe. This trend has a hoary ancestry. Even before World War II, the Dutch scholar J. C. van Leur complained about the way Indonesian history before the arrival of Europeans was written from an Indonesian perspective, but once the Dutch arrived, the angle of vision swung around and Indonesia was seen only through Dutch eyes. As he noted, there was "something unsatisfactory" about this.[4] The attempt to write from the view of the colonized has continued since this time, albeit with some reversions to ethnocentric perspectives, in which the rest of the world is measured against Europe and usually found to be lacking. Today, to accuse a work of being "Eurocentric" or "Orientalist" is automatically to condemn.

To write world history, let alone world-system history, is to fly in the face of a currently fashionable tendency to deprecate this sort of metanarrative. Postmodernists would, I think, claim that my efforts are too totalizing to take adequate account of the real lives of most of the people in the place and period I write about. I am aware of this potential problem, and have done my best to avoid a metahistory that privileges any particular group, especially, say, white European males. In fact, many of us have been trying to do this for years. I remain convinced that a macroview is valid, even essential. We do need, now more than ever, "a global explanation of the past which gives sense to the present and guidance to the paths of the future," or, in Marc

Bloch's words, "the only true history, which can advance only through mutual aid, is universal history."[5] Similarly, Stephen K. Sanderson cogently argues that human history "has long-term and large-scale patterns, and that it is important, both intellectually and politically, to comprehend these patterns."[6]

This book is about the east coast of Africa, the location of people known as Swahili, in the early modern period. I investigate a series of structures, enduring phenomena, and analytical categories. Some of these themes run through more than one chapter. Gold is a recurring matter, as are relations and connections between coast and interior. Much of the empirical data comes from east Africa, but my ambition is to use this—some of it quite familiar to historians, archaeologists, and anthropologists—in a much wider context, where I hope my analysis is enriched and improved by reference to cognate studies grounded in western India and indeed much further afield than this.[7]

Much of what follows is suggestive rather than definitive, indicating what seem to me to be useful new approaches and problems, but not presuming to write the final word on any of them. Scholars working on other areas and times may find some stimulation and new questions from this geographically and temporally limited study. One should see this book as a humble can, with an opener provided. When it is opened, we find that the can is full of many things, and different scholars will find different parts of its contents of more or less interest. I hope all readers will find at least one item that raises questions for them, something that may even provide, out of either acceptance or rejection of what I have written, an organizing principle for their own work.

I have been a shameless magpie in my reading and writing. Whatever was interesting, relevant, or provocative has been picked up and used, though not always explicitly. To give a few examples, the account of Islam and conversions in east Africa draws on recent analyses of the same phenomenon at the same time in southeast Asia, and to an extent in India and west Africa. The account of the Portuguese is illuminated by a broad knowledge of their wider imperial effort, and of the activities of other Europeans in Asia at this time. To be specific, east Africanists have coined the term *transfrontiersman* to describe someone who has crossed over a frontier, as opposed to a *frontiersman* who straddles it. The term could be used to describe Portuguese in areas outside of the Portuguese empire, such as in the Bay of Bengal. Joseph Conrad's *Lord Jim* is one of many other examples of Europeans who, as the Orientalists used to say, "went native."

The discussion of port cities owes much to analyses by geographers, urban historians, and economists, but also to analyses of such apparently remote areas as Canton in the late eighteenth century and the large literature on tributary relations in imperial China. It draws on some familiarity with port cities from all over the world, from Brazil to Europe to Japan and southeast Asia. As one specific example, A.J.R. Russell-Wood notes the problem of differentiating these from other cities when the context in Brazil is that until the mid eighteenth century, there were no other cities at all; all urban centers were coastal.[8] This comment applies to the east African coast also, to very late in the nineteenth century. I only touch on the issue of slavery, but my account is illuminated by a modest acquaintance with the vast literature in this field. My knowledge of the Mughal state in India, and other tributary empires, helped my analysis of the Mutapa state. Gold from this area can be satisfactorily analyzed only in terms of worldwide flows of bullion at this time. In order to understand the Portuguese attitudes to gold, one must have some idea of the context in which they were enmeshed, that is, knowledge of Spanish successes in the Americas. Portuguese relations with both the Mutapa ruler and with the Swahili city-states must be seen in the context of their contacts with many other states and cities over much of the world in the sixteenth century. In the broadest terms, readers will often note the influence of several major authors: Eric Wolf, Immanuel Wallerstein, K. N. Chaudhuri are perhaps the most obvious here, but many others have contributed also.

Chapter 1 is a description of the place of the Swahili coast in the maritime world to its east, that is, the Arabian or Afrasian Sea, and the Indian Ocean generally. The concern here is with the validity and utility of maritime history, and of the concept of a distinctive littoral or coastal society. Can we see the seas and shores of the Indian Ocean as being a discrete unit that can be investigated like a state, or a city, or a ruler? My account draws, sometimes silently, on maritime studies from the other oceans of the world, beginning with Braudel's classic account of the Mediterranean, and later studies by other *Annalistas*. I investigate elements binding together the people living on the west coast of this vast expanse of water.

To claim that littoral people have some commonality of life and society is to set them off from their own landed interiors. Chapters 2 and 3 are an analysis of this matter of connections between coast and interior. My empirical concern is to delineate ties between port cities and their interiors. In my discussion of these Swahili city-states, I use a more self-conscious terminology than has been usual. In particular, I show that the commonly used term *hinterland* is too wide ranging to be analytically useful. It needs to be replaced by more specific terms, namely *foreland, umland, hinterland,* and *entrepôt.* I hope that my preliminary discussion will be taken up by other students of port cities; indeed, my own account draws heavily on the now burgeoning literature describing port cities in other places and at other times.

Connections between the coast and the interior lead us into another general area that is very much on the scholarly agenda today. Chapter 4 deals with the political economy notion of a world-system or, more precisely, of the nature of world-economies before capitalism. I review some political economy analyses of east Africa, and then focus on recent world-system literature that attempts to flesh out Wallerstein's rather sketchy initial description of the situation before capitalism and the modern world-system. The precise question is which areas of east Africa, if any, were linked to an India-centered world-economy. My analysis of this matter investigates the connections between coast and interior, and contributes to the ongoing debate over the characteristics of world-economies before capitalism, and especially whether these can be seen as sharing the three constituent parts that Wallerstein finds characteristic of the capitalist modern world-system, that is, cores, peripheries, and semiperipheries.

Chapter 5 includes coast-interior and maritime themes, among others, for it is an analysis of the Portuguese presence on the Swahili coast. I draw here on recent accounts of the Portuguese presence all over the early modern world. My central theme is a familiar one, namely, that while the Portuguese had vast aspirations, they fortunately failed to achieve most of them. This is then a matter of relativism, or, perhaps, a denial of exceptionalism at least for these first Europeans, for what we find is that the mere presence of Europeans in other parts of the world did not ipso facto "make a difference." My discussion delineates precisely where the activities of the Portuguese changed things, and where they fitted into existing social and economic networks. Although there are many points of comparison with Portuguese activities elsewhere, in one or two aspects their east African experience was, for them, an exceptional one.

This chapter raises openly the central matter of how we look at the early modern world. One theme of this book is my attempt to look at the Afrasian Sea and its coasts in its own terms. It may be true that the greatest event in the world over the last few millennia has been industrialism and capitalism, leading to the creation of rich and poor worlds, and that this process was beginning in western Europe, especially England, in this early modern period with which I am concerned. It is important, however, to avoid a teleological analysis which uses the past to ratify the present, which essentially sees the rest of the world waiting passively to be taken over by a newly industrialized western Europe. The titles of two much-acclaimed books, *Asia before Europe* and *Before European Hegemony*, show this sort of lapse, even if the actual texts do better.[9] I try to avoid the sort of triumphalism that invalidates writers as diverse as Adam Smith and Karl Marx, and, more recently, Eric L. Jones (see his revealingly titled *The European Miracle*) and other economic historians. Seeds were being sown in early modern western Europe, but the portentous results that occurred when they sprouted belong to a more recent period. In the conclusion, I sketch what this meant for east Africa. But for the early modern period, it would be a gross distortion to write the history of my area only as a refraction of or counterpoint to the more "successful" history of western Europe.

This is not to say that this was some precolonial golden age on the coast; of course not. The point is that the area had its own autonomy, its own achievements and failures, and these had little to do with the beginnings of industry in another part of the world. It participated in a vast seaborne world stretching to east Asia and the Middle East, but was little affected by nascent developments in one tiny appendage in the far west of the vast Eurasian land mass.

Sources and Methods

I come to the history of the Swahili coast after a long experience in the early modern history of India and the Indian Ocean. It could even be that as a novice in east African studies I have been struck by some event or interpretation that, by reason of familiarity, the old hands would not notice. I believe that both methods and empirical data from India can enrich our understanding of east Africa, and vice versa. For the sake of comparison, I draw on some Indian material in order to make more pointed the themes with which I am dealing. This is an obvious thing to do; after all, India was just across the Afrasian Sea, and it had a long history of contact with the east African coast. In some aspects, its historiography is more advanced, and so it can contribute usefully to better analysis of east Africa. In other areas, the reverse is true. My ambitious aim is to show that both sides could profit by more acquaintance with the literature and methodology of the other.

There is a strong contrast in the sources available for these two areas. This has resulted in opportunities to be creative as well as in difficulties. Looking first at standard documentary materials, on the Indian side we have thousands of years of original documentation. For the early modern period, the most useful are in Persian, the literary and administrative language of the Muslim rulers. We have copious European records from the end of the fifteenth century, first Portuguese and then, from the late sixteenth century, English and Dutch. Because the English and Dutch traded on a basis of equality, they took more notice of local conditions. Together with Persian and some other indigenous sources, we can recreate in some detail and with some sophistication the world of Surat, its brokers, its merchants, and its hinterland of Gujarat, the region in India that had the closest ties with east Africa.

The case of east Africa is very different. Before we get European documentation, that is, from the very late fifteenth century, the only sources are some travel accounts, and a few Swahili chronicles, which are notoriously difficult to use.[10] J. C. Wilkinson has provided a useful overview of the general difficulties of using, and interpreting, the Arab and Swahili sources available for the period before 1500.[11] An excellent idea of the usefulness of these documents can be gained from G.S.P. Freeman-Grenville's compilation.[12] Neville Chittick has investigated the chronicle of Pate. This was first written down in the early twentieth century, and claims that Pate was at its height in the fourteenth century. Chittick investigates the chronicle in its various versions, and decides that archaeological evidence shows it was at its height in the seventeenth century. This conclusion is unexceptional, and is supported by much European documentation. However, Chittick also casts aspersions on the general reliability of the chronicle, dismissing it as fairy stories of no use at all to the historian. Randall L. Pouwels has confronted this claim, and shows that there is indeed usable information in this chronicle, albeit not necessarily the sort of traditional names and dates found in other sources. Pouwels wrote before Marina Tolmacheva's definitive study of the various recensions of the chronicle, but his general point is still well taken. Swahili chronicles can provide invaluable information about many historical matters, most particularly about the self-perceptions of the Swahili people.[13]

Arab nautical treatises are well covered by George Hourani and by G. R. Tibbetts.[14] An example is the "Poem of Sofala," edited by Ibrahim Khoury. The editor establishes a text, and provides a translation, of Ibn Magid's poem on Sofala, which gives navigational instructions for going from India to east Africa and southern Arabia. The detail on sailing seasons and celestial navigation shows how extensive was knowledge of navigation, both deep sea and coastal, from India to east Africa. Yet, as D. N. Beach also notes, while this chronicle may be the best available, it still is of little use for the historian.[15] An example of the usefulness of other Arabic sources is B. G. Martin's article, which shows that much more can be done than we suspected using Arabic sources from the Hadramaut and Yemen.[16]

Oral traditions have been of some use, and Beach has used them for the Zimbabwe Plateau. In a recent, somewhat self-indulgent, book, he provides a detailed discussion of Shona oral traditions, and of his own personal use of, and battles with, them. His book is a vivid account of his thirty years of collection and reflection on Shona traditions. In one example, northern Shona oral traditions tell how the Mutapa dynasty began late in the seventeenth century, which is of course two centuries too late.[17] Clearly, they must be used with care. In particular, the work of D. P. Abraham, which was influential at one time, has now been heavily discounted as his use of oral sources was dubious at best.[18]

In India, some Europeans worked alongside, on a basis of equality with, residents of the coast or inland. The documents they generated are invaluable sources for us. In east Africa, the situation was different. For the sixteenth and seventeenth centuries, we have, apart from very sparse references in Dutch and English sources, only the records of the Portuguese, who knew rather little of the northern coast, and who were trying to dominate the southern one. As a result, the official accounts of this effort obviously must be used with great discernment. Some Portuguese penetrated far inland, or traded along the coast like anyone else, but many of these pioneers were independent, not forming part of the official Portuguese presence. Thus, their lives remain unknown. What we do have are quite copious official accounts, from both Crown officials and religious. Many of these Portuguese sources have been translated in a project that presently reaches nine volumes and the year 1615.[19]

The result is that we can deal with my main topics reasonably well in India; indeed, they have been already. When we turn to Africa, we are constantly hampered by inadequate sources. Of the topics I cover in this book, the one we can treat most fully is the Portuguese and early colonialism. Ironically, my conclusion is that their role was minor. In other words, we have reasonable documentation to demonstrate a negative.

There is, however, one area where Africanists have been much more enterprising than have those working on India. This is the discipline of archaeology. It may be that archaeological work is more important for Africanists precisely because of the paucity of other sources, while those working on India have a wealth of textual sources for the last three thousand years or so. Nevertheless, the results of archaeological work and their use for Indian historians is a matter that should be considered.

In terms of methodology, archaeology has been one of the most vigorous disciplines since the 1960s. The so-called new archaeology broadened the field considerably and made it much less antiquarian.[20] In particular, scholars often combine archaeology, anthropology and history; some throw in other disciplines, too. This is particularly the case when scholars use archaeology and history together to write on medieval or early modern historical periods. A flyer for a new book claims that "medieval and early modern archaeology has in the past focused on small-scale empirical contributions to the study of the period [in Britain]. The approach taken here is both wide-ranging and more ambitious. The author breaks down the dividing lines between archaeological and documentary evidence to provide a vivid reconstruction of preindustrial material life and of the social and mental processes that came together in the post-medieval period in the transition towards modernity."[21] Another example of the use of history and archaeology is a recent book that shows the relevance of *Annalista* history, especially that of Braudel, for archaeology.[22]

These trends have percolated into east African studies. This is very clearly seen in the case of Great Zimbabwe. Eurocentric scholars, and from 1965 to 1979 the racist regime of Ian Smith, could not believe that such impressive works could have been created by Africans. Archaeological investigation, among which Peter Garlake's work stands out, has shown clearly that this was in fact an indigenous Shona civilization.[23] More recent work reported by Graham Connah and Paul Sinclair has had the effect of revising upwards population estimates for this site, to well over 10,000, and of suggesting that the site may have been occupied longer than Garlake thought.[24] Even more recently, Sinclair and others have used site catchment analysis and have come up with important conclusions about the nature of the economy.[25]

Much recent work has been concerned with the Swahili coast. There has been some excellent analysis, quite fundamental for our understanding of the port cities and Swahili culture. Older work has been revised as new techniques and concepts are used, and it seems African archaeologists are more up-to-date with modern techniques than are their Indian colleagues. "With the influence of modern cultural ecology, geography and sociobiology, settlement analysis has been transformed into a concern with environmental and ecological processes. Settlements are part of a complex integration of culture and ecology within a regional environment. As a result, settlement analysis in archaeology must attend not only to the physical layout of the environment, but also to the social and historical aspects of environmental interaction."[26] Using these techniques, Henry Mutoro, George H. O. Abungu, and W. Howard Brown have put forward important claims about the nature of contacts between the coast and the interior.[27] In particular, archaeology in the 1980s and beyond shows clearly that the viewpoint of Chittick and James Kirkman, namely, that the coast was cut off from the interior, is quite wrong; there were intricate connections between coast and interior. The *makaya* (fortified villages) and data from the Tana River both show "that the coast of east Africa was a region of autochthonous dynamic social and economic integration, rather than simply a dependant of middle eastern and oriental external influence."[28]

Now that peace has returned to Mozambique, we can expect much more work from the group based at the Universidade Eduardo Mondlane. A preview is in the work of Ricardo Teixeira Duarte, for example, his preliminary work on Somaná Island, a site that may tell us much about the orientation of Swahili port cites, whether to the land or the sea.[29]

New work is often published in *Azania*, and the work of its editor, J.E.G. Sutton, and his own contributions, are very important. From time to time, useful surveys of the field are published in the *Journal of African History*. The most recent was written by Paul Sinclair in 1991.[30] Connah provided a readable overview, though one that is now a little dated, and the same applies to Richard Wilding's comprehensive bibliography.[31]

One constraining factor affecting archaeological work is that it is expensive. The work of historians is notoriously cheap, needing little more than access to a decent library and a word processor. Digging requires much more investment and patronage. Luckily, for some years funding was available from Sweden for the important and widespread project Urban Origins in Eastern and Central Africa, which is now concluded. Preliminary reports on their work can be found in *Mvita*; it is published from the Fort Jesus Museum by George and Lorna Abungu.

Archaeology in Africa even makes the news. Recent work has pushed back the dates of the first mosques; it has told us much about the time of the arrival of Islam and its spread in the existing proto-Swahili port cities. The general problem here is that the existing literary sources are all Arab or Swahili, and so privilege Islam. Archaeology, being more value free, can question this. Archaeology also renews itself, as new diggings and new methods of interpretation provoke new paradigms. Thus, a standard history has a date for the arrival of Islam in east Africa that subsequent archaeological research shows to be incorrect. J. Devisse and S. Labib claim that Arabs arrived in east Africa in the twelfth century,[32] while the authoritative *Encyclopedia of Islam* says that the first certain notice of Muslims in east Africa dates from the tenth century.[33] However, M. C. Horton has found a small mosque in Shanga dating from the late eighth century,[34] presumably for the use of visiting or even resident Arab merchants; the local population was converted later. More recently, on Pemba Island, his team has found a mosque dating from at least the tenth century, and probably the early eighth century.[35] They claim that this may show that Pemba acted as the initial bridgehead for the spread of Islam down the coast all the way to southern Mozambique. This finding is, in conjunction with other work, quite revolutionary, for it puts back the arrival of Islam to a much earlier period than was accepted only recently.

Even in the period after the arrival of Europeans, archaeology still has a role to play. For example, Henrick Ellert has produced useful descriptions of goods found at the sites of the trade fairs of the sixteenth and seventeenth centuries. There is a mixture of Portuguese and Chinese pottery, ivory, and many other finds. This would tend to counter claims that the Portuguese relied entirely on Indian goods for their inland trade.[36] These sorts of studies show clearly how valuable archaeology can be for the early modern historian.

South Asian archaeology has not shared in these developments. Over the last 150 years, the great feats of Indian archaeology have had to do with very early periods; the Indus Valley Civilization comes to mind immediately. The discipline has been little used for the medieval and early modern periods, except for essentially architectural studies of extant monuments. A survey volume in which were represented many of the important names in the field was restricted to such older periods, and F. R. Allchin, a very senior figure, listed seven "Problems in South Asian Archaeology," all of which had to do with the pre-Christian era.[37] Significantly, Allchin's most recent book is called *The Archaeology of Early Historic South Asia: The Emergence of Cities and States*.[38]

Standard Indian histories for both the Hindu and Muslim periods do not cite much archaeological work. The bibliography in the current standard history text lists archaeological works only for the Indus Valley period: once written sources are available, these are used exclusively.[39] A. L. Basham's classic work on pre-Islamic India similarly lists archaeological sources for the chapter on prehistory, but none for the later period, for which texts are freely cited.[40] We would expect to find archaeology much used in urban histories, but this is not the case. Gavin Hambly's *Cities of Mughal India* lists a few archaeological works, but has no footnote references to them. Stephen P. Blake's excellent study of the Mughal capital lists some archaeological works, but they have played little part in his account, which is based almost entirely on literary sources.[41]

It could be that the richness of the Indian written sources has meant that historians have ignored the usefulness of archaeology, yet it seems that it could provide a host of new insights. Perhaps this sort of change is beginning. A large collective work on south Asian archaeology had about two-fifths of its contents devoted to what could be called historical topics, such as coins, a sixteenth-century tomb in Sind, and the important site of Hampi, though I do think these studies still tend to be too "archaeological," and do not draw insights from other disciplines.[42] Work on Hampi, the site of the capital of the great Hindu empire of Vijayanagara from the fourteenth to the sixteenth centuries, shows what could be done.[43]

Another potential example of what could be done is Champanir, capital of the independent state of Gujarat in the early sixteenth century. We have available on this planned capital some Portuguese accounts, brief mentions in Persian histories, and numerous accounts of the surviving monuments, especially in the annual reports of the Indian Archaeological Survey. These last deal with architecture rather than any social aspects. Some archaeological work has been done already, and a site plan has been established. A modest dig would supplement nicely these other data, and this would be relatively inexpensive as many buildings have survived to foundation or plinth level, and the site has not been built over since it was abandoned some 450 years ago. This site, and no doubt a host of others, awaits full investigation, and certainly were it done it would cast new light on the layout, and social dimensions, of this planned Muslim capital.

History and Politics

African historiography is in a state of flux and change. This is part of a general trend in the profession. Scholars are becoming more aware of the ramifications of their work, and they are beginning to be much more self-conscious about how and what they write. We need not just new sources and new books but a total reorientation and a much more self-conscious use of our sources. No doubt the influence of postmodernism, or more generally cultural studies, has been important. In the case of Africa, the new trend was well summed up in an announcement for a recent conference, part of an "Africa Year" at the Australian National University. One of the organizers noted that "Africa" is now seen as a colonialist construct. Similarly, "tradition" was often shaped, constructed, and filtered by its colonialist recorders. "Hidden biases and unconscious assumptions regarding the nature of knowledge permeate Western societies." Scholars need to take account of indigenous worldviews and notions of historical discourse, that is, to write from the inside out, and remember that cultural knowledge is not universal. There are excellent African accounts of Europeans, the colonizer as viewed by the colonized.[44]

In the broadest terms, the political process of decolonization has led to these sorts of reevaluations. However, politics intervenes in other more specific ways. For example, to investigate connections between coast and interior is to enter an essentially nonacademic debate over the place of the coastal Swahili people in the modern nation-states of east Africa. The older historiography, arguably unconsciously influenced by imperial divide-and-rule notions, wrote of the coast as being "foreign," "different," quite distinct from the interior, with ties going east and north across the oceans rather than west to the interior. These scholarly works connected with, maybe even validated, more overt communal claims in newly independent African states that saw the Swahili as insufficiently "African." Some new African states indulged in strident nationalism. The voracious demands of the nation-state for loyalty led to efforts at homogenization; in consequence, the Swahili have often been located outside the African mainstream. They were seen as essentially foreign, Arab descendants of slave traders and collaborators with colonial powers, whether these were Omani or European. All this has unfortunate resonances with other areas of the world today that suffer, often in much more extreme forms, from ethnic rivalries and conflicts and the ultimate barbarity of "cleansing."

I want now to expand on this matter and sketch covert and overt political influences that have affected the writing of history. Some data from India, where over the last ten years the matter has become one of pressing concern, will help us when we look at the matter in an east African context. In both areas, and indeed in many others, as the ongoing debate over "history standards" in the United States reminds us, history has been located in current debates over views of the past, in which professional historians have been forced to respond to claims and views that come from people with definite political agendas. This is not to say that there is a "correct" history that trained historians can reveal to the public. Postmodernism has reminded us of what we already knew, namely, that all history writing is subjective, a creature of its own time and place. Two of the old clichés still stand as warnings: "Before you read the history, first know the historian," and "Each generation must write its own history." The history of east Africa will be written one way by a person who has served in the British Colonial Service; in another when the author is one who shared in the liberal American euphoria about the prospects for independent Africa in the 1960s; in yet another way by someone who has lived through the agonizing process of decolonization in Mozambique; another when the author is committed to African, or maybe Kenyan, unity; and yet another by an historian who grew up in New Zealand, trained in the United States, has lived in Australia for twenty years, and comes to Africa in midcareer after long experience in the history of India and the Indian Ocean. All historians have their own individual sociologies of knowledge, their own codes of conduct, their own standards, and these will determine how they write history, what sort of history they write, and what topics they will chose to study.[45] Even those who claim merely to be "telling a story" are immediately making a choice, for what story they tell is a matter of selection, and this selection is not value free.

The oral sources noted above are the best, because most extreme, example of this. They have been filtered through generations of recipients and transmitters, with each adding, modifying, and deleting according to what was important or significant at a particular time. Indeed, oral sources can be seen as subsumed by the present, whenever that may be. History as written by historians is always a dialogue between past and present, but oral traditions are totally presentist. They are the supreme illustration of relativism in historical sources, yet the same can apply to even such an apparently "scientific" source as archaeological diggings. Early work on Great Zimbabwe was rendered nugatory by the racist assumptions of the archaeologists concerned, while the current stress on coastal archaeology in many areas of east Africa is far from a neutral decision. The same concerns are true for sources somewhere in the middle in terms of apparent "objectivity"; these include Arabic chronicles, Portuguese records, and Swahili accounts.

Even if we accept relativity, there is still a difference between "good" history and "bad" history. If Clio is used for an overt political purpose, to reinforce a particular political point of view, then this is bad history. In a sentence that has become a cliché, Lord Acton wrote that "Power tends to corrupt and absolute power corrupts absolutely." He went on, in the same letter to Mandell Creighton, to say, in fine high-Victorian style, something about history:

> The inflexible integrity of the moral code is, to me, the secret of the authority, the dignity, the utility of history. If we may debase the currency for the sake of genius, or success, or rank, or reputation, we may debase it for the sake of a man's influence, of his religion, of his party, of the good cause which prospers by his credit and suffers by his disgrace. Then History ceases to be a science, an arbiter of controversy, a guide of the wanderer, the upholder of that moral standard which the powers of earth, and religion itself, tend constantly to depress. It serves where it ought to reign; and it serves the worst better than the purest.[46]

The divide is malleable, slippery, impossible to define precisely, yet I hope in the succeeding discussion to show that there is a difference between the subjectivity that all historians need to acknowledge and partisan history that pushes a particular agenda.

Relations between coast and interior in east Africa are ostensibly an academic discussion, yet this topic shows an uneasy intersection between politics and history. What follows is a preview of the more detailed discussions of this matter of interior and coast connections that occupies much of the rest of this book. In this section, I refer to the whole Swahili coast, that is, from Mogadishu to Delagoa Bay and present-day Maputo. Later, I sometimes use a notional division between the north and the south, the divide being at Cape Delgado. This will be done for heuristic reasons, and should not be allowed to disguise a fundamental Swahili unity. This is not to say that there are not subdivisions. David Sperling notes a general language division around the present southern boundary of Kenya.[47] Justin Willis stresses, in an article called "Who Are the Swahili?" that they are very diverse, by no means socially, linguistically, or culturally homogeneous.[48] We cannot really talk of "Swahili this" or "Swahili that," "the Swahili do this" or "the Swahili believe that." Yet, there seems to be enough commonality for the broad term to have some utility, as indeed a recent archaeological study claims, for it finds ceramic similarity from the Lamu peninsula to southern Mozambique.[49]

The coastal zone from Mogadishu to Mozambique comprises 500,000 people today and it contains a very large number of sites.[50] A. I. Salim quotes an estimate that, from the ninth to the twentieth centuries, there were 173 coastal settlements between the Benadir coast and the mouth of Zambezi, while T. H. Wilson finds 116 from Mogadishu to the Tanzanian border.[51]

Are these people African, or were the coastal dwellers, the shorefolk, quite separate? The short answer must be that they were as African as any other Bantu from the interior. The new orthodoxy in Swahili studies lists a number of reasons for this. In a humble way, it is best summed up by a placard in the Zanzibar Museum, which stresses that once people said Swahili culture was foreign, but now it is accepted that it is African. There were coastal communities and settlements engaged in Indian Ocean trade long before Islam arrived. Contact with India dates to the beginning of the Christian era; contact with the Middle East long predates Islam. Pre-Islamic Persian ceramics have been found as far south as Mozambique. It may even be that the Swahili accepted Islam for internal reasons, rather than having their conversion imposed from outside. In any case, east African Islam is a distinctive variant, and one that owes much to its African roots. Even the names of the rulers were Africanized. What we have then are inland people who moved to the coast, and there were subject to more foreign influence than was the case with their Bantu kin who remained inland. Yet the Swahili remained fundamentally African. The language has borrowings, to be sure, but it is basically a Bantu tongue. The stress on Arab origins is a late phenomenon, having to do with the exigencies of life under the Omani rulers of Zanzibar in the nineteenth century. As Africans, the Swahili retained close ties with the interior from whence they came. True, Islam did not spread inland, but inland people continued to come to the ports and there intermarry and convert. In this sort of acculturation and change, the Swahili are in no way unique either in an African or world context. The self-contained, isolated village, much beloved of past anthropologists, is either a myth or at least very unusual. Thus, to be specific, Bantu people in the interior were also subjected to external influences, albeit maybe not as intense as those impinging on their fellow Bantu-speakers on the coast.[52]

The ports themselves were very often located with an inland rather than maritime orientation. Many were difficult to approach from the sea; most were located to give access to the surrounding countryside from where came most of their food. Social, political, and economic relations were all, whether friendly or hostile, advantageous or not, overwhelmingly with their fellow Africans to the west rather than with people and places across the sea. Being urban and coastal, these port cities were more cosmopolitan than the inland, so that for example by 1570 many of the inhabitants of Malindi had some Portuguese language, yet these foreign accretions were not the dominant cultural form in the towns. The presence of foreigners with political designs was most unusual, and whether Portuguese or Ottomans, they were mere squalls that had no lasting impact. The Portuguese failed to take over the plateau gold mines. Their *prazos* (estates) on the Zambezi were thoroughly African. In their port cities, they intermingled with local people, and were dependent on them for supplies and labor. Often they ruled through local sultans, and by no means dominated them. They may even have contributed to Africanization by hindering what links there were with the centers of Islam to the north.

There were links up and down the coast on local ships using the monsoons, but most routine and continuing ties were inland. There was constant reciprocity between the near hinterland and the ports. Trading connections went far inland, not only in the south along the river valleys but also in the north. Swahili Muslims penetrated the south, even if not the north, and made converts far up the Zambezi Valley and into the Zimbabwe Plateau. Of the Swahili towns and settlements on the coast, most were humble villages engaged in agriculture and fishing. In the small number of larger port cities, we have until recently been bewitched by the handful of large stone buildings, "palaces," and mosques, but the bulk of the population lived in thatch and mud dwellings closely akin to inland structures. The population of the towns was African. Some, it is true, were the offspring of resident or more likely visiting foreign merchants, but even the foreign-born merged into the Swahili African milieu over a generation or two, just as did newcomers from the inland.

Finally, there are a few specific observations to be made regarding the myth of Shirazi origins of the Swahili cities and Swahili language. The first, of course, is part of the "Swahili are foreign" notion. It was believed that several of the rulers of the port cities were Persians, indeed from Shiraz, and that they introduced culture and civilization to the barbarous coast. The Kilwa dynasty, established in the ninth century, is one example.[53] Now we realize that what was really happening was that the rulers of these port cities, often people with mercantile backgrounds, had a tendency to invent or have invented for them impressive "foreign" genealogies the better to show their elite status.[54]

The matter of language is rather similar. Once it was thought that Swahili was hardly an African language at all, for it had many Arabic words in it, and cultured Swahili people spoke Arabic. The notion was that Arabic culture enriched and civilized a previously primitive African language. It is now accepted that Swahili is emphatically part of the Bantu language family, and it is different from other Bantu languages only in that it has been more open to borrowings from other languages. One would expect this of a language located on the coast, and so much more exposed to diverse languages than was the case for inland Bantu languages.

There was an identifiable Swahili language before Islam arrived. The language spread from north to south in the ninth and tenth centuries, a century or so before mass conversions. The vast majority of the borrowings were from Arabic, although the original words were often greatly modified as they acculturated. In any case, most of these borrowings from Arabic occurred during the last two centuries, as a result of the period of Omani rule.[55] There are some Hindi-derived words, though these also are probably of recent origin. Some European words have also been acquired, as one would expect, although studies of words of Portuguese origin show surprisingly few examples. A. Pires Prata has a list of about 110 words, but in fact many of even these are dubious: for example, he claims the Swahili *yaya*, "a nursemaid," comes from the Portuguese *aia*, but one would think the Hindi *ayah* is much more likely as the original word. Similarly, *nahota*, the "commander of a ship," comes not from the Portuguese *nauta* but rather from the Arabic *nakhoda*. *Cha*, "tea," is surely from the Hindi *chai*. What he misses is that the Portuguese picked up many Sanskrit-based terms in India, and took them to Africa with them, and some of them then passed into Swahili.[56]

The conclusion that the Swahili are African may owe something to current politics, at least unconsciously. Concern about threats to African unity, or the continuing viability of diverse African nations, the whole tendency towards fissiparousness on the continent, may have influenced the studies that stress unity. However, the older paradigm, which stressed that the Swahili were of foreign origins, being derived from Arab and Persian merchants, shows a much more overt and unfortunate intersection between history and politics. An older generation of (mostly British) historians and archaeologists, who stressed the separation notion outlined above, contributed to this distortion. Maybe unconsciously, they wrote of African divisions. Their studies contributed to this marginalization of the Swahili in several ways. Their work finds a precise and unfortunate parallel in India. Here, British historians perpetrated a series of claims in the nineteenth and twentieth centuries that put forward a case for Indian disunity, and for the consequent beneficent results of British rule. The eighteenth century was presented as a time of troubles, from which India was rescued by the British. It was claimed that the preceding dynasty, the Mughals, were much more tyrannical than were the British, and that British rule brought a rise in prosperity for the common Indian. Indian society was factionalized and divided along racial, caste, and religious lines.[57] All this contributed to solidifying British rule and to underpinning the division of India at the time of independence. In an Orientalist way, they created categories and stereotypes. The Sikhs were martial but stupid, the Bengali clever and devious, the *banyas* (Gujarati merchants) and *chetties* (south Indian merchants) weak but ruthless in business. The whole notion of caste that used to dominate discussion of Indian society was to a large extent a British creation, a result of their mania for classification and pigeonholing, which is seen most clearly in the early Indian censuses.

It is in this light that we need to see the claims of Swahili distinctiveness and separation from the interior. Kirkman was merely more outrageous than some other imperialist historians when he wrote of the "set-up of town and country—one semi-foreign, renegade, expatriate, as you will; the other pure, untamed, barbarous."[58] The notion was that around the year 850 foreigners brought in a sophisticated new culture, so that Gedi, for example, is described by Kirkman as an Arab city. Later, Arab culture in this city was diluted and made crude by increased African influence.[59] Even studies of Islam contributed to libels against Africa, as in J. Spencer Trimingham's comment that "By adopting Islam the African entered into history."[60]

The alter ego of the "Swahili as foreign notion" is one that finds the "real" Africans to be "primitive." Reginald Coupland wrote "with respect to East Africa, the history of Africa was a history of its invaders, while the majority of Africans formed a black background to the comings and goings of brown men and white men on the coast."[61] T. Hoffman claimed that the creation of the Zimbabwe culture was entirely a result of foreign stimulus: "The Zimbabwe Culture can be described as an indigenous reaction to an external stimulus—the East Coast gold trade."[62] Even the notion of a kingdom or empire was foreign. In the fifteenth century, "it was precisely the Arabs who . . . conceived and implanted in the mind of the Rozvi king a desire for empire."[63] In fact, even the term "empire" is an example of European attempts to impose their categories onto Africa. The Portuguese were fascinated by the "empire" of Monomotapa, yet in fact this was a greatly attenuated congery of loosely controlled tribal groupings.[64]

These older scholars claimed that the rulers of the city-states were immigrants, and looked back to their homelands in Yemen or the Hadramaut or the Gulf for their religion and their political legitimation. These states also looked to the Middle East or India for trade and commercial contacts. They were even racially different from the black, and, in one version, barbarous, inhabitants of the interior. The preferred elite language was Arabic. The Swahili port cities were outposts strung along the east African coast; they were urban and civilized; apart from location, they owed nothing to the inland. A substream of political economy theory within this paradigm found the Swahili and their Arab masters to be the first of many foreigners who underdeveloped Africa; they were followed by a succession of European powers from the late fifteenth century.

Early Europeans are given a greatly magnified role by many of these "colonialist" writers. The Portuguese in particular are seen as inaugurating a new era for the east African coast.[65] Histories of the Portuguese that make no attempt to locate them in the African context in which they operated can no longer be seen as satisfactory, indeed as permissible.[66]

Other historians have found other foreigners to be influential in east Africa. There is a regrettable strain in Indian historiography that produces versions of Greater India, of India in the past having a major colonizing and civilizing role all over the Indian Ocean area. This is a crudely nationalistic view of history, often written in reaction to denigration from British writers. Many of these studies have to do with the Indian colonization of southeast

Asia, but there have been others that address east Africa.[67] Some foreigners have also magnified the role of Indians in east Africa in our period, perhaps influenced by their undoubted prominent role in later centuries. R. B. Serjeant seems to give Indians far too large a role on the coast around 1500.[68] However, the person who most exaggerated the role of India was Cyril Hromnik in a Ph.D. dissertation, in two articles, and especially in a notorious book. The latter, significantly, was published in apartheid South Africa, and so hostile was the reception that his promised later books have never appeared.

His dissertation set out to show that Indians, and especially Canarins, Goan Christians, from 1501 to 1752 played a much larger role in Mozambique than anyone had previously realized. It is ostensibly a large, well-researched piece of work, running to 497 pages, and with a twenty-eight-page bibliography. However, his use of evidence is all too often extremely suspect. To avoid prolixity, I will give only a few examples of the way he magnifies the role of the Canarins in the Zambezi Valley. "It is a well documented fact that at the end of the fifteenth century Christians from Malabar were able to navigate their boats along the coast from Cochin and Cranganur as far as Malindi, Kilwa, Angoche, Moçambique, and most probably Sofala also." "Since all Christians were included together in general figures, specific references to Indians in Mozambique are generally to be found only in a few personal documents and then the reference is usually to non-Christian Indians only." He uses this to justify seeing all Christians as Canarins, while of course many were nothing of the sort, being either Portuguese or African. In October 1560, a Jesuit, Father Gonçalo de Silveira, arrived in Sena. He found it to be a very large town "where there are ten or fifteen Portuguese settlers, with some Christians from India. Since a very large town could not have been composed of the houses of fifteen Portuguese, there must have been many more Canarins than Portuguese." Hromnik then states that Silveira got the Christians to marry their concubines, and suggests this must mean that most of the Christians were Canarins. He claims that Indians had resided in Sena since the twelfth century, "and in later centuries the town must have resembled a Goan village more than anything else as Canarins were its primary occupants."[69] No need to belabor the obvious: All of these claims are entirely fanciful; his use of evidence is totally flawed.

His two articles are derived from his thesis, and suffer from the same problems.[70] His book, however, is much more wide ranging, and overtly racist. Again, I will restrict my comments, partly to avoid being redundant, and partly as several reviews can be consulted to see what the experts thought.[71] Among other things, he claims that Great Zimbabwe is not African at all, and that "Africa owes its system of trade and currency, its metal technology and iron tools, and the terminology to express this entire complex of cultural development to India, Indonesia, China, with later contributions from the Muslim world and Europe."[72] Among his evidence for an Indian presence, even dominance in east Africa before 1500, are the Indian carved doors to be found in Lamu. In fact, none of those that survive predate the nineteenth century.[73] Indian gold mining on the Zimbabwe Plateau began around 1000 A.D. No need to spend more time on this work, except perhaps to say that I have often been accused or congratulated for being "India-centric," but Hromnik is ridiculous.

This magnification of the role of foreigners is a distortion that runs contrary to the more recent trend that stresses the autonomy of African history. However, the notion of the Swahili as foreign is much more malign. This perception of history has contributed to giving the Swahili an invidious position today, which was reinforced by events in the nineteenth and twentieth centuries. The role of the Swahili at this time led to popular suspicion of the community and reinforced the notion of them as being foreign. Inadvertently, the Swahili contributed to their future problems. In the Omani period, status was closely linked to Arab origins, and many Swahili manufactured them in order to thrive. They also played a large role, under the sultanate, in the slave trade, for the first time venturing far inland to pursue this odious occupation. Traditional Swahili accounts of slavery are quite matter of fact. For example, one story discusses the merits of taking a female slave as a concubine, a *suria*. This had its pragmatic advantages. "Some people prefer a suria to a wife, because they say that a suria is a piece of luggage, meaning that if you travel you take your suria with you; but a wife, first you have to persuade her, and then you have to consult her parents before you take her on a journey."[74]

In retrospect ill-advisedly, but at the time understandably, the Swahili continued to stress their foreignness into the twentieth century. Indeed A.H.J. Prins, using data now some forty years old, noted that on the coast most people did not call themselves Swahili, but rather either Arab or Shirazi, though they referred to an inferior as a Swahili.[75] At least in the British colonies, the general notion of the rulers was that no African could produce civilization. Thus, the coastal people had to claim to be foreign, or non-native, if they wanted to be civilized. Many did claim to be Arab and of foreign origin, and were rewarded by the British by privileges in education and taxation, and were allowed to avoid compulsory labor duties.[76] "The Swahili, therefore, unlike other 'Negroes,' were provided with a legal loophole through which some of them could escape the scourge of their nativeness, if they so desired."[77]

There is also the delicate matter of what may at first appear to be Swahili contempt for their African neighbors. On the surface, this looks like racial superiority. The experts note the use of particular terms to set off the Swahili from others. One word for culture is *usta-arabu*, "being like an Arab."[78] *Waungwana* means "free, civilized, urban people," that is, Muslims; and *washenzi* are "barbarians from the interior."[79] Pouwels writes about Swahili fear or contempt for the interior. There is their town, representing order, civilization (*ungwana*), and predictability, and the world outside it, the interior, which represents chaos, barbarity (*ushenzi*), and the fearful unknown.[80] In Jan Knappert's collection of Swahili myths, there is an example where "white" people are seen as better than "black."[81] A Kenyan scholar notes that Swahili society is patriarchal, that is, the lineage of offspring goes through the father regardless of the ethnicity of the mother (who, given the shortage of Arab women, was often African). "An informant remembers his grandmother [in Lamu] reserving in her sitting room a wooden stool for one of her visitors whose husband had African blood from his father's side, in distinction from other guests who sat on padded chairs."[82]

This may not be merely crude racism. J. de V. Allen writes of Swahili values, and says that "Pre-eminent among these values was a certainty that they, as townspeople and Muslims (usually in that order), were superior to the rural dwellers who lived outside their settlements and further away in the interior. This superiority was based, not on race or tribe, but on culture, which to them—as to so many societies in history—was an urban prerogative, something which country dwellers altogether lacked."[83] We are asked to believe that the prejudice against their inland neighbors was the result of an urban-rural tension and differentiation, not racism. This explains the Swahili reluctance to venture into the "bush." As a traditional saying puts it, "Why go inland and have a lot of trouble in the bush?" The attitude to the inland traders who came to the coast with goods was scornful. A Swahili story tells how as soon as one group, the Nyamwezi, get to a town and civilization they will be drunk for six or seven days, and then will trade. At first, "Their idea of business is that for each tusk they should receive the whole contents of the [Indian] shop; but the Indians understand the business" and beat them down mercilessly.[84]

All of these matters have interacted to make the Swahili something of an anomaly in recently independent and strongly "Africanist" states. In all the states of east Africa they make up a small minority. They still have a whiff of the collaborator, whether with the colonial powers or with the Arabs, about them. In extreme cases, Swahili loyalty to the new, black, Africa is questioned, and they are discriminated against. All too often today they are economically marginalized and stigmatized as foreign. Their attempts to set themselves off from their fellow Africans as a result of threats and inducements under both Omani and British colonialism have now backfired in a most distressing way.[85] Yet, ironically, in both Kenya and Tanzania the Swahili language is the official tongue.

A courageous young archaeologist, C. Makokha Kusimba, has addressed the problem directly. In an account of an address he had given, he "decried the relentless destruction of archaeological sites on the Kenya coast. . . . Relying on the premise that false conceptions of Swahili culture and identity influenced government policy on the Swahili, especially Muslim Swahili, I argued that the current destruction of Swahili sites and monuments and systematic appropriation of Swahili lands can only be understood from the perspective of the manner in which their history had been researched, analyzed, written and marketed to the masses." Among other things, he noted the "repatriation of cultural objects; destruction of sites and monuments; under-investment in human power; and ethnic and religious discrimination . . . [and] described the processes of destruction as they are manifested in the so-called development of the Swahili culture and heritage. I argued that policy decisions aimed at increasing investment and economic development have sometimes reduced the Swahili to mere observers of the destruction of their sites and monuments."[86]

Since independence, corrupt nationalist politics, notably in Kenya, have exacerbated the situation. Presidents Kenyatta and Moi, especially the latter, have engaged in dubious ethnic politics, a divide-and-rule tactic even more malevolent than that pursued by the British, in order to safeguard their own positions. The term used is *majimboism*, in theory a federal system based on ethnicity, but in reality the same as ethnic cleansing and forced relocation. The past Swahili role in the slave trade is stressed. Swahili people claim that government officials say that one day they will be "driven back to Arabia." A recent book writes of "generalized Swahili dispossession . . . Swahili peripheralization in the political, economic and educational spheres of Kenya's national life . . . internal colonization." They have been dispossessed and "otherized" by rampant black African leaders who have taken their land, and denied their Africanness.[87] This has tied in to corrupt politics, where favorites are given the right to clear away Swahili remains, even Swahili people, in order to make way for "development" on the coast, and in particular the construction of facilities for foreign exchange–bearing tourists. It is earnestly to be hoped that the new academic orthodoxy will percolate down to popular consciousness and that this, allied with a new form of government dedicated to national reconciliation and unity rather than covert ethnic cleansing, will create a climate where the Swahili can be seen as different but the same, a distinctive but thoroughly African group within the nation, and one which has much to offer within the rich kaleidoscope of east Africa and its people.

In India also communal politics in recent years have undergone a disturbing recrudescence, and this has meant that the discipline of history has been manipulated by people with a political agenda. Certain politicians, especially those associated with the revivalist Hindu party the Bharatiya Janata Party (BJP) and its even more chauvinist offshoots, have manufactured history to suit their own, communal, political purposes. Communal history is not new in India. Such works have been around for at least the whole of this century, as in the writings of Hindu nationalists like V. D. Savarkar, but they have recently gained a most distressing currency and popular credibility. After independence, P. N. Oak wrote a series of books that tried to show that nearly everything that had happened in India was due to the Hindus, not, as had been incorrectly thought, the Muslims. Two samples are *The Taj Mahal Is a Hindu Palace*, and *Who Says Akbar Was Great?* The Taj of course is a monument to a Muslim empress, while Akbar was notorious for his religious tolerance.

In the 1970s, these books were considered a joke; indeed, I bought several of them just for fun, or to use to show students how bad history writing could be. What is very threatening is that Oak's reputation now stands high, and he is considered to be a major and important historian. The full implications of this sort of history were seen in the disastrous struggle in Ayodhya, which culminated in December 1992 when a mob of some 200,000 Hindu militants destroyed a sixteenth-century mosque because it was claimed that it stood on the place where the Hindu god Ram had been born. The growth of Hindu chauvinism in Indian politics, such a retrograde step after the broad tolerance and humanism of Jawaharlal Nehru; the "othering" of the 11 percent of the population who are Muslims; and the rise of the BJP party as the partially acceptable face of this wave of communalism, seen most recently in the elections of May 1996, has been accompanied by, even ratified by, history at the beck and call of unscrupulous politicians. Those who insist on tolerance, or attempt an objective history, are marginalized or even silenced.

The profession of history in India has mostly performed heroically in the face of these threats. For most historians, it is quite possible to have differences with one's colleagues on matters of fact or interpretation, even if there may be an inadvertent communal tinge in the discussion. An example from our own period is the communal composition of brokers, who played a vital intermediary role in the economy, and in particular whether a Hindu broker would service a Muslim merchant or vice versa. Three senior historians, K. N. Chaudhuri, Ashin Das Gupta, and Tapan Raychaudhuri have each stressed a lack of cross-communal business dealings, yet Irfan Habib, A. Jan Qaisar, and I all question this.[88] This is within the bounds of accepted academic debate.

It is quite another thing to write work that ratifies communal antipathy, as for example P. N. Oak does. Many senior historians have performed valiantly, have indeed put aside their own work and careers in an attempt to promote rational discussion. Several collections have tried to spread light rather than heat.[89] We can only hope that the discipline of history in India will be able to resist the pressure to become the plaything of politicians, as is too often the case in dictatorial states, and more immediately that the dangers so clear in India will not be allowed to influence what is also a perilous situation in east Africa, and especially in Kenya.

Slaves carrying ivory and cloth. Reprinted from Carl von der Decken, *Reisen in Ost-Afrika* (Leipzig, 1869).

Killing an elephant. Source unknown, but before 1800. Reprinted from Victor Giraud, *Les Lacs de l'Afrique equatoriale* (Paris, 1890).

Portuguese on board a ship, and using local labor. Reprinted from Theodore de Bry, *Tertia Pars Indiae Orientalis* (Frankfurt, 1601).

The Dutch Factory (trading post) at Surat. Reprinted from Isaak Commelin, *Beginn ende Voortgangh van de Vereenighde Nederlandtsche Geoctreerde Oost-Indische Compagnie* (Amsterdam, 1646).

Fort Jesus, Mombasa. Photograph by the author.

The Mutapa ruler. A seventeenth-century French print, from the Bibliothèque Nationale, Paris.

Chapter 2

The Swahili Coast in the Afrasian Sea

What of terminology relating to the coast of east Africa and its bordering sea? Frank Broeze suggests that the term "Indian Ocean" is inappropriate. He writes of "a string of closely related regional systems stretching from East Asia around the continent and across the Indian Ocean to East Africa (to which sea space a new generic name, such as 'the Asian Seas,' might well be given)" and then notes that the Swahili coast "constituted the southwestern facade of 'the Asian Seas.'"[1] While the term "Indian" Ocean may be a little ethnocentric, an "Asian" sea excludes east Africa. The Great Southern Ocean obviously does not fit our area. What of the Arabian Sea, a commonly used term for the stretch of water between east Africa and western India, extending up to the southern shores of the Middle East? This seems to give Arabs a role much more prominent than is appropriate. Some years ago, people began to write about Eurasia, the idea being to stress connections rather than the artificial separation between a reified (and successful) Europe and a timeless (backward, even redundant) Asia. We were reminded of millennia of contact, especially between the eastern Mediterranean and the Arabian Sea. Now, some have urged us to go further still. In what seems to be the ultimate uniformitarianism, the desire to show "one world" before capitalism, to stress links between areas long before the European voyages, and to avoid the perils of the Four Civilizations model for the precapitalist world, the term Afrasia has been suggested. This would make up a vast area, with western Europe to be seen as a tiny appendage on the western edge. But this also is controversial, for it is stretching things to see most of sub-Saharan Africa sharing in the history of Eurasia before the European voyages. This, however, does not apply to the Swahili coast. I suggest that the appropriate term for what used to be called the Arabian Sea is the Afrasian Sea.[2]

The geographical limits of this sea would be relatively easy to define, much more so than is the Indian Ocean.[3] Very simply, the Afrasian Sea can be identified as a unit for study, an area that, at least heuristically, has some unity, beginning at Sofala and extending right around the coast down to the southern tip of India, Kanya Kumari. Once the Portuguese arrive, the

African southern limit goes right down to what they called the Cape of Good Hope. Both the Gulf and the Red Sea are included, and of course this area has intricate links with much further areas.

Several scholars have claimed that the Swahili coast shared fully in this maritime world, indeed was much more linked to it than to the interior. By 1500, Swahili culture was "a child of its human and physical environment, being neither wholly African nor 'Arab,' but distinctly 'coastal,' the whole being greater than the sum of its parts."[4] Neville Chittick suggests that "this has resulted in [the Indian Ocean] constituting what is arguably the largest cultural continuum in the world during the first millennium and a half A.D. In the western part of the basin, at least, the coasts had a greater community of culture with each other and with the islands than they had with the land masses of which they form the littorals."[5] Similarly, from D. Nurse and Thomas Spear: "While the Swahili lived in widely scattered communities, each characterized by its own dialect, culture and history, they also lived within a single larger community, knit together by their mutual involvement in the Indian Ocean world."[6]

J. de V. Allen also tries to locate the Swahili coast in an Indian Ocean world and to define an Indian Ocean civilization, or culture. Like most of his work, the attempt is provocative, and frankly careless and muddle-headed.[7] The main link is "maritime Islam," and thus Sri Lanka, Burma, and Thailand are excluded as they are not Muslim, but on the other hand, confusingly, south India is included. Another element of unity is claimed to be the Malay people. In summary, he finds three common elements: a racial one provided by Malay and other migrations; cultural unity radiating out from India; and religious unity provided by Islam.

These claims raise several crucial questions having to do with coast-interior relations, and how Swahili people fit in African history. They will be addressed in detail below. For now, I want to raise the matter of littoral society. Littoral society can be seen as related directly to maritime history, to the history of the Afrasian Sea. Ashin Das Gupta writes of coastal Gujarat, which is marshy, irregular, and includes river estuaries and tidal flats that were submerged at high tide. This zone was peopled "by the truly maritime men who fished and who sailed the vessels on which trade depended. The coastal cities usually stood back a little."[8] John Middleton takes a similar view on Africa: "Part of the coast is the sea: the two cannot be separated. The Swahili are a maritime people and the stretches of lagoon, creek, and open sea beyond the reefs are as much part of their environment as are the coastlands. The sea, rivers, and lagoons are not merely stretches of water but highly productive food resources, divided into territories that are owned by families and protected by spirits just as are stretches of land. The Swahili use the sea as though it were a network of roads."[9]

Littoral society is usually considered to be the same as coastal society. J. C. Heesterman stresses that it is transitional, permeable: "The littoral forms a frontier zone that is not there to separate or enclose, but which rather finds its meaning in its permeability."[10] In an article published in 1985, I sketch the case for identifying such a society, which has certain links and a commonality to do with society, religion, and economy.[11] Fernand Braudel writes evocatively about coastal society, stressing that it was as much land-oriented as sea-oriented. The life of the coast of the Mediterranean "is linked to the land, its poetry more than half-rural, its sailors may turn peasant with the seasons; it is the sea of vineyards and olive trees just as much as the sea of the long-oared galleys and the round-ships of merchants, and its history can no more be separated from that of the lands surrounding it than the clay can be separated from the hands of the potter who shapes it."[12] Another great *Annalista*, E. Le Roy Ladurie, describes mid-sixteenth-century Normandy peasant-fishermen, who were always keen to get back to land "to get on with the more serious matters—looking after the cows, cutting the corn, laying down apple juice."[13] Braudel once flippantly remarked that the Russian economy centered on a "landlocked heart, which means a bad heart—the good hearts are the maritime ones."[14] But what exactly is a maritime or littoral economy or society, and is it necessarily different from a landlocked one? Is it only coastal? A moment's reflection will show first that littoral society is very similar to some land-bounded societies, and second, that the littoral is not restricted to the shores of the ocean.

Camels are often called the ships of the desert; indeed, we should see deserts as similar to oceans, with their long-distance trade and communication, and oases like islands, and towns on the fringes like port cities. Thus Timbuktu is like Kilwa or Aden. In a stimulating fashion, Philip D. Curtin identifies three "coasts" for sub-Saharan Africa: the south side of the Sahara, the Indian Ocean, and the Atlantic.[15] Indeed, it is easy to see that long-distance land trade, whether or not over deserts, is functionally similar to sea trade. K. N. Chaudhuri notes that "The caravan trade in particular was wholly dependent on the existence of urban centers, providing a mirror image of the co-ordinates that bound together port-towns and sea-lanes." Among the caravan cities were Aleppo, Timbuktu, Baghdad, and Samarkand, and "The port or caravan town in Asia was the valve that regulated the flow of trans-regional trade in Eurasia."[16] My own study of the pilgrimage to Mecca showed that a *cafila* (caravan) can be either a land caravan or a sea convoy.[17] There were cost differences, to be sure, however, the same goods could be moved by land or by sea, and sometimes one could choose which method. Trade in the Red Sea from Mocha to Jiddah could be carried on by either means. Similarly with the itinerant *banjara* (trader) community in India, which traveled long distances all across the subcontinent, camping out and from time to time putting in to cities/ports to trade.[18] Sea travel at this time was dependent on the monsoon winds, but the seasons also governed, to a considerable extent, long-distance land travel. For example, during the rainy months of June to September in India land travel is difficult, just as is sea travel off the west coast of India.

There is, however, one important difference. If both land and sea transportation were available, all else being equal the sea would be chosen. Sea navigation at this time had a pronounced cost advantage over other forms of transport. Chittick claims that one needs, roughly, the same energy to move 250 kg on wheels on a road, 2,500 on rails, and 25,000 on water.[19] Similarly, and related to the matter of deserts as inland seas, it has been calculated that a *dhow* (lateen-rigged boat) can travel the same distance as a camel caravan in one-third the time; each boat could carry the equivalent of a thousand camel loads, and only one dhow crew member was needed for several cargo tons, as compared with two or more men for each ton in a camel caravan.[20]

The second point about littoral society may be more obvious. If we are writing about a littoral society that is characterized especially by its proximity to water, then lakes and large river systems must be included. The best example of the latter is the vast and complex Zambezi River system. M.D.D. Newitt describes this system, and he notes that between the two main settlements of Sena and Tete, respectively 260 km and 515 km from the sea, is the dangerous Lupata Gorge, where goods had to be portered. Above Tete are the Cabora Bassa rapids, which are a major block. He happily notes that "The valley of the Zambezi . . . is in many ways like an extension of the coastal zone, a finger of low veldt extending 300 miles [480 km] into the interior." Thus, what we are used to conceptualizing as port cities, Kilwa, Sofala, Angoche, and Quelimane, shared very similar roles with Sena and Tete.[21] The best term for Sena and Tete is "inland port cities," or maybe "fluvial ports." Indian counterparts would be Patna, Varanasi, Allahabad on the Ganga. It is hard to separate Tete, for example, just because it is more than 500 km inland, from Cambay, Kilwa, Calicut, Aden, and a host of other port cities.[22]

António Bocarro described how, in the early seventeenth century small ships called *almadias* sailed right up to Tete, presumably with a porterage at the Lupata Gorge, and each carried a not inconsiderable cargo of 25 *fardos* of cloth.[23] With 25 *corjas* to each fardo, and 20 pieces of cloth in each corja, this is a total of 12,500 pieces of cloth on each boat. In a letter dated 1511,[24] another contemporary described an extensive trade to 6 leagues (about 30 km) upriver to a chief called Mongualo. The merchants paid customs duties there, and then went further upriver 20 more leagues (about 100 km) to a mountain called Utonga, where there was a large settlement of African and Muslim merchants.[25] So also with the port city of Braboa, north of Angoche. Although it was located half a league from the sea, it was on a river and so was visited by Gujarati ships; it also had extensive contact with the interior and with the Mutapa state as well as a large coastal trade to Sofala.[26]

Similarly, islands in the rivers can be seen as making up little littoral societies all their own, even far "inland." Dos Santos described an island in the river of Sofala, 4 leagues above the fortress, called Maroupe, 8 leagues in length and 1.5 in width at its widest.[27] Around 1570, Monclaro noted many islands in the Zambezi system before Sena. There were two big ones: Caya, 12 leagues long and 2 wide, and Inhangoma, 5 leagues by 2. Both had their own villages and rulers.[28] Thus, when we write of littoral society we must extend our scope considerably.

Littoral people, as Das Gupta notes, should be seafarers, but in fact Swahili people engaged only in coastal and river navigation. There is no evidence of them sailing in their own ships across the Afrasian Sea or beyond. Early in the sixteenth century, Tomé Pires found in the great port city of Melaka, among many others, men of Kilwa, Mombasa, Mogadishu, and Malindi, but he implies that these people in fact were foreigners from the Swahili coast, not themselves Swahili, and in any case it is clear that these people did not travel in east African–based ships.[29]

The structure of trade, and the monsoon regime, which we will investigate shortly, seem to have militated against the Swahili people needing to travel far by sea. Like many other Muslim people, they had pronounced normative hostility to the sea. To aphorisms from the landed elite of Muslim India ("Wars by sea are merchant's affairs, and of no concern to the prestige of kings") and Ottoman Turkey ("Merchants who travel by sea are like silly worms clinging to logs") we may add a Somali traditional poem that states that "A man who has been to sea has had a bewildering experience which will be difficult for him to explain."[30]

What sort of ships were used on this coast, both to sail up and down the coast and to link the coast with other coasts far away? The coastal craft, today generically referred to by foreigners as dhows,[31] were small, less than 50 tons capacity, undecked, with one mast and palm-leaf mats for sails, and held together with coir rope.[32] Dos Santos distinguished between three types, depending on size. Big ones were called *navetas*; middle-sized, *pangaios*; and small ones, *luzios* or almadias.[33] It was these last which sailed far up the Zambezi River, and we have noted that even these could carry 12,500 pieces of cloth.

Larger ships engaged in the international trade were called *sambuks*, these being smaller than those called *naus* ("great ships") by the Portuguese. These would be over 50 tons capacity, and some as large as 200 tons and more, thus making them considerably larger than the ships used by the Portuguese in their early years. Dom Manuel, king of Portugal, described them to the king of Spain. In Malindi, Cabral found three naus from Cambay, each of 200 tons. "These naos have the superstructure built of cane and their hulls bound with ropes and caulked with pitch for the lack of nails; all the naos of these parts are fashioned so; they sail always with the wind astern for they cannot sail into the wind, and they have a quarter-deck."[34] A member of Vasco da Gama's first voyage noted that "Their mariners have Genoese needles [i.e., compasses], by which they steer, quadrants, and navigating charts."[35] These ships were able to cope with the lack of good harbors on most of the coast. Rather, they were beached at high tide, repaired and unloaded at low tide, and then floated again on the next tide. Thus, the long coral reef off most of the Swahili coast is ideal, as it provides sheltered sandy beaches with a low surf behind the coral reef.[36]

Who were the members of this littoral society in east Africa around 1500, the people Richard Wilding aptly calls the "shorefolk"?[37] We have very little information on the fishers, hunters, and peasants living in the coastal zone away from the towns, though we must remember Le Roy Ladurie and see these people as oriented both to land and sea activities, with a pronounced privilege to the former. We know quite a lot more about the inhabitants of the port cities, the jewels in the necklace of the whole coast. Like other port cities, they were notoriously heterogeneous in their composition. No doubt the bulk of them were humble people—laborers, peasants, menials, slaves—most of them by now Muslim, yet of Bantu stock. We know little of them either, for their dwellings were made of mud, wood, and thatch and so, unlike the stone buildings so beloved of archaeologists, have not survived to tell us of their lives.[38]

The great traders and merchants, however, were a mixed lot. The origins of these men is a matter of historical and contemporary political concern, yet in many ways it is anachronistic to categorize them as "foreign" or "local." In an age before the all-encompassing demands for loyalty of the modern nation-state were in effect, notions like "foreign" or "citizen" had no currency. People were grouped and divided on quite different criteria: ethnicity, occupation, religion, or wealth. Nevertheless, something can be said about the origins of these people. Most of the resident merchants were Swahili, speaking the language and often of "pure" Bantu origin. Others were mixed, the result of unions between local women and visiting or resident "foreign" merchants, nearly all Muslim, and deriving from the Red Sea area, the Hadramaut, a few from the Gulf and many from India. Some settled merchants may have been "purely foreign," in other words, men born outside Africa, although the majority of these men were sojourners only, coming in for trade and returning again on the next monsoon.

Another element in the total population was comprised of visitors from India. Most of these were Muslim, but there is copious evidence of Gujarati Hindus trading, and settling, in some of the Swahili ports. The Portuguese often mistook them for Christians, so eager were they to find coreligionists in the area, but it is clear that these people were Hindu, or just possibly Jain, men then who had not been constricted by the normative prohibition on sea travel for Hindus.[39] João de Barros noted them in Malindi in 1498, "such devout followers of the teaching of Pythagoras that they will not even kill the insects by which they may be infested, and eat nothing which has life."[40] Another account noted significantly that they did not eat beef.[41] In 1507, another visitor to Malindi wrote of some people there who lived "a frugal life. Called Gujarati, they are very withdrawn and sparing of conversation. Many of them will eat no living thing; by that I mean anything that must be killed and has blood. By another name they are known as Brahmans."[42]

There is a question about whether these Hindus were settled in these towns, or merely sojourners. Certainly Gujarati *banians* settled in other Muslim areas, even in the Red Sea.[43] One account says that they "lived" (*morão*) in Malindi,[44] but an eye-witness account describes how the Hindus in Mombasa "are only temporary residents, and are held in much subjection, they not being allowed to do anything except by the order of the Moorish King."[45] We know that the ruler of Malindi was much more sympathetic to foreigners than was the ruler of Mombasa, as evidenced in the contrasting receptions the two rulers gave to da Gama and other Portuguese. Thus, it is quite likely that Hindus were allowed to settle in Malindi, but not in Mombasa.

There is much confusion over who were the rulers of these Swahili port cities. It used to be thought that they were all foreign dynasties, coming from Persia (the Shirazi origin claim) or from Arabia. This is now generally discounted. In the nineteenth century, many Swahili tried to attach themselves to the prestige of the Omani rulers of Zanzibar, and claimed, or manufactured, a pure Arab origin. Similarly with the rulers, who, like many other Islamic leaders invented elaborate and prestigious genealogies, frequently designed to connect them with Arab ruling houses and also with the Prophet himself. Many of the rulers no doubt were descended from Muslim foreigners, but probably not from politically elevated men.[46] Most of the rulers' lineages went back to a merchant ancestor. The mixed origins of these rulers are clearly demonstrated by the way an Indian Muslim became ruler of Kilwa in the early sixteenth century, in this case, courtesy of the Portuguese. One Muhammed Rukn al-Din al-Dabuli, called Muhammad Ankoni by the Portuguese, was put in charge of the treasury at Kilwa in 1502; later, he became ruler of this declining port city. He certainly was Indian, though there is some confusion over his town of origin, which may have been Daybul, on the Indus River, or Dabhul, a major Deccan port.[47]

These port cities competed vigorously with each other for dominance, something of which the Portuguese were able to take advantage. Wilding writes of "the kaleidoscopic political mayhem of Swahili life."[48] At different times different cities were prominent. Kilwa was at its height between roughly 1250 and 1330, and in this period was richer than any other city. Its prosperity was based on its control of the gold exports from Sofala further south. The early-fourteenth-century palace complex, the Husuni Kubwa, was "as spacious as any roofed stone building south of the Sahara until modern times." It extended over about 150 meters, and included a large hall, a pool, and domed roofs. The existing stone mosque was also massively enlarged at this time, reaching dimensions of about 12 meters by 30.[49] Uniquely on the coast, Kilwa even minted copper coins, and recently three gold ones have been found.[50]

Kilwa declined later in the fourteenth century and by the time the Portuguese arrived Mombasa seems to have been the dominant town. An account of Francisco de Almeida's voyage says that Kilwa had 4,000 people, while Mombasa had 10,000, including 3,700 soldiers.[51] However, it is but one indication of the difficulty of our sources that another Portuguese source, a letter from Diogo de Alcaçova to the king in 1506, claimed that the whole "lordship" of the ruler of Sofala came to 10,000 men, and 7,000 men answered to his drums overnight, while in Kilwa, apparently including Sofala, there were more or less 30,000 men.[52] A further difficulty is that the local chronicles often tend to exaggerate the importance of their particular areas, and so must be used with caution and their claims reinforced by reference to archaeological finds. One good example of this is Pate, in the north, whose chronicler claimed a very large role in the fourteenth century. On the basis of his digging, Chittick thinks the town was important only in the seventeenth century.[53]

This is how the Kalabari people of the Niger Delta reacted when they first saw white men, around 1500. "The first white man, it is said, was seen by a fisherman who had gone down to the mouth of the estuary in his canoe. Panic-stricken, he raced home and told his people what he had seen: whereupon he and the rest of the town set out to purify themselves—that is to say, rid themselves of the influence of the strange and monstrous thing that had intruded into their world."[54] Once the Portuguese reached the west African coast south of the great caravan routes, they entered a real (for Europeans, and also for Muslims) terra incognita. Contrast this with the situation on the east coast. Even if the Swahili did not travel, they were still linked to a very wide world. When the Muslim sultan of Mozambique found out that da Gama was a Christian, he reacted in a way conditioned by centuries of Muslim-Christian antagonism in the Mediterranean, that is, with hostility. The coast was already linked to a wider Indian Ocean world, and the newcomers had little to offer. Once the Portuguese had finished their fort at Sofala, they tried to enter the gold trade by offering the same goods as they had used for decades to buy gold in west Africa, "but the negroes of Sofala did not care for it, as they wanted articles which the Moors procured from India, especially from Cambay."[55] However, the Portuguese did introduce some new products, such as tobacco, pineapples, sweet potatoes, corn, avocado, and guavas.

Swahili tombs and mosques often have objects embedded in them. These may be wine bottles or even a chamber pot.[56] These are usually local, but it is another indication of how far-flung, how cosmopolitan, was this world that at Takwa, on Manda Island, a blue and white sixteenth-century Portuguese dish is set into the base of the cistern beside the mosque, that is, the ablution trough.[57] Another example is a bronze lion statuette, which was found at Shanga and that dates from around 1100. It is a real puzzle, for it seems clear it was used in Hindu *puja* (worship), and this means it would hardly be sold or used by a non-Hindu. But mosques in Shanga date from around 800. It might have been part of some regalia. The conclusion reached by M. C. Horton and T. R. Blunton is that, taking account of extensive contacts across the Indian Ocean, "the Shanga lion must therefore not be so much 'Indian' or 'African' but 'Indian Ocean' in attribution."[58] We can now turn to a more focused discussion of links across the Afrasian Sea and even beyond, looking in turn at political, economic, meteorological, and religious connections.

Before the arrival of the Portuguese, the east African coast was not subject to any foreign political control. In the south, there certainly were relations with inland states, first that centered on Great Zimbabwe, and then with its successor, the Mutapa state, but the relationship between inland power and coastal city was reciprocal rather than dominating. It seems that each needed the other, and the Shona states had no need, or it seems even desire, to extend what was, in any case, very disarticulated rule to the coast. External trade played a small role in their economies, or their ethos. While many of the rulers of the port cities claimed, or manufactured, genealogical links with the Arabian and Persian world, these were tenuous in the extreme and implied no political role for Middle Eastern states in east Africa.

The only other impingement of external politics on the coast before 1500 came from China, and this was a very temporary matter. Chinese wares, mostly bulk porcelain, have been found in east Africa from at least the ninth century, long before the famous voyages of Zheng He (Cheng Ho). In return the Chinese acquired ivory, which being softer they considered was preferable to Indian tusks; ambergris, which they called dragon spittle; and rhinoceros horn to use as an aphrodisiac.[59] This, however, was not a matter of a direct economic linkage between these two distant regions, for this was an indirect trade done via the Gulf or India. Direct contact came from two of Zheng He's seven expeditions in the early fifteenth century. In 1417–19, his ships got as far as Malindi; some of his ships were a massive 3,000 tons and over 100 meters long. And in 1431–33, he traveled to Mogadishu.[60] Many historians have speculated about what would have been the consequences if he had kept going, rounded the Cape, and colonized Europe. However, whatever tribute relations were imposed on the Swahili rulers, if any, did not survive the end of the Chinese voyages in the 1430s.

This situation changed dramatically with the arrival of the Portuguese and their claims to be able to monopolize trade in some items and control and tax all other trade. While before 1500 the coast had been linked to a great international *trading* world, now it was linked to a much larger *political* world. This world was centered in Goa, and then in Lisbon, and extended also to a fourth continent, that is, to Brazil, from where the Portuguese brought new crops to Africa and Asia. While the economic links changed little, for the Portuguese traded on the coast, both as regards imports and exports, in Indian Ocean products, international, political links were created for the first time. These links are symbolized in the letters from the Portuguese king in far-off Lisbon or Madrid to his officials on the coast. The Portuguese presence drew in other Europeans as they also entered the Indian Ocean. English and French traders visited the coast in the seventeenth century, and the Dutch even attacked Mozambique.

Middle East political interest in the coast was in part a reaction to Portuguese policies, though the Ottoman empire was expansionist anyway, and even without the Portuguese may well have taken an interest in the area. Their main thrust was in the 1580s, and was hardly a full-scale effort. Long before this, the Portuguese had been worried about their intentions, for they feared, rightly, that any Turkish expedition would receive support from local people. In 1542, João de Sepúlveda undertook a punitive expedition to the north coast, as far as Mogadishu, as there had been rumors that the Turks were coming, and without a show of force "all the said coast would have risen in their favour."[61]

This is precisely what happened during two small, but very successful, expeditions led by Mir Ali Bey in 1585–86 and 1588–89. These were as much privateering as official conquest attempts, though the contemporary Diogo do Couto claimed that the main objective was to get access to mangrove poles, lumber being in short supply in the Red Sea area.[62] On the first occasion, Mir Ali Bey had one very cranky old ship and fifty men, yet he still managed to give the Portuguese a major fright. He also demonstrated how disliked they were, for all the local rulers, except that of loyal Malindi, rose in his favor. His second expedition had five ships and again achieved great success. He made an attempt to establish a permanent Turkish base in Mombasa. Such a base would have been catastrophic for the Portuguese, who responded by paying much more attention to the north coast than they ever had before. They built Fort Jesus in Mombasa, begun in 1593 and completed many years later.[63] It was the Portuguese who had introduced the notion of client sultans and direct foreign conquest of particular port cities, but they would not permit the Turks to emulate this pattern.

The Ottomans were followed, from late in the seventeenth century, by the Omanis. An early sign of their success was their epic siege of Fort Jesus itself. This major setback for the Portuguese, signaling the end of their influence on the north coast, began in March 1696. The fort finally fell in December 1698, despite massive attempts to succor it from Goa. Thus, the Portuguese were succeeded by a Muslim power based in Oman, and later Zanzibar, that impacted much more dramatically on the area. The key point, however, is that from the time of da Gama the coast was linked into a wider political world that provided an overarching commonality all around the littoral of the ocean. The fall of Mombasa to the Omanis was really just one sea power replacing another.

The trading network in which these Swahili port cities participated was complex. Here, I concentrate on the seaward, Afrasian Sea, aspect, leaving connections with the interior for chapter 3. Some idea of the seaward connections, and of the major role Gujarat played in it, can be gained from the descriptions by Duarte Barbosa, one of our best observers of the coast early in the sixteenth century. Barbosa wrote of Zanzibar and Pemba that the elite "are clad in very fine silk and cotton garments which they purchase at Mombaça from the Cambaya merchants." Mombasa had a large trade, "and also great ships both of those which come from Çofala and those which go thither and others which come from the great kingdom of Cambaya and from Melynde."[64] When Almeida sacked Mombasa, he found "a great number of very rich cloths, of silk and gold, carpets and saddle-cloths, especially one carpet that cannot be bettered anywhere and which was sent to the king of Portugal."[65] In Malindi, Barbosa claimed that the Muslim inhabitants "are great barterers, and deal in cloth, gold, ivory, and divers other wares with the Moors and Heathen of the great kingdom of Cambay; and to their haven come every year many ships with cargoes of merchandise, from which they get great store of gold, ivory and wax. In this traffic, the Cambay merchants make great profits and thus, on one side and the other, they earn much money. There is great plenty of food in this city," including wheat imported from Cambay.[66]

Barbosa hints here at a trade in necessities. In this category, we have wheat from India, lumber taken to the Red Sea, and rice grown locally but not for local consumption but to sell to the Portuguese.[67] Nor was wheat eaten by these coastal Africans. When da Gama was in Malindi, he asked for wheat, but the king told him this was not a trade item. The Gujarati merchants imported it, but only for their own consumption. When Pedro Alvares Cabral reached Malindi in 1500, he found that the helpful sultan had imported wheat from Gujarat especially for them.[68] Similarly, the Portuguese on Mozambique Island, at least at the end of the century, had to import their own grain and rice and corn from India.[69] Perhaps the best known of the long-distance trades in an essential product was the lumber trade from the northern Swahili coast to the lumber-deficit Red Sea and Hadramaut areas. This humble trade has been ignored by most historians, who have preferred to concentrate on gold, ivory, and slaves, yet the economic and political consequences of it were profound.[70]

Most trade in necessities did not take place over long distances. As one would expect, there was a large trade in foodstuffs and necessities all up and down the coast. Many of the port cities were food-deficit areas and relied on supplies brought either by land or sea. Even water had to be imported to Mozambique Island sometimes. In 1591, Sir James Lancaster, the first Englishman in the area, while cruising around Mozambique came across small local boats laden with such homely items as grain, maize, hens, ducks, and water.[71] Generally, this humble, and essential, trade has been submerged in the records by the more glamorous long-distance items, to which we now turn.

In this period before massive slave trading, ivory ranked with gold as the main export. African ivory was considered by consumers in both India and China to be especially workable, and well patterned, much to be preferred over Indian or Sri Lankan ivory. The trade was large indeed. We analyze in detail where the product came from in chapter 3. Suffice for now to note figures generated by P. F. Thorbahn, who lists ivory exports from Sofala and Mozambique for several years over the two centuries. Broadly, these ran from 23,000 kg in 1520; to 121,000 in 1546; 39,000 in 1552; 44,000 in 1609; and 110,000 in 1679.[72] Goa's great savant, Garcia da Orta, claimed a total importation to India of 330,000 kg,[73] a figure which seems extraordinary. However, it may be that he, unlike Thorbahn, was trying to include illegal, unofficial, imports as well as that quantity counted by the officials. In other words, he may have tried to estimate the total trade done by locals and by Portuguese, rather than just that done under the auspices of the Portuguese state.

Comparatively vast quantities of cloths were taken into east Africa from Gujarat. Again, I present data to give an impression of quantities, in order to show this part of economic linkages across the ocean. As one example, in the early seventeenth century the Portuguese found the cloth market in the Zambezi Valley was over-supplied, so they proposed limiting imports strictly to 700 *bars*. This one region, then, imported 280,000 pieces of cloth.[74] More generally, when Almeida sacked the greatest city on the coast, Mombasa, in 1505, "great wealth was burned, for it was from here that the trade with Sofala and Cambay was carried on by sea. . . . And there were in the city quantities of cotton cloth from Cambay because all this coast dresses in these cloths and has no others."[75]

Cloth was a vital component in the trade all up and down the coast, and far inland too. In this nonmonetized world, it, along with weights of gold, often served as currency. However, the relativities are also important. These imports were vital for east Africa, but in their place of origin, Gujarat, the trade to east Africa was a rather minor one. Tomé Pires noted, in a much-quoted passage, that "Cambay chiefly stretches out two arms, with her right arm she reaches out towards Aden and with the other towards Malacca, as the most important places to sail to, and the other places are held to be of less importance."[76] E. A. Alpers has estimated that only 4 percent of the total export trade of western India was with east Africa.[77]

Gold is a rather different sort of trade good. Only gold traveled long distances and was affected by very distant market forces; only gold was a truly international commodity. This is not to say that gold from east Africa made up a large part of new supplies in the total world economy, but it was still significant.

We have some amazing estimates of gold production before the arrival of the Portuguese. Duarte quotes Ian Phimister as saying that the total pre-Portuguese gold production from the Zimbabwe Plateau was between 6 and 9 million ounces.[78] This estimate seems to be quite fabulous, for if we convert at one ounce to 28.3 grams, then we have between 170 and 254 tonnes, though it should be noted that this is over a very long period. Production began slowly at the start of the tenth century, or perhaps earlier, and was at its height in the eleventh to fifteenth centuries; it then declined drastically. Placer mining, that is, washing from alluvium, was most common at first, but later, quite sophisticated reef-mining techniques were also employed. This gold was exported through Sofala but marketed at Kilwa, up to 10 tons a year before the decline late in the fifteenth century.[79] A well-informed Portuguese claimed in 1506 that when the land was at peace at least 1 million, and up to 1.3 million, *maticals* of gold were exported each year from Sofala; another 50,000 came from Angoche, bringing the totals to a maximum of 5,744 kg (that is, 5.7 tonnes).[80]

What data do we have for gold exports in the sixteenth century, once the Portuguese had arrived and we get slightly better figures? Vitorino Magalhães Godinho quotes with some skepticism a figure for exports from Sofala and Kilwa of gold originating inland in the Mutapa state of 8,500 kg a year. For later years, he quotes the following figures for kilograms of gold from these mines being exported to Goa: 1585, 573 kg; 1591, 716 kg; 1610, 850 kg; 1667, 1487 kg.[81] Manuel Lobato provides some confirmation, for he finds about 830 kg coming to Goa around 1600.[82] A Portuguese calculation of 1614 said the trade was worth about 400,000 *pardaus*, in other words, a little over 1,000 kg.[83] S.I.G. Mudenge claims the following: 8,000 kg in 1500, falling rapidly to 6,000 around 1510, 3,500 at 1550, less than 1,000 in 1600, a slow rise to 1500 kg around 1670, and then a decline again.[84]

What is beyond doubt is that gold exports that came to the attention of the Portuguese fell very rapidly soon after their arrival. Chittick claims that in 1512–15 the Portuguese got only 12,500 maticals (53 kg) a year.[85] This decline was mostly a result of "smuggling," and its prevalence in the sixteenth century means that official Portuguese figures need to be used with caution, as they are certainly too low to show total exports.

C. R. Boxer claims that in 1511 three-quarters of the gold exported from Sofala evaded the purported royal monopoly.[86] A year earlier, a Portuguese official wrote that the king had received no gold from Sofala this year, but the unofficial and so illegal trade amounted to over 30,000 maticals (128 kg).[87] Bashir Ahmed Datoo noted copious smuggling by both local Portuguese and by Swahili traders. The Gujarati traders often paid for the gold with cloth. The cloth was imported to the northern Swahili coast by Gujaratis, traded in ports not controlled by the Portuguese, and then taken south of Cape Delgado by local craft, especially to Angoche.[88] As noted, it was not only local traders who exported gold "illegally"; Portuguese did, too.

J.E.G. Sutton has recently raised the matter of demand for this gold.[89] He claims that European demand for gold was at its height from about 1250 to 1350, as states transferred to a gold standard. Subsequently, a slump in Europe, caused largely by the Black Death, reduced demand, which revived again only in the early fifteenth century. I would agree that demand, even for gold, can vary, as fluctuations in its price show. However, Sutton's focus on European demand seems misplaced. Rather, we should be looking for variations in demand, if any, in the Indian Ocean area, and especially in India itself. A more obvious international dimension was Spanish discoveries of gold, and then silver, in the Americas in the sixteenth century, which made east African gold less competitive; for this reason gold declined, as we have noted, and ivory became much more important.[90]

We can make few generalizations about the size of gold exports because the figures are so sparse, and the amount of smuggling so indeterminable that any broad trends are obscured. If we take a lower figure than Boxer's, say 50 percent, for smuggling during the course of the sixteenth century, and if we estimate, with a huge margin of error, exports that the Portuguese knew about at 6,000 kg in 1510 and 1,000 in 1600, we then would have perhaps 12,000 kg a year being exported at the beginning of the sixteenth century, and 2,000 at the end. It must be noted that Godinho produces a much lower estimate, for he says that exports never fell below 500 kg between 1500 and 1650, and were never more than 1,500 kg.[91] However, these are amounts which the Portuguese knew about, and take no account of "smuggling." My conclusion here is fairly close to Mudenge's estimates noted above.

Finally, it is important to note that all this gold stayed in the Indian Ocean area.[92] What was collected by the Portuguese was taken to Goa, and thence presumably flowed to other Asian areas. Given Goa's massive trade with Gujarat, most of it probably ended up there or was taken from there to north India. We have no records of the Portuguese taking any gold back to Portugal. Similarly, exports outside the Portuguese system must have gone to Gujarat, or to the Red Sea area.

We can compare these very crude figures with data from other areas to put it into some sort of perspective. In the peak years of west African gold production, from 1500 to 1520, the Portuguese received about 700 kg a year.[93] Two centuries later, from 1712 to 1755, the Portuguese exported well over 10,000 kg a year from Brazil to Portugal.[94] Spanish American exports in the sixteenth century were also large: about 900 kg a year in the 1510s, 2,500 in the 1540s, and a high of 4,300 in the 1550s.[95] In the later seventeenth century, Japan also exported large quantities of gold: 4,000 kg a year in the 1660s, 11,500 in the next decade, and then a steady decline to 3,000 in the 1680s.[96] A. Kobata's figures for total world production of gold per year in the period from 1521 to 1640 produces a rough average of about 7.75 tonnes a year.[97] The most we can hazard by way of conclusion is that exports from the Mutapa state were substantial, and that, so far, they have not been adequately discussed in the literature.

We have described a vast exchange of Indian products with those from east Africa. What is interesting about this exchange is that it was relatively localized, when we take account of the extent of the Indian Ocean. East Africa's exports came mostly only from the south of the area, though we will have to look more closely at ivory exports from the north presently. The great market for ivory was India, though an unspecified amount also went to the Middle East and to China; we have no way of knowing how much. The other main export, lumber, seems to have been exclusively consumed in the wood-deficit Hadramaut and Red Sea areas. As for imports, it is remarkable how dominant were Indian goods: textiles, and not just cotton cloths, and beads. We have almost no record of significant imports from any other area to east Africa.

Monsoon winds are often cited as a unifying force around this ocean. All sailing ships must dance to the same tune, their voyages dictated by the prevailing, invariable, winds. No ship can sail off the west coast of India during the southwest monsoon, from June to September. The passage from India to east Africa must be undertaken when the northeast monsoon is prevalent. We are told there are wider implications, particularly that the predictability of the winds and so the voyages dictated that merchants leave agents in the port cities of the Indian Ocean, who throughout the year could buy when the market was low rather than be constrained by the need to buy a cargo quickly so as not to miss the return monsoon.

Abdul Sheriff, an historian, and Datoo, a geographer, both people who have lived on the coast, have produced the two most detailed accounts of the monsoons. Many authorities stress the divide of the coast at Cape Delgado, which is just south of the mouth of the Ruvuma River, which forms the boundary today between Tanzania and Mozambique. (I use this divide when I refer to the north and south Swahili coasts.) As a rule of thumb, down to Cape Delgado is one monsoon from Arabia and India; south of there, there are two. The northeast monsoon, called the Kas Kazi in Swahili, starts in November and one can leave the Arabian coast at this time and reach at least Mogadishu. However, the eastern Arabian Sea has violent tropical storms in October and November, so for a voyage from India to the coast, it was best to leave in December, by which time the northeast monsoon was well established as far south as Zanzibar, so that a rapid passage of twenty to twenty-five days could be expected. By March, the northeast monsoon was beginning to break up in the south, and by April the prevailing wind was from the southwest, known as the Kusi. This was the season for sailing from the coast to the north and east. At its height, in June and July, the weather was too stormy, so departures were normally either as this monsoon built up in May, or at its tail end in August. Vasco da Gama, fortuitously, was able to leave Malindi for India at exactly the right time, that is, April 24, and consequently had an easy passage of twenty-seven days to Calicut. It is important to note that both monsoons prevailed longer the further north on the coast one was. Lamu, for example, had excellent reliable winds.[98]

The documentation is full of incidents that demonstrate the practical effects of this regime. As one example, in March 1612, the Portuguese were worried that the Dutch might attack Mozambique, so they brought troops from Tete to defend it. The troops stayed until October, and then went back upriver for the Portuguese knew the monsoon for reaching Mozambique from the south, the southwest monsoon, had passed.[99]

All sailors knew of these winds. Arab geographers produced sailing directions to advise when to sail to where; the Portuguese produced comparable *roteiros* (sailing guides), the northern Europeans their rutters.[100] These were written by experienced sailors, yet even so they can be misleading. There are two problems: first, that the winds are not quite as regular as these books say, and, second, that it really depends what you are trying to do on the monsoons: Different people need different monsoons.

The depiction of an almost mechanical regime, one you could count on, does not always apply, as contemporary documentation makes clear. In particular, in the south, the southwest monsoon is not nearly as strong and predictable as one may expect if one believes the writings of landlubbers. The important Mozambiquean archaeologist, Ricardo Teixeira Duarte, an experienced sailor, says that the much-fabled southwest monsoon is only useful when there is a cold front in the south. Up to Mozambique Island there was really no monsoon. Square-rigged ships had to wait for the occasional cold front from Antarctica, take it until it petered out, and then wait for the next one.[101] Even in Lamu, the winds vary from day to day, and from hour to hour within the day. There are seasons to be sure, but they vary greatly. The Indian experience is similar; every time we read of a bad monsoon in India, this means that the winds have not behaved in the clockwork-like fashion the books tell us they should.

Second, different monsoons suit different people. In particular, the Portuguese not only had to cross the Afrasian Sea but they had to get around the Cape of Good Hope into the Atlantic. This, along with other factors, dictated their interest in Mozambique, for ships coming from the Atlantic could call there to get supplies and then sail on to India much more easily than they could by calling at the alternative, Malindi, which for Portuguese purposes was too far north. Mozambique thus became an important trade center, much more so than it had been in pre-Portuguese times. As François Pyrard de Laval put it picturesquely, "You might call it a sentinel or a bulwark at the entering in of the Indies, or a kind of hostelry for the refreshing of the Portuguese, worn out with a long and toilsome voyage."[102] Letters from the king frequently describe Mozambique as "one of the most important bases I have in India," both as a way station and as a base to pursue the chimera of an El Dorado in the interior.[103] The Dutch equivalent, after 1652, was their settlement at the Cape of Good Hope.

Two other geographical matters further modified the role of the monsoons and determined when and where sailing ships, the main links joining the shores of the ocean, could operate. One was sea currents. Horton notes that the east African coastal current, which travels all year at about 2 knots, turns east into the Indian Ocean close to Lamu. In order to avoid this current, ships from the Middle East would terminate their voyages there. Their cargoes were taken on in smaller ships that could avoid these currents by sailing close to or inside the coral reefs.[104] Sheriff provides a rather different account. He claims that the current is seasonal. Around April, it hits the coast near Cape Delgado, and splits to a strong north-flowing current that is good for going north, and a south-flowing one that hinders sailing north from, for example, Mozambique.[105]

The final modifier was the nature of the coast itself, which interacted with wind and current to determine when and where ships could sail. Keep in mind the great length of this coast, some 3,000 km from Inhambane to Lamu, or from 2 degrees north latitude to 16 or even 22 degrees south latitude. By contrast, the west coast of India, from Kanya Kumari (Cape Comorin) to Cambay is only 1,500 km. Coral reefs shadow the coast most of the way and extend as far south as Inhaca Island, off modern Maputo. These reefs are not continuous, and gaps in them have made it possible for coastal craft to sail inside the reef, hugging the coastline and avoiding the worst of the monsoons. Yet the reefs can also be hazardous for an inexperienced navigator. It has been claimed that Sofala was not favored by the Portuguese in part because reefs made it a poor anchorage. On the other hand, the reefs compensated for the general lack of good harbors on the coast, for inside them was calm water, and even large ships could be beached, unloaded, and then refloated on the tide.

I have described how small boats sailed far up the Zambezi River, but this, apart from the Tana River, was the only river in our area navigable for any distance, and it will be remembered that there was a gorge between Sena and Tete, and past Tete the impassable Cabora Bassa rapids. For that matter, the entrance to the river was a hazardous one, for the area is low-lying marshy delta country, with endless mudbanks and shifting navigation channels. To find the right one, one that did not end in a mangrove swamp, was a task for an experienced navigator. Yet, the general interaction between many factors can be seen right here. On the one hand, the Zambezi was difficult to navigate, and was located too far south to be reached on one monsoon, but on the other hand, the river gave access to the gold, ivory, and slaves of its vast basin, and thus the difficulties had to be overcome. Conversely, the ports of the much more favorable northern coast provided easy access, but they acted only as redistribution areas because comparable products were not available in the interior.

If geography provided both a link and an obstacle for the coast, so did Islam. Several authors have found religion to be the great common denominator of the coast and of the wider maritime world of Asia. While this is often asserted, it is surprising how few attempts there have been to draw on the work of scholars working in related and comparable areas, both with respect to the process and meaning of conversion, and to the implications of these conversions for creating unity around the shores of the ocean. In particular, Islam was spreading in the Malay world at the same time as in east Africa, and the process of conversion shows some remarkable parallels, which can serve to show the advantages of comparative research.

There are several main themes of research on the Islamization of southeast Asia, including a substantial literature devoted merely to trying to work out when and where the first conversion occurred or the first mosque was built.[106] Other scholars have stressed the worldwide dimensions of the religion and the importance of the central focus of Mecca. Islam is described as a uniquely centralized religion, where holy men and scholars from the center had much prestige in outer areas, while people from outer areas strove to visit the holy cities. All this is tied up with the role of the surprisingly large numbers of Muslims who in the early modern period visited Mecca either to make the hajj, or to study for long periods, or both. Another area of southeast Asia studies accounts for how the religion spread through the mediation of traders. Muslim trading groups would take with them their own spiritual preceptors, called *caciz* in the Portuguese documentation, and these men, often members of *sufi* orders, would not only service their own merchants but also would spread the faith. This was true with all traveling Muslims, for it would be incorrect to see a clear role differentiation between a proselytizer and a merchant; rather, men oscillated between one role and the other, depending on circumstance.

Related to this theme is the way trade and politics intersected. Frequently, the controller of a southeast Asian port city would be pressured to convert by visiting Muslim merchants, who might even threaten to trade elsewhere unless this were done. Hence, the elite converted, the religion trickled down to the other residents of the ports, and then spread to the countryside. Finally, there are numerous southeast Asia studies that focus on the quality of Islam. This is a dubious matter indeed. Scholars, often not Muslims but rather western Orientalists, erect a scaffolding of "pure" Islam, based on the Quran and such claimed fundamentals as the "Five Pillars" of the faith. Islamic practice in southeast Asia, and all over the Muslim world, is then measured against this ideal yardstick, and deviations are roundly condemned as being un-Islamic or syncretic. Ironically, these rigid interpretations of Islam by westerners have been joined in the last few decades by equally rigid and dogmatic interpretations by Muslim revivalists.

There has been considerable public interest in the date of the first conversions and the beginnings of an Islamic presence in east Africa. Archaeologists have found a public role as they find earlier and earlier mosques. The record shows that there were trading contacts from the Arab world to east Africa before the beginnings of Islam. For the first century of the Christian era, the famous Greek nautical guide, the *Periplus of the Erythrean Sea*, mentions extensive contacts between east Africa and Yemen, and also notes that there was extensive intercourse and intermarriage between these Arab traders and the locals. Pre-Islamic ceramics from the Middle East have been found in both Somalia and Mozambique. These are mostly Persian of the Sassanian period. While it is true that Sassanian styles continued after Persia was converted, it seems clear that some of this pottery is pre-Islamic.[107] As these traders converted, they kept on trading, to east Africa among many other places. The very earliest mosques, dating perhaps to the mid or even early eighth century, were constructed to service these itinerants, some of whom may even have settled. The mosques were very small, and made of nondurable materials: wood or wattle and daub. Horton's work on Shanga shows that the initial phase of mosque building there was late in the eighth century.[108] More recently, Horton claims that an early mosque on Pemba Island is probably from the early eighth century.[109]

The early Muslim accounts of east Africa indicate that the locals had not converted. The tenth-century collection of Arab stories, *The Book of the Wonders of India*, describes "Zanj" as a strange wild place, with sorcerers, cannibals, strange birds, and fishes.[110] In the early eleventh century, Al-Biruni still seems to find east Africa a wild, strange, and largely un-Islamic place.[111] The locals were converted from the later eleventh century. Only then can we talk of a Swahili civilization, that is, if we follow Middleton and see a defining characteristic of the Swahili being that they are Muslims.[112] During the eleventh century, wooden mosques at Kilwa were enlarged and constructed in stone. By around 1300, the main mosque at Kilwa was some 12 meters by 30 meters, implying a very large Muslim resident population.[113] H. T. Wright has pointed out that all the larger communities seem to have accepted Islam at roughly the same time, that is, primarily in the twelfth century and a few years on either side of this. He suggests that Islam was spread not by settlers from the Middle East, nor by missionaries, but rather that the origins of Swahili Islam are endogenous to the coast, the result of some common factor in the larger Swahili communities.[114] Whatever this may have been, his discussion raises the second matter outlined above, namely, the international dimension of Islam in east Africa and worldwide.

John Obert Voll has reflected on the world-system debate. He suggests that we should get away from what he sees as an overemphasis on material exchanges and look at other elements that tie different areas together. An example is the Muslim world from about 1000 to 1800, which he calls "a special example of a large-scale human group."

> This pattern of communication in the Islamic world is not primarily based upon exchange of goods, coordination of means of production, or a large network of economic activities. Instead, it is built on the shared sources of the Islamic experience, which provide the basis for mutually intelligible discourse among all who identify themselves as Muslims within the Dar al-Islam. . . . The Muslims might be said to have created the "Islamic world-system," identified by a distinctive set of sociomoral symbols for the definition of proper human relationships. . . . I am suggesting that both [the modern world-system and the Islamic world-

> system] are relatively comprehensive social systems that can qualify as world-systems, even though the primary identifying characteristics are drawn from different dimensions of the social system as a whole.[115]

The cosmopolitan, international, aspect of Islam has often been cited as a prime motivation for conversion. Coastal people especially find their indigenous beliefs, localized and very specific, to be inadequate as their world expands. When they are exposed to a universal faith, in this case, Islam as represented in their foreign business partners, the attraction is obvious and can be widely seen all over the Malay world at this same time. Nurse and Spear put this well for the Swahili:

> Many townspeople . . . operated in a wider world than the microcosm of the village, living in towns with other peoples, sailing from town to town along the coast, and trading with people from across the Indian Ocean. These people lived in a macrocosmic world inhabited by peoples speaking different languages, having different ancestors, and working in different occupations. In this world the beliefs of the microcosm were too parochial; what was needed were beliefs that were universal. And so townspeople began to adopt Islam, and in so doing they adopted a set of beliefs and a framework for action that were held in common by others in the town, by people in other towns, and by people from the whole Indian Ocean world.[116]

After Islam became established, links to the center became very important. The center can be political, or religious, or both. The most obvious center is Mecca itself, and this is most clearly symbolized by the way Muslims face toward Mecca when they pray, and by the pilgrimage. Unfortunately, I have found no evidence of Swahili people at this time undertaking this pious obligation, but it would be extraordinary if they did not. What we do have are indications of other connections with the wider Islamic world. In Kilwa in 1331, Ibn Battuta found that *sharifs* (religious specialists) came from Iraq and the Hijaz to profit from the pious generosity of the sultan.[117] In 1507, the Portuguese tried to communicate with the ruler of Oja, in the Tana River area, but he refused communication with those who cruelly persecuted peaceful Muslim traders going about their lawful business. His only overlord, he defiantly proclaimed, was the caliph in Cairo. This demonstrates a far-flung Muslim network, and a local ruler who was very well informed on power and authority in the wider Muslim world.[118] In the fourteenth and fifteenth centuries, Hadrami *sayyids* (prestigious Muslims) were influential, which meant that Muslims on the coast were predominantly influenced by the *shafi'i* school of law, and this continued despite the influence of the Omani rulers from the eighteenth century.[119] B. G. Martin has done an excellent study of flows and interaction and movement back and forth of holy men and others between east Africa and Yemen and the Hadramaut.[120]

Within the Swahili world itself there were recognized prestigious scholars and saints, men who had area-wide reputations. Around 1570, Monclaro noted that "a Moorish caciz, the greatest in the entire coast," resided in Pate.[121] In Malindi, da Gama's expedition found a sharif, whom they equated, slightly incorrectly, with a priest, and they also captured some "books of the Law," presumably a Quran.[122] A sharif in Zanzibar in 1591 was described as a priest; he was very much respected by the local king.[123]

The Portuguese were vehemently opposed to Islam, and they struggled to decrease its influence, at least at the official level. Seizing the "books of the Law" is one example of how they operated. It is possible that their activities hindered contact between the Islamic heartland and the coast. If so, this in turn would tend to increase the indigenization of Swahili Islam. Certainly this seems to be implied in an account of 1588. A traveler claimed that "the Mahometans that at this present doe inhabite those Countries [Sofala], are not naturally borne there, but before the Portugals came into those quarters, they Trafficked thither in small Barkes, from the Coast of Arabia Felix. And when the Portugals had conquered that Realme, the Mahometans stayed there still, and now they are become neither utter Pagans, nor holding the Sect of Mahomet."[124] This was reversed in the eighteenth century with the rise of the Omanis, for as their influence spread, the wider Islamic world had a strong impact on the coast.[125] In any case, it seems that here, as in many other areas, there is an important difference between the northern and southern Swahili coasts, with the divide at Cape Delgado. In the north, the Portuguese were less successful, especially in the Lamu area. In the sixteenth century, Pate continued to have close ties with the Islamic heartland, and Islam there was strengthened by the arrival of religious leaders from southern Arabia, the Red Sea area, and the Banadir coast. Pate was a center of the faith, of conversion drives further south, and of opposition to the activities of the Augustinians who operated on the north Swahili coast. Consequently there was no church at Pate.[126]

The notion that east Africa was colonized by Muslims, who created trading or even political empires on the coast that had nothing to do with the interior but rather were foreign enclaves looking outward across the ocean, has been dismissed over the last few decades. Current theory sees the Swahili as intrinsically and completely African. Yet this can go too far, as perhaps Horton does in the following analysis: "The East African coast was always inhabited by African communities, who in time gradually absorbed the culture and teachings of Islam as they were drawn into contact through commercial dealings and missionary activities. . . . [The visitors had] no interest in either conquest or settlement but rather in the establishment of reliable local trading partners. . . . But for direct settlement by these traders there is no evidence. . . . Asiatic colonisation of the East African coast remains . . . an unlikely and unproven hypothesis."[127]

We can look at the question of settlement. Colonization implies dominance, and is certainly not an appropriate term for east Africa at this time, but the records do show that Middle Eastern traders settled in, and indeed were influential in, the Swahili towns. From their ranks came rulers, and it was their presence that encouraged the spread of the faith. Monclaro, himself a religious specialist and therefore keen to know the enemy, claimed there were three divisions among the Muslim population of the coast around 1570: "All the Moors in this coast are white-cap Moors, there being three castes in India, some wearing a coif [*carapuça*], others a cap [*barretinho*] and others a toque [*touca*]. The latter ones are of better quality." Later, in Sena, he described ten Muslims *de touca*, honored and rich men.[128] Muslims of Indian origin also resided in east Africa, as da Gama found in 1498. He captured a Muslim agent of a great trader, and this captive, who hailed from Cambay, led them to Sofala.[129]

The Portuguese distinguished between sojourners and indigenous people. Fernão Lopes de Castanheda's account of da Gama's voyage noted many Arabian Muslims in Malindi; he calls them *estrangeiros*, "foreigners," as opposed to *gente natural*, or "natives."[130] An eyewitness account of this same voyage found, in Mozambique, well-dressed local Muslim merchants, who "have transactions with white Muslims." Four vessels belonging to the latter were in port at the time.[131] Yet the contemporary chronicler Barros claimed that in Mozambique "the inhabitants were Moors from other parts."[132] Portugal's national poet, Luís Vaz de Camoens, glossed this in an even more extreme fashion, claiming that they told da Gama, "We are foreigners here too, and having nothing in common with the natives. They are pagans, and uncivilized. We are Moslems of the true faith, like the rest of the world."[133] To add to the confusion in our sources, another contemporary writer described the Muslim grandees in Mozambique as the children of local Africans and white Muslim merchants, who had traded for many years in all these lands, and had become natives.[134]

Writing about Sofala in the early sixteenth century, Barbosa says: "These

Moors are black and some of them tawny; some of them speak Arabic but the more part use the language of the country." In Kilwa, a much wealthier town, the Muslim population were olive, some black, some white, and very well dressed: "These Moors speak Arabic, they believe in the legend of the Alcoran, and are great worshippers of Mohamed, which is their sect [*seita*]."[135] Another account from early in the century says that Kilwa was a big town. The natives were black, the foreigners white, and all spoke Arabic.[136] In the 1580s, J. H. van Linschoten said of Kilwa: "This Island is inhabited by Mahometans, and they are all most white apparelled in silk and clothes of cotton wooll: their women weare bracelets of gold and precious stones about their neckes and armes: they have great quantitie of silver workes, and are not so browne as the men, and well membered: their houses are commonly made of stone, chalke, and wood, with pleasant gardens of all kind of fruit and sweet flowers."[137] Yet, around the same time, another source describes the ruler of Kilwa as being black.[138] The same distinction between foreign and local was made early in the century with reference to Angoche. A Portuguese official said that the Muslims of this area were a real worry because they continued to trade outside the Portuguese system. The problem was not the local converts, "those of the land here in Mozambique," for they were primitive people. "These others who do the damage are merchants and foreigners, one from Ormuz, another from Aden, others from other parts and they are men of knowledge who have traded all their lives and these are the ones who should be expelled."[139]

Knowledge of Arabic was one way to identify a settler from the Middle East, or someone thoroughly assimilated to Islam, as compared with a recent convert. It is significant then that an early Portuguese voyage came across twenty-five Muslims in almadias and, though they had many interpreters, they could not understand them.[140] As they must have had an Arabic-knowing interpreter, these people must have been local converts speaking Shona or some other Bantu language. To add to what is a very complex situation, in 1570, Monclaro wrote of Malindi that the Muslims were very friendly to the Portuguese, "and in their condition and features there is no difference from our people; many of them speak Portuguese very well, this being our chief centre of trade with them."[141]

The link between trade and conversion is mentioned occasionally in the sources, though they are not as informative as are comparable ones from southeast Asia. We cannot, for example, reconstruct the history of Kilwa as we can what may well be its analogue, the port city and Islamic center of Melaka. Similarly, Horton has suggested that Pemba may have acted like Melaka, as the great diffusion center for its region, but we have no firm evidence of this yet. Several of the accounts we have already quoted note the connection between trade links and conversions, and the Dutch observer Linschoten set this out very clearly. He noted of the local people that "Many of them hold the law of Mahomet, that is to say, such as dwell on the coast of Abex or Melinde, and round about those places, as also in Mosambique, by reason the red sea is so neere unto them, together with the Arabian Mahometans, with whome they dayly traffique."[142] In a related matter, this time conversions to Christianity, we find fascinating echoes not only from southeast Asian history but also from Japan, where Catholic priests did very well in the sixteenth century because it seemed to the *daimyo* (feudal barons) that they opened up access to trade. In 1559, a Jesuit claimed that the son of the king of Inhambane was very eager to convert for he was keen to have dealings and commerce with the Portuguese.[143] So also for conversions to Islam in east Africa.[144]

The final matter is the quality of Islam debate, where text-based scholars erect normative standards and then measure real people against them. In the case of east Africa, J. S. Trimingham was the main culprit. He used his version of "pure" Islam to test and condemn east African Islam. He found no indigenous input. "Islam in East Africa . . . bears many of the characteristics of a foreign religion." In the creation of the Swahili, "African culture was the passive element, and Islam brought the vital cohesive element." He sees Islamic institutions as "unyielding," and notes, astoundingly, that "By adopting Islam the African entered into history."[145]

The situation on the ground seems to have been a much more relaxed and informal one, where we can see at least dimly the development of a distinctively Swahili version of Islam. Much of our information for this period comes from censorious Portuguese missionaries, who took a malicious delight in finding fault with the observance of Islam on the coast. In March 1498, the ambassador of the king of Malindi was "a white Moor and sharif, that is priest, and at the same time a great drunkard."[146] On one occasion, a Jesuit father went to the mosque at Mozambique to debate with a man who had already been chosen as their future grand imam (*cacis o maior*). He claims to have routed this Muslim, for he was very ill-informed. Among other things, he thought Muhammad was the first man created by God.[147] Later in the sixteenth century, another cleric said the sailors on the coastal craft were very fond of wine, "and are only Moors in name and in the practice of circumcism, as they neither know nor keep the creed of Mohamed that they profess."[148] Francis Xavier, in Malindi in 1542, was told by the chief caciz that the locals were very slack. Once there had been sixteen mosques, but now there were only three, and these little frequented and badly served.[149]

These depictions may be the beginning of the evolution of east African Islam; on the other hand, they may be examples of partial conversions. These people were "neither utter Pagans, nor holding the Sect of Mahomet." Among local converts there was little clear differentiation between the converted and their Shona or Bantu fellows. Dos Santos wrote about this in some detail, and complained that local Christians similarly retained many *Kaffir* ideas and customs.[150] Indeed, a rather promiscuous mingling of Muslims and Christians, and people who were neither, is much commented on, and no doubt should warn us not to categorize people too sharply at this time.[151]

Whether or not these people followed some idealized normative version of Islam, they were still, even if sometimes tenuously, tied in by their religion to a wider world, one that stretched all around the shores of the ocean, all of these places being connected to the center in the Hijaz. Thus, traders and travelers from all over the Muslim world, of whom Ibn Battuta is the most famous, found a familiar environment on the coast. This final link, along with political and economic ties, may reinforce the notion of a distinctive and differentiated littoral society.

Chapter 3

The Swahili Coast and the Interior

The Swahili ports had relations with three distinct areas: the interior, the coast, and those countries and peoples across the ocean. So far we have looked at the last two; it is now time to look westward in order to investigate connections between coast and interior. Three separate areas can be illuminated by such an investigation. First, the connections between the Swahili people on the coast and their fellow Bantu-speakers in the interior, as discussed in chapter 1, have important implications for modern politics and for the position of Swahili people in independent African countries. Second, the rather empirical and economic matter of establishing how, if at all, the port cities of the coast were geared in to the interior is the subject of this chapter. Finally, this matter has a powerful resonance when we turn to political economy analyses of the Indian Ocean in the early modern period, and this, especially world-system theory, is addressed in chapter 4.

There are several ways in which a discussion of connections between coast and interior is a comparative exercise. By drawing on some low-level theory, or at least more rigorous attempts at definition, one can demonstrate the utility of comparisons when they are modestly underlaid by some general concepts. The comparisons are between India and east Africa, and also between the north and south coasts of east Africa. The concepts have to do with the burgeoning literature on port cities.

The comparisons in the literature are plain to see. From the Indian side, there are many attempts to investigate the mechanisms by which goods from the interior were brought to the coast. These are not merely a matter of transportation but of the economic structures evolved in India over many centuries.[1] This sort of work is not possible for east Africa, at least not yet. It is in part a matter of the sources, which are so much richer for India from 1600, thanks to massive English and Dutch documentation, which supplements longer standing Persian sources. Nevertheless, I hope I will be able to use east African sources in a slightly more rigorous and illuminating way than has been the case so far.

The Indian studies that trace the mechanisms by which goods reached the coast or the market have a particular relevance for the southern Swahili coast. In the north, that is, north of Cape Delgado, there are now many claims that the port cities traded far into the interior. I investigate this important matter presently, but there can be no question that the interior in the south was much more linked to the coast than was the case in the north. This has to do with geography as much as anything, but it seems that the difference with India lies in the relative sophistication of trade mechanisms and the development of commercial techniques and expertise there as compared with Africa.

In the Indian scene, the vital link in the economy generally, and especially in linking the interior with the coast, was the figure of the broker. Brokers were especially important in integrating foreign merchants in port cities with the prevailing commercial norms of the port in question. In his seminal article on brokers, A. Jan Qaisar says that they show "the purchaser where to find the goods he requires, and the seller how to exact his price." Qaisar concludes that, "the whole commercial world in India during the 17th century was set in motion by brokers."[2] Ashin Das Gupta depicts the varying roles of brokers in his fine study of Surat. He notes that foreigners needed them more than did locals, but says, "There were in general two kinds of brokers. Every important merchant would have a general broker who took care of the entire range of the merchant's sales and purchasers. It was the function of the general broker to put his principal in touch with another kind of broker who dealt with specific commodities."[3]

Given the vital linking role of brokers in India, it is strange that we find no evidence of their existence in Africa. The only hint I have found in modern works is John Middleton's assertion that "the role of mercantile broker linked culturally to both sides has been filled by the Swahili."[4] There is an immediate problem with this claim. Cultural links must mean links between Muslims, but the Muslim Swahili interacted with non-Muslims in the interior, and to an extent on the coast. I find no evidence of brokers on the Swahili coast. The mechanisms in Africa appear to be much simpler, with producers often merely bringing their product to a market and selling directly to a buyer, or more likely engaging in nonmonetary transactions of simple exchange. It is significant that gold was coined in India, but it was merely exchanged, with the value dictated by weight, in Africa.

This relative lack of sophistication is also to be seen in the matter of political organization. While it can be fruitful to see both Mughal India and the Mutapa state as embedded in tributary modes of production, there can be no question but that the latter was much less articulated, efficient, and penetrative than was its Indian contemporary. The Mughals built on existing precedents to establish a relatively efficient administration, which provided sophisticated methods of extracting revenue from its peasant population. They were able to take a substantial share of rural production as land revenue, a third or even a half of the total product; in most areas, this was collected in cash. As a consequence, the market penetrated right down into rural society in India. As compared with this taxation, the Mutapa state (if indeed this not be too grand a term for a very loose agglomeration) simply demanded tribute, albeit at high rates, from elephant hunters, gold diggers and washers, and traders. The methods involved in extracting this levy were more or less ad hoc, so far as we know, with nothing of the relatively articulated, even bureaucratic, paper-based methods used by the Mughals and other Indian states. The fact that Africa exported only raw materials but imported manufactures has important political economy implications (see chapter 4), but this also points to little need in Africa for the complicated chains of credit provision, bills of exchange, and specialization within the production process that prevailed in India.[5] The fact that the literature on India is more sophisticated than that for Africa appropriately reflects the sophistication of the two economies themselves.

There is another related comparison to be made before we get to specifics. Intermediary or hinge groups in Africa linked the Swahili coast and the interior. These included the Mijikenda, the Vumba, and a host of others. We can delineate quite specific zones and layers of their operation. Some of these have to do with urbanization, for the Swahili are often distinguished from other coastal and near inland inhabitants by the fact they lived in towns. There were no towns in the northern interior, and those in the south, especially those on the Zambezi River system, such as Sena and Tete, should be seen as more coastal than interior. Possibly as a reflection of much greater political disarticulation, there are clear divisions between coast and interior; we will treat the connections presently.

Religion provided another divisor, for the vast majority of east Africa's Muslims were coastal residents, while in India Muslim merchants on the coast had fellow Muslims living inland, and indeed ruling most of India. Thus, in India there is no clear difference between coast and interior. A resident of Surat or Cambay was no different from one who lived in Ahmadabad or Gwalior, and indeed they would have overlapping caste, kin, or occupational connections with people in the interior cities. There were no hinge groups that connected coast and interior. Brokers functioned inland and on the coast, their roles in no way differentiated by location. Merchants in Surat financed production in the interior just as did merchants living inland. While the Indian ports were certainly more cosmopolitan than the inland cities, due to the presence of many foreign merchants, Indian society was much more connected, and hence homogeneous, than was African society. J. C. Heesterman asserts that "the littoral forms a frontier zone that is not there to separate or enclose, but which rather finds its meaning in its permeability."[6] This seems to apply much better to India than to Africa. Indeed, the Indian littoral was so porous, permeable, and open as to hardly be a frontier at all, while in Africa there were very clear divisions.

Our concern now is not with the largely maritime littoral, but rather with the jewels strung along the coast, that is, the port cities. Much has been written about Asian port cities; but until recently not in a helpful way. Many were autonomous, not ruled by the landed empires on whose shores they were often located. Examples include: Hurmuz, Calicut, Aden, and Melaka. Others, however, were fully governed from a distant center: Those in Gujarat are good examples. The autonomous port cities, obviously most directly comparable with Swahili city-states, lived from trade and visiting merchants. Fair conditions, security, low taxes, and considerable autonomy for visiting merchants were characteristic of all of them. This was necessary for there were alternatives. A port city that did not meet the basic needs of visiting merchants would soon be deserted, and would whither away. Most of these autonomous port cities were mere redistribution centers, for they lacked productive inlands, unlike those located within large empires such as those in Gujarat. There was no strong identity between government and merchant as in such European examples as the Hanseatic League or the Italian city-states. In Asia, rulers traded, to be sure, but most of the merchants were "foreign," unlike in Europe where foreigners were increasingly discriminated against.[7]

Over the last decade or so, terminology developed from European studies has percolated into investigations of the Asian port city. The result has been a more self-conscious and productive use of concepts that contribute to comparison and analysis rather than description. The general problem is to be more precise about the frontiers of the sea and the port cities. Years ago, Fernand Braudel wrote poetically about this: "The circulation of men and of goods, both material and intangible, formed concentric circles round the Mediterranean. We should imagine a hundred frontiers, not one, some political, some economic, and some cultural."[8] More recently, S. Arasaratnam has noted that the problem for historians of the Indian Ocean has been to work out "where the coast ends and the hinterland begins and how much of the hinterland is relevant to an understanding of the coast and the ocean." In the 1980s boundaries for maritime historians were pushed inland. "It was now realized that ports and the coast were not isolated areas in which extraneous activity was carried out but that these were integrated in various ways with the states where they were located."[9]

Four concepts have been used in European studies, and have now been taken up by Asianists. First is the geographers' term *umland*. This is defined as: "formerly applied in a general way to surroundings, and included in hinterland; now more precisely applied to an area which is culturally, economically and politically related to a particular town or city."[10] Umland, then, is the immediate surrounding area, directly connected to the city, frequently because it provides foodstuffs for the city. Richard Fox has coined the word *rurban* to describe Indian towns; these surrounding areas, the umland, may be best seen as transitional between the dominant town and the pure countryside.

Port cities have relationships both to the sea and the land. For the former, the term *foreland* is used. The foreland is the areas of the overseas world with which the port is linked through shipping, trade, and passenger traffic. It is separated from the port city by maritime space. The *hinterland* radiates out from the port city inland and so begins at the end of the umland. It is the landed area to which the port's imports go, and from which come its exports. To try and be more specific than this is difficult, as an early attempt showed. A. J. Sargent, writing in 1938, said a general definition is difficult, though one can be quite precise by using statistics for any particular city. One could say that the hinterland is "an area of which the greater part or a substantial part of the trade passes through a single port."[11] Later, I supply data to show the extent of the hinterlands of the Swahili port cities. While all cities have umland and hinterlands, only port cities also have forelands.[12]

Some port cities may have an umland but no hinterland. Rather, they draw on a vast foreland. These ports, mentioned above, are usually referred to as entrepôt ports, and they manage redistribution. A modern example is Singapore; one from our period is Melaka. Aden and Hurmuz may have functioned as entrepôt ports, too. Such ports draw little or nothing from the interior, but rather repackage, break up, and send on foreign goods to a foreign destination. In east Africa, Mombasa may have been such a port city, but we must investigate first whether it exported local products or merely re-exported foreign goods.

A rigorous use of these four terms can contribute to a focused discussion of port cities and their relations with the interior. Indeed, several recent discussions could have profited from this sort of differentiation. One example is Justin Willis's book on Mombasa. His terminology is far too vague and unspecific. He writes of Mombasa's "local hinterland" and then notes that "The people of Mombasa themselves, like those of other ports and borders, needed access to the products of the hinterland: both because the coast was not particularly productive of foodstuffs, and in order to realize their potential as traders. The viability of the domestic economy in the hinterland was intimately involved with the control of access to the coast, and therefore to the products of other zones; and wealth and authority on the coast were similarly bound up with access to the hinterland. Those who sought wealth or power in either coast or hinterland were, therefore, reliant to some extent on accommodation with their neighbours."[13] Here, both "local hinterland" and "hinterland" seem to be Mombasa's umland, while the vague "other zones" are in fact the hinterland. I have similar concerns about A.J.R. Russell-Wood's short but stimulating discussion of Brazil's port cities. He raises several important questions. One is the matter of how one distinguishes between port cities and cities that are not ports, particularly in a context where all cities were also ports, as was the situation in Brazil until the mid eighteenth century. This situation applies to east Africa until the end of the nineteenth century. All the cities of these two areas have forelands. This changed after the rise of São Paulo, Kampala, Nairobi, and other non-port cities. What is the difference between a port city on an island, as opposed to one on the coast; or between a fluvial port city and a coastal one?[14] So far so good, but then he discusses hinterlands, and it is here that different terminology would add analytical rigor to his argument. He tries to differentiate between primary, secondary, and even tertiary hinterlands, but I think the term umland would have helped here. He then claims that because of its close ties with Brazil, west Africa should be seen as part of its hinterland; the concept of foreland, areas linked over water, is preferable in this context.[15]

We use these four terms to describe relations between the Swahili coast and the interior. There were some divisions within the broad region of the Swahili coast. The monsoons contributed to this. We have already noted that the northern coast could be reached on one monsoon, while those in the south could not. Yet it was from the south that the main exports, gold and ivory, came. This meant that the northern ports became important redistribution centers for these products from further south. The standard division of the coast is based on a northern coast, down to Cape Delgado, just south of the present boundary between Tanzania and Mozambique. Scholars of the Swahili language usually divide northern and southern variants at this point, too. M.D.D. Newitt notes three divisions. The Banadir coast extends from the Horn of Africa to the Lamu archipelago. Apart from brief mentions of Mogadishu, this region will figure little in our discussion. There follows the Mrima coast, from Lamu to Kilwa, often seen as the heartland of Swahili culture. The third region goes south from Kilwa, passing by the mouths of major rivers like the Rovuma, Zambezi, Sabi, and Limpopo, and ends at Inhambane, the limit of seaborne commerce before the arrival of the Portuguese.[16] Yet there is also an overarching unity, so that coastal people from Somalia to Mozambique, and the adjacent islands, should all be seen as sharing a common culture to some degree. This then includes the coastal inhabitants of five modern African states: Somalia, Kenya, Tanzania, Mozambique, and the Comoro Islands.[17]

While the monsoons played their role in enforcing this separation, it has been claimed that the geography of the interior also did. The main concerns here are the presence of rivers, and the nature of the land behind the coast. As Newitt notes, the southern rivers can be navigated some hundreds of kilometers inland. In the north, modern Tanzania has no navigable rivers at all. For Kenya, the only river of any consequence is the Tana River in the north, which is navigable for some 300 km by medium-sized craft, and for 500 km by very small craft. The others are mere rivulets, such as the Kilifi, Mtwapa, and Kilindini creeks, which can be navigated only for a very short distance and only in very small boats. However, even the possibility of navigation on the Tana is rendered nugatory by the fact, so we are told, that the surrounding countryside is the famous *nyika*, or "wilderness," a dry barren region.[18] This nyika extends behind the whole Kenya coast; further south, it is more broken, and it virtually disappears in southern Tanzania.[19] Merrick Posnansky states the implications of this very strongly, claiming that not only was access to the interior difficult in the north but also that the interior had little to offer as compared with the interior of the south. The Tana River merely penetrated desert, while further south, the Ruvuma and Rufiji Rivers were rendered useless by coastal swamps and meandering streams.[20]

These geographic factors contributed to an earlier perception that the coast, particularly the northern coast, had nothing to do with the interior. We have already dealt with the political implications of this in chapter 1. Neville Chittick was one of the great exponents of this view: "The people of the coast of East Africa were oriented to such an extent towards the ocean that their social and cultural interaction with the peoples of the interior before the nineteenth century was very slight." Or, "the impact of this [Swahili] civilisation on much of the mainland coast was slight, and inland non-existent."[21] The most extreme statement of this view comes from James Kirkman, who, in a classic Orientalist vein, inexcusably wrote that "The coast of East Africa . . . was brought into the Asian commercial system, to provide raw materials and curiosities for the more sophisticated countries across the sea." He described the "set-up of town and country—one semi-foreign, renegade, expatriate, as you will; the other pure, untamed, barbarous."[22]

Some scholars however had hesitations. Sheriff noted that the nyika was not an absolute barrier, but rather put a premium on the cost of communication between coast and interior.[23] Indeed, as I have traveled by train from Nairobi to Mombasa I have found myself wondering what all the fuss is about. Certainly it is not very hospitable country, but it is far from impenetrable. Graham Connah also questioned the dichotomy of an attractive coast and an unattractive hinterland, and notes "Problems of overland communication . . . have probably been exaggerated in the past." He adds that "it is likely that, as research progresses, increasing evidence will be found of close contacts between the inhabitants of those [inland] areas and the peoples of the coast."[24]

Indeed, this shift in thinking has occurred. These claims are either implicitly or explicitly part of the trend toward seeing the Swahili as intrinsically African, not foreign. There thus may well be a political agenda here, as I noted in chapter 1. The present task is to look more closely at this matter, using original sources. I investigate not only economic but also political connections as well as the penetration of Islam in the south.

To delineate the hinterland of the north coast port cities is a difficult task, given the fragmentary sources and uncompleted research. It is helpful, however, to look at political relations between the coastal cities and their umland, merging into hinterlands, and then to look at the evidence for trade and exchange both with the areas immediately contiguous to the cities, and with more distant areas.

In looking at the political context, we find that port cities controlled neither land nor sea. From time to time, they were threatened from both directions. This was the case in the 1580s in Mombasa and Malindi. At this time, these two towns were subjected to attacks and threats and help from four different external groups: from the sea, the Portuguese and the Ottoman Turkish fleet commanded by Mir Ali Bey; and from the land, by the Zimbas and the Mossequejos. The latter, the Mossequejos, more correctly the Segejus, were a newly arrived group who lived in the interior of Malindi.

In 1588, Mir Ali Bey was invited back to the Swahili coast by the local Muslims. After receiving support all down the coast, he was beaten off when he attacked the Portuguese ally Malindi, and so moved on to Mombasa. Soon, he was besieged in the port city by the ferocious Zimba. In March 1589, the Portuguese arrived and attacked from the sea. The Turks could not hold out, and prudently decided to surrender to the Portuguese rather than to the Zimba.[25] The Portuguese then sacked Mombasa yet again. The Turks then disappeared from the coast.

Meanwhile the Zimba, still hungry after having eaten all their Turkish captives, moved on to Malindi. They were close to taking this city when 3,000 Mossequejos arrived to help the sultan. The Zimbas were heavily defeated and vanish from our story. They returned south and merged with the Maravi group. Mombasa then attacked Malindi, was defeated by the Malindi-Mossequejo alliance, and retreated. The allies followed, took Mombasa, and from then, with help from the Portuguese, it was ruled by the sultan of Malindi, who was moved from Malindi to take up his new post.[26] Once established in Mombasa, the Portuguese took on the traditional obligation of the ruler of Mombasa to pay a tribute, or more accurately protection money, to another interior group, the Mozungullos, a different group from the Segeju, who lived around Mombasa.

These sorts of dramatic matters, leading to changes in control of major port cities, were rare enough. There were, however, continuing political and military relations between the port cities and the surrounding tribes, in which the merchants of the cities bought off the non-Muslim tribes who dominated their umland.

The Segeju, the Moceguejos of the Portuguese records, have had a rather bad press, thanks especially to a much-quoted account from Monclaro in 1570:

> The Moors of this place [Malindi] have as their inland neighbours some Kaffirs who are utterly different from those in the entire coast; they are called moceguejos, and the name itself proclaims their barbaric condition. They have no fixed land or home. Their abode is in the fields and forests, and they put on their heads stinking clay for the mixture therewith of sundry oils, and they do think it a rare aroma. They own much cattle, the milk and blood thereof being to them as food; they eat the flesh raw without any other manner of ordinary food, as it is said, and they bleed the oxen every other day. They are very warlike and the report goes that in their fights they are wont to cut off the foreskins and swallow them, and that when they appear before the king they do cast them out again from their mouths so that he may make them knights. They wear animals' skins and have sundry other barbaric customs. The Moors there are very much plagued by these Kaffirs, and so that they may not damage their harvests and wage war against them they redeem their vexation with clothing and other things they give them, but their general costume is skins, as I said.[27]

Couto tells a similar story; he may have copied from Monclaro. Writing in the 1590s, he claimed they were recent arrivals to the area, used to be cow herders, and still lived from this occupation.[28] In the seventeenth century, they apparently moved south to the present-day boundary of Kenya and Tanzania.[29] Their eruption on the stage was then a brief one, and they are known only for their role in the events of the 1580s and 1590s.

So also with the Zimba, whose reputation among European observers then and now was also a low one. Several scarifying Portuguese accounts of their reputed cannibalism have led to them attracting much morbid, and quite "Orientalist," notice. There is an implication that this is what Africans were "really" like, and hence European influence and control are to be seen as having the beneficent result of stopping this sort of barbarity. It is generally accepted today that the Zimba have some connection with the larger group known as Maravi. People identified as "Zimba" came up from the south, leaving havoc and devastation in their wake. They are reputed to have sacked Sena, Tete, Kilwa, and a host of other places, and eaten whatever people fell into their hands. It was around this time, or soon after, that they may have coalesced with other groups, including the Cabires and the Mumbos, to form the Maravi, who played an important role in Zambezia from the late sixteenth century. It is unclear whether their cannibalism was a routine matter, or rather a result of famine. In any case, as one African historian points out, cannibalism is one way to get protein.[30]

The history of the third group, the Mozungullos, is still rather obscure. They may have been an advance migration of Nyika people, that is, the people today called Mijikeṇda, or they may have been a separate group who were absorbed by the Nyika as the latter came south in the seventeenth century. Today these people, so Hamo Sassoon tells us, are called Liangulu (also Langulo, Ariangulu, or Walangulo), live on the upper Tana River, and speak a language related to Oromo (that is, Galla), which means they are Cushitic speakers, not Bantu.[31] In the 1630s, we have records of these people interacting vigorously with one of the port cities, in this case the Portuguese city of Mombasa. The Portuguese built three small forts to keep them out of the town, this effort being foreshadowed earlier by a wall which the rulers of Mombasa had built before the Portuguese conquest. The puppet ruler also gave the Mozungullos a portion of the customs revenues which the Portuguese allowed him in order to try and buy their neutrality. In the 1630s, they were described as having "neither law nor king nor any other interest in life except theft, robbery and murder." There were about three or four thousand of them. Although described as timid, they were formidable users of poisoned arrows, so that Mombasa was always afraid of them. In theory, they were vassals of the ruler of Mombasa, but "their submission was mainly obtained by giving them cloths. They were in reality quite different from vassals." Indeed, the Swahili inhabitants of the coast north and south of Mombasa are described as being "like prisoners of the Mozungullos Caffres, because they have to pay them a large tribute in cloth in order to be allowed to live in security."[32] The total picture is unusual: a city being held in thrall by the rural inhabitants of its own umland.

Later in the seventeenth century, the Mozungullos were absorbed into the Mijikenda confederation, and their activities now are included with those of the Mijikenda. They continued to play a role vis-à-vis the port cities, now often in opposition to the Portuguese. In 1698, the Omani besiegers of Mombasa persuaded the Mijikenda to cut off supplies to the Portuguese garrison in Fort Jesus. In 1729, Mombasans and Mozungullos drove the Portuguese out of Mombasa again, after their reoccupation in 1728.[33]

The Mijikenda have been much studied.[34] Willis has written a totally new interpretation. He claims that to use the term "Mijikenda" in the sixteenth and seventeenth centuries is anachronistic, as it was only used from the 1930s, was created out of a particular context during the colonial period, and before then had no currency. He sees the evolution of the term, and its people gaining some sense of solidarity, deriving from their experience in Mombasa in the colonial period. He suggests that there is no evidence of their living in *kayas* (more correctly, *makaya*) at this time. Thomas Spear disputes all these claims, which is not surprising as Willis's interpretation runs directly counter to his. It is odd that Willis uses so little archaeological evidence, for this certainly reinforces the more standard view.[35] The accepted version still seems to be valid. The Mijikenda moved south in the sixteenth century, having been driven out by the Oromo, often now called Galla. Once established behind the coast in southern Kenya, they built makaya (plural of kaya), or fortified villages covering about 10 hectares, which also had important sacral roles, to defend themselves from further attacks from the Oromo. These are located behind the coastal plain, which in this area is 3 to 8 km wide and leads into hills and valleys and then a range of hills up to 900 meters. The nyika, the desolate wilderness, begins about 20 km from the coast.[36] To the west of the makaya lay territory controlled by the Oromo and other pastoralist groups, to the east lay the Swahili and the coast.

The Mijikenda played a large role in the lives of the port cities in the seventeenth century, especially in Mombasa.[37] They often raided both Portuguese and Swahili settlements, and on occasion would block supplies to the towns.[38] However, usually relations were reciprocal, as indeed one would expect of relations between a town and its umland. During the seventeenth century, different groups among the Mijikenda formed alliances with other groups both among the Oromo and the residents of Mombasa.[39]

This is an example of the Mijikenda acting as crucial hinges between the coastal Swahili and interior tribes. The nine groups comprising the Mijikenda formed close relations with the twelve Swahili communities that inhabited Mombasa. "Each Mijikenda people was allied with a specific Mombasa community, conducted its trade through that community, and received annual tribute payments from them. Mijikenda were invited to the installation of Mombasan Sheikhs and fought along side their Mombasa allies in coastal disputes."[40]

A very similar political nexus between town and country prevailed on the mainland opposite Lamu. The Swahili inhabitants had close relations with the various groups who controlled the mainland over the years. Indeed, when a mainland controlling group was expelled by newly arrived peoples, they often took refuge on the islands with the Swahili people they had known for so long, and in time would merge into Swahili society.[41]

Further south, in Kilwa, we are fortunate to have Portuguese documentation, during their brief overlordship of the port from 1505 to 1513, that provides another illustration of relations between a northern Swahili port city and its umland. In 1507, the Portuguese deposed the existing puppet sultan, Ibrahim, and chose a new one. However, the father of their new protégé had been killed the year before, and he was keen to avenge this immediately. The person blamed was the ruler of an area called Tirendikunde, a kingdom on the mainland north of Kilwa, and he in turn was a relative of the deposed Kilwa sultan. The new sultan allied with another interior chief, a non-Muslim, and the Swahili forces attacked from the sea while the tribesmen attacked from the land. Their attack was successful. However, it was the tribesmen who did best here, not the Muslim Kilwa forces, and indeed the tribesmen captured large numbers of Muslims from Tirendikunde, including their women. Using interior tribesmen against one's fellow Muslims was a risky business. These events show how people from the interior or umland could be enlisted in and indeed profit from divisions within a Swahili port city.[42]

Northern Swahili townspeople had to keep their wits about them. There often was no one stable group controlling their umland with which they could establish permanent and durable relations. Rather, the political situation in their immediate environs was extremely unstable as one group after another came in, became dominant, and then were either replaced or moved on. The Mozungullos merged into the arriving Nyika, forming part of the Mijikenda. The Segeju moved south. The Oromo came down from the north and remained, moving around in the interior. The Zimba came from the south and then returned there, their brief moment on the coast being merely a thunderstorm. Richard Wilding claims that the interior was much more unstable in the sixteenth and seventeenth centuries than it had been before, and this meant the Swahili had to give up their mainland farms and retreat to their island towns.[43] There is little doubt that the port cities had complex political relations with their immediate neighbors, varying at different times between cooperation, uneasy alliances based on payments from the towns, and occasional hostility.

Yet we should not overemphasize difficult relations with the interior. Recent studies have suggested that the port cities were located so as to give access to the land rather than the sea; in other words, that their umlands and hinterlands were more important that their forelands. T. H. Wilson has investigated 116 Swahili sites from Mogadishu to the Tanzanian border, and he finds that, of these, 16 had no anchorages at all. Of the 100 that did, 13 could be classified as good, 47 as fair, and 40 as poor.[44] The location of the major town of Gedi is apposite here. In the fourteenth to sixteenth centuries, Gedi covered some 18 hectares within its outer walls, which were 3 meters high. The largest building, dubbed the "palace," was about 25 by 35 meters. Yet this town was 6 km from the sea and 3 km from the nearest creek.[45] To my knowledge, no convincing explanation for its location has been put forward. One could possibly find answers in the changing courses of nearby rivers. Or, there may be a political explanation, that the founders of this town for some reason had an especial fear of attack from the sea, and so built inland.

It is more likely that it is simply an extreme example of Wilson's analysis, that is, that its concerns and connections were much more with the land than with the sea. If this were the case, it would tend to support W. Howard Brown who, on the basis of his work on Siyu, finds that the port cities were more oriented to the land than to the sea. He claims that the notion that they chose city sites on islands because they were afraid of attacks from the land is untrue. Only about 25 percent of sites are located on islands. The much-noted fact that access to many of these towns is difficult from the sea proves the point: They were much more worried about attack from the sea than from the land. Brown even claims that the coastal locations of these port cities has nothing to do with the sea, but rather with fresher well water on the coast, and the availability of the best building material, coral, there. Coral is too heavy to carry inland, hence they built on the coast.[46]

It is important to disentangle this matter of whether port cities were land oriented or whether they were more connected with the sea. It seems that the land-oriented writers are, consciously or not, engaged in an otherwise commendable tendency toward Africa-centrism. That is, a sea orientation equates with foreign, a land one with indigenous. If the argument is restricted to politics, then Brown, Wilson, and others seem to be in trouble, for they ignore the vital fact that none of these towns was ever attacked from the sea before the arrival of the Portuguese. By this time, most of these towns had been established for some centuries. They all, on the other hand, had at times been threatened from the land. However, if we look at social and economic connections then the land-oriented argument is powerfully reinforced, for we find the social connections, and economic interdependence, we would expect to find in an umland area.

It is clear that there were copious social interactions between the Muslim Swahili and their umland neighbors. Influences went both ways, though it must be stressed that one of the prime differentiators, Islam, remained urban. However, the character of northern Swahili Islam was being formed all through this period by the interaction between the existing community and newcomers, who often added their own beliefs to those already found in the towns. Many of these people became Muslims as a result of conversion after marriage. Wilding, in a powerful reinforcement of the land-oriented argument, stresses that Swahili merchants were much more likely to marry their daughters or sons to influential interior families than to seaborne foreigners, whether Arab or Persian, let alone Indian or Portuguese.[47] Other people intermarried with the people they lived among, that is, the slave populations who cultivated Swahili farms on the coast.[48] More social connections, and often conversion, resulted from the shifting power patterns of the interior. Groups who were displaced took refuge with people they already knew, the townspeople, and over the years merged into their society. Thus, Swahili Islam and its wider society evolved with powerful influences from the Bantu people of which they were part.

In the southern part of the northern zone, that is, Kilwa, things began to change in the late sixteenth century. In pre-Portuguese times, Kilwa had almost no relations with its interior, for it lived by controlling the gold trade from Sofala far to the south. However, as the Portuguese tried to block this trade (indeed Sofala had escaped from Kilwa's control before the arrival of the Portuguese), Kilwa began to look inland. This contact was accomplished by a long-established far-interior trading group, the Yao, who set up a regular trade route from northern Zambezia to Kilwa.[49] E. A. Alpers has some very interesting comments on this matter: "New ideas from the coast must have been entering the mainstream of Yao life from the very beginning of Yao trade to the coast [in the sixteenth century]. These initial contacts accordingly influenced individuals, men who had been to the coast, rather than society as a whole. It is impossible to determine the total effect of these individual contacts on Yao customs and habits during this period, but it seems unlikely that it was marked before Swahili traders began to enter Yaoland in the last quarter of the eighteenth century. Thereafter, the style of the coast was more readily observable." This is seen, for example, in late-nineteenth-century conversions to Islam; this had not happened before. There seems to be a problem with this argument for late social influence. Earlier in this article, Alpers quotes a traditional source that says, "in the old days the Yao were great travellers, for they used to say 'He who knows foreign parts is a man worth knowing . . . ' he who knew other countries was always listened to with respect, the people hanging on his words delighted." This records an early penetration of coastal exotic ideas inland, in this case carried not by coast people but by Yao travelers who had returned.[50]

Economic relations with the umland were similarly reciprocal. It is impossible to imagine a society as urban-oriented and specialized as the Swahili not having close relations with the surrounding countryside; they were essential. Two sorts of goods were being traded. The countryside produced the foodstuffs to feed the towns, but some umland production was also destined for export; the manufactures of the towns, especially cloth, were seldom exported but rather went to local markets.

Several recent studies have elaborated on these connections. In the case of Pate, Lamu, and Siyu, we find close ties between the port cities, in these cases located on islands, and the immediate interior. This is direct exchange by the Swahili; unlike the long-distance trade with the further hinterland, here the Swahili interacted with the producers. Indeed, many of the mainland plantations were owned by Swahili from the towns, and they used slave labor. This is the area that Randall L. Pouwels calls the *bara* (surroundings), and which we can consider as being identical with the umland.[51] In the early sixteenth century, Duarte Barbosa noted the characteristic mixture of war and economic symbiosis that characterized relations between Pate and Lamu and the coastal people: "These carry on trade with the inland country, and are well walled with stone and mortar, inasmuch as they are often at war with the Heathen of the mainland."[52] Brown's thesis elaborates on Siyu, on Pate Island. He may go too far in his stress on a land rather than sea orientation, but this could be because Siyu fits this notion much better than some of its neighbors. He stresses that the port city was inaccessible to large dhows, but it was located in a rich agricultural area. Its residents cultivated land on the mainland, and returned to their island home in the off-season. On the mainland the Siyu people interacted with the Boni from Somalia, who once were pastoralists and now were hunters and gatherers. Siyu's mainland cultivation area overlapped with the traditional hunting grounds of the Boni, so there was mutual interaction. The Boni received food and cloth in exchange for ivory, timber, and honey. They helped to plant and cultivate crops, and married with the rural Swahili slave population, and sometimes with the Swahili.[53] A similar situation may have existed in the region around the mouth of the Tana River, where at least today several different groups interact. In the wetlands areas, the land is used by the Pokomo and Swahili for agriculture, by the Orma for grazing, and by the hunter-gatherers for exploiting wild resources, including animals.[54] Similarly with Lamu, where in fact, due to the infertility of Lamu Island, most food seems to have come from the mainland, and here again the townspeople interacted with various mainland non-Muslim people.[55] Pate seems to have been a little different; it was not just an entrepôt but also an important center of local production. I pick up this matter in chapter 4; for now, it suffices to say that fine-colored cloths and oceangoing vessels came from this port city.[56]

Excellent information documents the situation in the immediate interior behind Malindi and Mombasa. Barbosa described Mombasa in the early sixteenth century. "This Mombaça is a land very full of food. Here are found many very fine sheep with round tails, cows and other cattle in great plenty, and many fowls, all of which are exceeding fat. There is much millet and rice, sweet and bitter oranges, lemons, pomegranates, Indian figs, vegetables of divers kinds, and much sweet water. The men thereof are oft-times at war and but seldom at peace with those of the mainland, and they carry on trade with them, bringing thence great store of honey, wax and ivory."[57] The reciprocity between the city and its umland was described in the mid nineteenth century, in a saying that applies for many centuries earlier: "The inland tribes [i.e., the Mijikenda] cannot exist without their supplies from the coast, and the tribes of the coast cannot subsist without the produce of the interior."[58] Henry Mutoro provides a more complete list of exchanges between Mombasa and the Mijikenda. The Swahili received grain and other food from the Mijikenda, and the Mijikenda in return got cloth, beads, fish, cowrie shells, porcelain, glass, and wire.[59] Connections in this area around Mombasa were facilitated by creeks that linked several coastal towns, including Mombasa itself, with what Willis calls the "immediate hinterland," that is, the umland. These creeks could be navigated by small craft up to the foot of the main ridge.[60]

Wilding provides a broad statement that serves to introduce a discussion of long-distance trade:

> The Mijikenda obtained cattle from the Oromo of the hinterland, and used these animals not only for subsistence but also for trade with the

> Swahili settlements of the coastline. This function of commercial middlemen is visible in several other important trade commodities. Mijikenda also passed to the Swahili from the plains behind the coast incense, ivory, rhinohorn, rockcrystal, carnelian and small stock, in return for metal goods, cloth, beads and wire. They also traded their own hunted and gathered goods into the Swahili settlements, including gum copal, honey and hardwoods. The grain surpluses which they were able to produce on the fertile hills were also traded into the coastal towns. This commercial symbiosis was recorded physically by the spread through the Mijikenda settlements of the coconut palms, used for copra, wine, nut flesh, cooking oil and frond roofing tiles."[61]

The Swahili acted as intermediaries between the Indian Ocean world and Africa, but they depended on another layer of intermediaries for part of this exchange, that is, from the interior to the coast.

The extent of links between these two distant zones has been much discussed in the literature. The older version of no contact has been vigorously challenged. Yet the revisionists have merely asserted that there were these distant links: We have very little hard data to show either export goods coming from far inland or imports being sent long distances to the west. Yet the matter is crucial, for if these sorts of exchanges were minor, then we have to see the northern port cities as more or less entrepôt, with vast forelands but little in the way of an hinterland. This, however, would not reinforce the Swahili are foreign argument, for we have already demonstrated close connections with non-Muslim people in their umland and even near hinterlands.

Again, the way monsoons function is important. Large foreign ships were unable to travel all the way to the south in one season. The northern ports, first Kilwa and then Mombasa, had a central role, for it was here the foreign cargoes were broken up and sent on south. Perhaps this fortuitous, and very profitable, export trade may have provided more than enough living for the Swahili elites. Collecting goods from the interior would be arduous and risky, and would not be undertaken while easy profits were to be made from an essentially compradorial role. In other words, the cities could thrive as entrepôt, and they had no need of an hinterland. At first sight, Kilwa, the greatest port city of the northern coast before the fifteenth century, supports this position. Its relations with its hinterland were sparse and hostile. Kilwa appears to be purely an entrepôt. In fact, Kilwa was a port city at one remove, for its wealth derived from its control of the gold trade from Sofala far to the south. It was thus connected with its hinterland, the Zimbabwe Plateau from where the gold came, at one remove, via Sofala, in other words, by an extensive foreland.[62]

Given this compradorial role, one would expect such fortunately located port cities to levy high taxes, and indeed they did. It has been generally assumed that the wealth of Kilwa, for example, seen in the vast "palace" and mosque, was derived by rulers from the profits of taxing trade. Yet there is considerable confusion in the sources over the role of these ministates in trade, and especially how and if they taxed it. Barros presents a version of a state of nature in Mozambique when da Gama arrived. The Portuguese admiral was greeted by a native of Fez, which indicated how international the trade was. This person told da Gama that the custom of the sultan "was when strange ships arrived to send and enquire what they sought; and if they were merchants they might trade in that country, and if navigators bound to other parts he provided them with whatever was to be had there."[63] This happy situation, if indeed it existed, was soon disrupted by the Portuguese.

Other evidence seems to show that some Swahili rulers had never even thought of taxing trade. Marina Tolmacheva, in her analysis of various versions of a Pate chronicle, notes that the chronicle says that the Portuguese said to the local ruler that "'Your kingdom is very great, but there is no profit. Why do you not make taxes?' So they made a customs house at a place in Pate harbour called Fandikani; in the language of the Portuguese it means 'customs.'" She points out in a footnote that *-ni* is only a locative postfix, so the word is in fact *fandikan*, that is, the Portuguese word for a customshouse, *alfandega*. Another version of the chronicle says that the word is *fundika*.[64] This argument suggests that the whole idea of levying customs duties came from the Portuguese. It might be that the wealth of the rulers, as well as the local merchants, came from participation in trade rather than in controlling and taxing it. However, the following account seems to show rulers profiting both from customs payments and from their own trade.

This is an account from 1506 of customs payments further south, in Mombasa, Kilwa, and Sofala. Any merchant who came to Mombasa and brought 1,000 pieces of cloth had to pay 1 matical of gold, and the king then took half the cloth, regardless of whether the merchant sold the cloth in Mombasa or was merely transhipping his goods further south. The king then sent his 500 pieces of cloth south to Sofala or Kilwa to sell on his own account. In Kilwa, the merchant had to pay 1 matical on 500 pieces of cloth; the king took two-thirds of the cloth; and the merchant's third was then valued and for each 1,000 maticals of value, he paid 30 maticals to the king. The merchant, with his by now considerably reduced trade goods, then went on to Sofala, and gave 1 piece of cloth in 7 to the king. When he returned to Kilwa from Sofala, he had to pay to the king 50 maticals for each 1,000 with him, and it cost nothing to go back through Mombasa. However, if on the return voyage the merchant did not stop in Kilwa, this 50 maticals was payable instead in Mombasa.[65] To summarize, if a merchant started off with 1,000 pieces of cloth, he would be left with only about 25 by the time he got to Sofala and was able to start trading, and he would have paid other levies also. While merchants' profits were very high, this account seems to be wildly exaggerated.

Let us look at the origins of the export goods, and first at ivory from the north. The data is extremely confusing. We have extensive evidence of ivory coming from the northern Swahili coast, some claims of it coming from further inland, and then evidence of ivory coming from the south and finding a profitable reexport market in the northern ports. We can assume that nearly all this ivory was exported, especially to India, although we need to remember that some was also used locally, in the port cities. The best-known example of this local use is the famous *siwas* (side-blown horns carved out of ivory) used for ceremonial occasions in some of these ports.[66]

One contemporary found the ivory coming from the coast. Thomas Kerridge claimed that "from the coast of Mellinda the Portingall do bringe great store, which they gett by trading with the blackamoores, thatt inhabitt all the [coast] alonge from Mosambique to Mangadore [Mogadishu]."[67] Many modern scholars have also assumed that ivory exported from the northern coast came from close inland.[68] Wilding, who has lived in the area for many years, claims that elephants abounded along the northern Swahili coastline until the late 1970s.[69] Several other scholars have claimed that there were no important economic connections with the interior until at least the late eighteenth century.[70]

The ivory from the immediate interior was collected, but apparently not hunted, by the Mijikenda, who then on-sold it to the Swahili towns, for there is no doubt that, before the nineteenth century, the Swahili did not travel inland. Indeed, they did not even travel to the contiguous Mijikenda area but rather waited for the goods to be brought to town. This matter has been much commented on. There was no need for the Swahili to venture inland, for to the extent that interior goods were important for their middleman role, they were adequately provided by people from the near or far interior. The Swahili, as the only urban people on either the coast or interior of northern east Africa, seem to have considered the interior to be threatening, dangerous, and alien. This was reflected in a late-nineteenth-century saying that embodies long-held attitudes: "Why go inland and have a lot of trouble in the bush?" Another account from the same period paints a bleak picture: "In the past the inland people and the people of the coast feared and robbed each other. If an inland person came to the coast with goods, he was robbed, and if the coast people went inland, they were robbed of their goods and murdered."[71]

Other scholars are less certain about the provenance of the ivory. It is claimed, for example, that the Mijikenda got their ivory from the Waata, but we are not told how far inland these last went.[72] Similarly, we are told that the Mijikenda operated in permanent markets behind the coast, such as Changamwe and Kwa Jomvu behind Mombasa and Kao behind Lamu. There, actual producers or hunters had close social and economic relations with the Mijikenda.[73] Mutoro even claims they made up caravans of two to three hundred people and traveled inland to get ivory, rhinoceros horn, cattle, hides, gum copal, and other goods.[74] Further north, the people of Siyu got their ivory for export from the inland Boni people.[75] Pate got its ivory first from the Pokomo people, and later from the Oromo. Both these collected their ivory from around the Tana River, where elephants were widely found.[76] W. R. Ochieng', contrary to his main thesis of no contact, claims there was some interior trade. For example, the Dorobo and Athi hunters were involved in long-distance ivory trade.[77]

Mutoro and George H. O. Abungu put these claims of very widespread connections between the coast and the far interior in a useful context. They discuss the old notion that the coast was really part of the "orient" rather than Africa:

> This assumption was due to the fact that many early researchers tended to assume that the northern coast of east Africa, and particularly that of Kenya, was never in close contact with its hinterland prior to the nineteenth century. This situation was attributed to various factors, ranging from: the coast being foreign, overseas-looking with nothing to do with the interior; the 'harsh' environment between the coast and the interior; the lack of enticing goods such as gold and copper in the interior to attract the coastal traders; to the restricted coastal zone as having been self-sufficient in goods required for the sustenance of this trade. The coast of Kenya was thus seen as sea-facing, cut off from the rest of the African continent, and more or less a province of the Middle East.[78]

Their evidence to support a rectification of this outlook is somewhat spotty. For example, they point out that pottery from Takwa shows contact not only with different coastal sites but also with the interior. So also in the Mijikenda sites. Ungwana, a large town on the delta of the Tana River from about 950 to 1600, is described as a center of trade for the lower and middle Tana River systems; the wells in the town seem to show inland influence. It is true that few foreign trade goods have been found in the interior, but this could be because many of them, most obviously cloths, were perishable. Also, foreign goods may have stayed in the port cities, and only local products from cities like Pate would be sent on to the interior.[79] Abungu has recently reported on his findings so far concerning the Tana River. This work is part of a continuing project on coastal and interior interaction in east Africa. Near the mouth of the river are several uninvestigated sites, that may be seen as "probable gateways to the interior and ports of passage to the outside world on the one hand, and as sub-systems in the wider coast/interior system on the other."[80]

Further work is proceeding that may flesh out these claims. In a sense, they are supported by a rather eccentric doctoral thesis by P. F. Thorbahn, completed in 1979. Thorbahn's argument is based on considerable archival research and a computer simulation; it is poorly presented. He puts forward what he considers to be the incorrect view, that is, that up to the nineteenth century ivory in the northern ports was all reexports from further south. However, he claims that there was direct trade from the south to India, so that the notion of sending the ivory north and then to India makes no sense. He seems to confuse Portuguese trade with total trade, for there is no doubt that there was copious trade outside the Portuguese attempted monopoly, and this would follow the traditional pattern of local trade to the north, where ships sailing on one monsoon would then buy the ivory and take it to the Middle East or to India, and, in some cases, on to China. The Portuguese records, as we will see, discuss this reexport trade. Thorbahn then presents evidence to show that the interior had been exploited long before the nineteenth century.[81]

There are other factors to consider. Philip D. Curtin points to the problem of disease, something often overlooked by historians. He claims that, due to the problem of tsetse flies, people were used for transportation in the area inland from the northern coast. He argues that no interior product was sufficiently profitable to cover these high transportation costs.[82] This claim may be problematic, for others have written that before colonialism African societies coexisted with this disease, which became a problem only when colonialism destroyed this balance.[83] There is no question that ivory was a difficult product to transport because it was so heavy. An average tusk weighed about 20 kg; some weighed 40. In the south, conditions may have been healthier, gold was much easier to transport, and the various river systems facilitated the movement of goods. There was a geographical problem, namely, that over time supplies from the coast diminished all up and down the shore. Once the interior had to be penetrated, the south provided far easier access than the north, as it was hard to find corridors through the nyika wilderness.[84] Newitt claims that ivory had not, before the arrival of the Portuguese, been a major trade item from anywhere south of Kilwa. However, once gold supplies dried up, the Portuguese expanded the ivory trade in their southern area, extending down as far as Delagoa Bay, the site of modern Maputo.[85] This new trade tended to undermine trade from the north, for the Portuguese traded from Mozambique to India directly and so may have been able to outcompete traders from the north, who in any case were hindered by Portuguese opposition and seizure of their ships.

It seems to be fair to say that very few imports to the north coast seem to have gone far inland. The main export was certainly ivory, leaving aside large supplies of mangrove poles from the coast. We have decent evidence of elephants being hunted along the coast, and some spotty claims of some ivory coming from further inland. However, this is by no means proven. In addition, we have some data that may undermine the whole claim of important quantities of ivory coming from the northern coast, let alone the interior, at all.

Evidence suggesting that ivory was a profitable import from the south to the north casts doubt on whether supplies existed on the northern coast, or in its interior. In 1518, António de Silveira told his king that ivory could be sent from Sofala to Malindi and make a good profit. It would sell for 140 *cruzados* the *bahar* (nearly 300 kg).[86] Its cost in the south would have been perhaps 40 cruzados. The great historian of Mozambique, Alexandre Lobato, constructed a table that showed that the best-quality ivory in 1530 cost 30 to 40 maticals in Sofala, and would sell for 120 in Malindi, or could be exchanged for cloth and other goods worth 160 maticals. The profits on medium and small tusks were comparable.[87] What we need is hard data that can conclusively show us where ivory came from in the north, and that also finds trade goods from the coast in the far interior. This issue is very much on the current research agenda, for the answers will tell us much about northern Swahili port cities and their orientation in the sixteenth to eighteenth centuries. In terms of the port cities concept, it is a question of whether they were oriented more to their umland and hinterland, no matter how deep this may have been, rather than to their foreland across the sea.

The area south of Cape Delgado is quite different. The geography changes; the monsoon pattern is more variable; and the coast is penetrated by several great rivers: the Zambezi, the Limpopo, and a host of others. Inland is the great Zimbabwe Plateau, high healthy country producing much gold. Relations between coast and interior are very different from what we have described in the north. Even so, the south shares a certain commonality with the north when we compare the two to India. There may have been large internal states in the south with which the port cities interacted, but these were still very loose agglomerations, and, economically, the port cities were still dealing in primary products from very primitive economies.

There is evidence that internal trade in the south was long standing. This internal trade provided the experience that made possible their extension of this trade to the coast. Discussions of this matter come out of a particular context, as J. F. Mbwiliza notes. In the 1970s, nationalist historians, to counter Eurocentric colonial writings, wanted

> to identify those areas in which Africans demonstrated their initiative by contending with, or responding to, new economic and political challenges. With respect to trade therefore, the main concern was to demonstrate that the development of long distance trade which linked the east African coast with its hinterland was not initiated solely by foreign traders, mostly Arabs and Indians and, in the case of Mozambique, Portuguese and French traders, but to show that the long distance trade developed as a consequence of the expansion of older and relatively localized trading networks dealing in foodstuffs and locally manufactured goods. It was through the widening sphere of economic operations in the hinterland that traders from the interior eventually came into contact with traders from the coastal settlements.[88]

This influence was perhaps most clearly seen in revisionist studies of the slave trade. In our case, the aim was to show the existence of abundant internal trade for centuries. In the older writings, these traders only entered history when they extended their routes to the coast and so came to the notice of foreigners. The new historiography was concerned to show that this perception was false and to give back to these people without history their autonomy and their story.

These studies have usually dealt with the southern area inland from the coast, where a denser population fostered trade and exchange, which, until the nineteenth century, was based on barter rather than money. One of the earliest known long-distance internal trading groups was the Yao, who dealt in essentials like salt, iron, and food. Salt may have provided the initial impetus, for their far inland homeland produced little of this essential commodity. Later, typically, they extended their trade to the coast, especially to Kilwa. In the seventeenth century, they brought ivory; later, they became the major slave traders.[89]

We can now turn to a discussion of the dimensions and nature of trade between hinterland and port city in the south. Four factors influence our discussion of the depth of the hinterland in the south. We can briefly look at where ivory came from in the south, and then consider people who penetrated inland from the coast, that is, Muslims and Portuguese. Then, we will look at how gold was traded from the interior to the coast, and at relations between the interior states and the traders who came inland to buy the precious metal.

A famous nineteenth-century saying mentioned that "When the flute plays in Zanzibar, they dance on the lakes."[90] Was this the case earlier? In other words, where did ivory come from to reach the south Swahili coast in the sixteenth and seventeenth centuries? One indication that the ivory trade of the south was much greater than that of the north is the fact that so many of the European observers commented on this trade, leaving us detailed accounts of how the elephants were hunted and killed.[91] Many of these accounts make clear that this was a discretionary activity, undertaken only when trade goods were needed. We also have data on Portuguese attempts to control this trade, and on the vast profits which were made. However, the present concern is to try and work out where the ivory came from.

This task is made more difficult by the fact that the sources write of supplies of ivory on the coast, but they do not tell us where it came from originally. For example, we have detailed records of Portuguese purchases in Sofala from January to September of 1515. Only a little came from Africans and from one Portuguese merchant who came from the interior. Most was supplied by the Muslim merchants of Sofala, but we have no idea where they got their supplies from.[92]

Ivory was readily available on the coast, from local supplies. An early Portuguese captain of Kilwa claimed that "a great quantity of ivory is to be had between Sofala and Kilwa which is valued at 15 maticals of gold the quintal and that in due time it will be worth 80 and 100 maticals the quintal in Cambay and that Your Highness may have as much as you want."[93] Barbosa noted that "On the mainland appertaining to these islands [of Mozambique] are many very great elephants."[94] His assertion is backed up by Ludovico di Varthema, and much later, in 1585, by Couto.[95]

We also have copious evidence of ivory coming from far inland, and this may point to coastal supplies being inadequate, for ivory, unlike gold, is a heavy product: transporting tusks weighing at least 20 kg through the tsetse-ridden lowlands was a difficult task. Another implication of this factor is that ivory was usually taken to the nearest port, and so several of the ports on the south coast participated in this trade. An important retrospective account from 1582 claimed that Sofala's ivory came from far inland, and it was brought to the coast by the local Africans.[96] In the second half of the sixteenth century, we are told that ivory came from an area 100 leagues inland from Sena.[97] The evidence does not allow us to be definite about sources of ivory in the south. It seems likely, however, that the expansion of this trade as a result of the intervention of the Portuguese meant that coastal supplies grew scarce later in the sixteenth century, therefore, supplies would have come from far inland.

The organization of this trade is similarly obscure. The hunters gave one tusk to the local chief, and sold the other. We have little information on who the buyer was in the earlier period, but certainly by the late seventeenth century, African groups, especially the Yao, drew their supplies from north of the Zambezi. They built on their existing experience of long-distance trade in the interior to expand their networks to the coast, especially to Kilwa.[98] The entry of African people into the trade seems to be a later development. In the sixteenth and seventeenth centuries, the main transmitters seem to have been people from the coast: Muslims (some of them Swahili) and Portuguese. We can now turn to this matter, and in particular try to determine who a Muslim in the interior was.

The main historian of the Zimbabwe Plateau, David Beach, has put forward a strong case for minimal coastal Muslim penetration of the plateau. He claims that the interior Muslims were mostly partially Islamized local converts who had no political ambitions, and while they traded in gold, they played no part in the productive process. While Swahili Muslim communities existed on the coast in the fifteenth century, on the lower Zambezi, they mixed with only partially Islamized Shona and Sena speakers, and there were no Swahili settlements on the plateau.[99] The coastal Muslims knew nothing of the plateau, and those whom the Portuguese called Mouros were in fact not Arabs or even Swahili but rather native Shona speakers.[100] It is possible that Swahili people, and even Arabs, visited the plateau, but we have no evidence of this. In fact, it is highly unlikely that any literate Arab or Swahili ever reached the plateau.[101]

The total number of Muslims on the plateau was not the often-accepted Portuguese estimate of 10,000, but rather perhaps 1,500 or 2,000. Beach claims that on the Zambezi in the 1570s there may have been 20 traders cum rulers who were Muslim, and they had about 800 Muslim followers.[102] Thus, the total in the sixteenth century on both the river and the plateau was a few thousand at most. The Shona rulers treated them as trusted strangers, *torwa*, just as they did the Portuguese, but their total influence was very small.[103] Beach has also made the important point that the dynamic may have changed. As the Portuguese took over the comprador role in the interior that the Muslims had held, there was less Muslim contact with the coast, and so Islam in the interior merged back into Shona beliefs.[104]

Beach's claims command respect, yet the available sources seem to demand that we revise some of his claims. This is possible despite the fact that the Portuguese documents are very difficult to use because of their imprecise terminology. The usual term for a Muslim is *Mouro*; the terms for an African were *Kafre*, or *Caffir*, or some other variant. Yet, Mouro is actually a generic Portuguese term for Muslim so such people could be Indians, Arabs, Persians, and/or part African.

Another example is the word *sheikh* (in the documents, *xeque*). One would assume that this term meant a prestigious Muslim, and indeed sometimes the Portuguese seem to use it in this sense.[105] In 1513, a Portuguese wrote of how in the interior, where the gold came from, there were established fairs "where are the sheikhs [xeques] here from Sofala."[106] But then we read of "hum xeque senhor dele que he cafre" (a sheikh, the ruler of it [a village] who is a kaffir).[107] This person is not a Muslim; if he were, the Portuguese would certainly have called him a Mouro. Another common prestigious Muslim term, *sharif*, is also used. During internal disorder in 1632, the Mutapa ruler was helped by the Portuguese, and also by a Muslim called *Xarife* (sharif).[108] To add to the confusion, the Portuguese often refer to "white Muslims."[109] This term may refer to Muslims not of African stock, or maybe to the evolving Swahili community, as compared with black converts. Another interesting case is that of "Pero a Negro turned Christian because he knew the Kaffir tongue and spoke Arabic well"[110] This seems to be an African who converted to Christianity but spoke Arabic.

In 1572, Barreto led the punitive expedition to avenge the death of Gonçalo de Silveira. Couto tells us that in 1569 on the coast they got preliminary information from Moors who knew the interior well, but Dos Santos tells the same story but says they were *kaffir* merchants.[111] Finally, Barros uses the word *Emozaidij* to describe Muslims in the interior. These followed the doctrines of the grandson of Ali, Zaid, who was condemned as schismatic. He and his followers were banished, and they spread down the coast of east Africa. Later Arabs drove these schismatics into the interior. They were called *Baduys* or *Baduijs*, "country people," by the coastal Arabs.[112] (Here, Barros is quoting the version of the Kilwa chronicle to which he had access.) Presumably these later Arabs are the Hadrami sayyids, who arrived in the fourteenth and fifteenth centuries and turned the coast into a predominantly *shafi'i* area.[113] Cyril A. Hromnik, in what is otherwise a very misleading dissertation, expands on this, claiming they were in fact followers of the sect of Said ibn Ali, a *shia* pretender killed in the year 739. They grew food for the coastal populations, and served as trade intermediaries. This implies that they were residents of the umland rather than the far interior. Hromnik claims there is a basic difference between the coastal Muslims, who did not go inland, and these people, the Emozaids. He correctly criticizes Alexandre Lobato on this matter, for Lobato glosses Barros's word *Emozaidij* as *omeziados*, that is, Portuguese renegades who had fled.[114] This matter awaits more research, but we can see the difficulties in identifying Muslims, and in deciding what sort of Muslims were to be found in the interior of the southern Swahili coast.

There are several accounts of the role of Muslims in the interior at the time of the Portuguese arrival. Vitorino Magalhães Godinho claims that they were found in the gold-producing areas, and H.H.K. Bhila asserts that Swahili traders, no less, operated bazaars in the interior from the tenth century.[115] In his description of Great Zimbabwe, Barros mentions the presence of Muslims several times; he claims that some learned Muslim merchants had visited the site before it was abandoned late in the fifteenth century.[116]

In 1512, António Fernandes found Muslims at fairs sixteen days' journey inland from Sofala, and others seven days' travel beyond the Mutapa state.[117] The only evidence we have of Muslims being restricted to the coast comes from the self-proclaimed, well-informed Diogo de Alcáçova in 1506, who said that Muslims who participated in the gold trade with the Mutapa state journey "into the interior [from the coast] some 4 leagues [about 20 km]; they dare go no further, for the Kaffirs rob and kill them, having no belief in anything."[118]

Monclaro's famous account of the expedition led by Barreto to punish those who had killed Silveira makes clear how many Muslims were trading and living far inland. He noted, for example, that they sailed 100 leagues (about 500 km) beyond Sena upriver to get ivory, on the face of it a rather extreme claim.[119] An earlier account indicates that Sofala's Muslims went far into the interior to trade, for a Portuguese official said that the local Muslims' trade was so drawn out "that the greater part of those who trade in this factory during my time will not be back until the time of another captain."[120] Portuguese captains usually held office for three years. Some Muslim traders from the coast had penetrated the whole interior, according to Couto, and some had even met traders from Angola, so that traders from the Atlantic met those from the Indian Ocean in the middle of Africa.[121]

While no one denies that Muslims were found far inland at this time, it is difficult to determine who they were: Were they Beach's partially Islamized Shona speakers, or Swahili, or something else? In 1513, a Portuguese factor said the people at the fairs inland were the "sheikhs [xeques] here from Sofala, the factors of these merchants [of Sofala],"[122] which seems to point to Swahili traders.

On the night of 15–16 March 1561, the intrepid Jesuit missionary Gonçalo de Silveira was killed at the capital of the Mutapa state. He had recently converted the ruler, the ruler's mother, and numerous other residents. His death was a significant event in the history of relations between the Mutapa state and the Portuguese. It should be seen in the context of the Portuguese attempt to do two related things: convert natives, and expel Muslims. For our purposes, the significance of this melancholy event is that contemporary accounts, of which there are many, tell us something about the Muslim residents at the Mutapa court at this time.[123] All the accounts agree that it was Muslims who turned the ruler against the Jesuit. This is hardly surprising for the Portuguese had made very clear their antipathy to followers of Islam. The records vary greatly. One, which seems to point to those responsible being only partially converted, said those responsible were "Moorish engangas—the greatest witch-doctors in the land, who read the future by means of four sticks."[124] This is, however, a confused letter, as the author also says that these *engangas* said "que o padre era moro" (the father was a Muslim), a surprising accusation indeed.

The much more detailed account of Luís Fróis indicates that elite Muslims were present at court. Fróis said that the people who incited the ruler were "certain rich and wealthy Moors who dwelt there and who were highly displeased at the king's conversion" and they had "ease of access to the king, and [were] on familiar terms with him." "In this conspiracy and malice a Moor from Mozambique, who is a veritable Mafamede was the most conspicuous. His name is Mingame and he is a priest [cacis] of the Moors."[125] The term *Mafamede* implies a prestigious, and possibly even devout, Muslim, while a *cacis* is a preacher, or a scholar, certainly an informed and influential Muslim. Another version calls the ringleader Mingamis, and says he was a native of Mozambique, in other words, almost certainly Swahili. With some prescience, this person told the king that he was in great danger, because Silveira was really an agent of the king of Portugal, and also his baptized subjects would now be a fifth column.[126]

Other accounts from this time describe "a leading Moor" (hum mouro honrado) trading far into the interior, to the gold fields on the plateau.[127] The various Portuguese compilers of the sixteenth century all use this sort of terminology. Barros relies heavily on Muslim accounts, and especially the Kilwa chronicle. It is clear he saw Muslims as very knowledgeable about this kingdom.[128] A missionary in the 1580s complained of Muslims traveling in the interior, buying people, and then converting them to Islam.[129] It is reasonable to suspect that such traders were not local converts.

On his way to the court and his martyrdom, Silveira wrote letters claiming that the interior was ripe for conversion, for there were no Muslims. Writing about Inhambane and its interior, he claimed that those Muslims who were to be found "practice circumcism which they say they inherited from an eminent Moor who came there some time ago, but they follow no other Moorish laws." He said that other inhabitants, especially in the interior, were ripe for conversion: "It is better than all the other Gentile nations to be found in these parts, most of which are corrupted by the infernal sect of Mohamed and even mixed with the pestilential Jews, but this nation is quite free from them because, except for the sea coast and some parts of it, it is a marvel if a Moor can enter it."[130] This optimistic estimate certainly does not apply to most areas inland, for it is clear that Muslims continued to be found far and wide.

Before the Portuguese arrival, and through the sixteenth century, Muslims continued to hold important roles in trade in the interior. To try and quantify this would be impossible, for we are working with very vague and confused evidence. There is only one contemporary estimate of numbers. António de Saldanha said "he has learned that in the land of Monomotapa there are more than ten thousand Moors spread out at random and that it is impossible to cast them out."[131] This claim has been much quoted, and we noted that Beach finds it fanciful. Mudenge, however, accepts it.[132] I believe that the evidence quoted above casts serious doubt on Beach's denigration of the quality and prestige of all Muslims in the interior: It seems clear that some were educated and influential men who had come inland from the Swahili port cities.

Another common claim is that the Portuguese had been able to drive the Muslims out of the interior by the seventeenth century. This had long been the Portuguese aim. In 1571, the Barreto expedition reached Sena, massacred the local Muslims, and then demanded, unsuccessfully, that the Mutapa expel all Muslims from his territory. When the Portuguese were more successful, they imposed an agreement on the weakened Mutapa that, among other things, insisted that all Mouros be expelled within one year, otherwise the Portuguese could kill them.[133] In fact, the Portuguese thought that they had achieved much of this even before this agreement. In 1608, the king, in pursuit of the Portuguese chimera of a new Potosí in the African interior, wrote that in earlier times "it was not possible to proceed with this because of the many difficulties which presented themselves in those days, as the land was unknown and occupied by the Moors who were a great hindrance to Portuguese trade. These problems no longer impede the conquest, since the Moors have left those parts."[134] At the same time, the Jesuits thought that the Muslims had lost their power: "Previously there were so many of them and they were so powerful, now there are only a few who are very poor, and they only live on what the Portuguese allow them and so they do not even have any influence over the King nor any power over the land."[135] One contemporary, António Bocarro, agreed, for in 1616 he found Muslims only near the coast, a mere five or six hours distant from Kilwa Kisiwani.[136] Yet, there is other evidence to show that some Muslims remained inland, though no doubt their connections with the coast were weakened by Portuguese hostility.[137] In the 1630s, a Jesuit cleric still found Muslims making converts far inland.[138]

There were indeed strong connections, based on religion and trade, between the coast and the interior. We cannot say that the interior participated fully in the rich Islamic life of the port cities, where, for example, visitors from the Islamic heartland were patronized by the ruler of Kilwa, but many of the Muslims inland were learned to a degree, and many also were of coastal derivation, acting on their own behalf or as agents of rich merchants on the coast. Here we have evidence of a powerful and important connection between coast and interior in the south.

From an African point of view, this discussion may be somewhat pointless, for from this perspective relations between Muslims and Portuguese were a matter of one torwa, or protected foreign community, fighting with another. In the later sixteenth century, the Portuguese penetrated far inland, though their numbers seem to have been fewer than their Muslim opponents. In the 1590s, fifty years after their arrival, there were still fewer than 100 Portuguese in residence in the river ports of Sena and Tete. Converts, many of them slaves, number more than a thousand. In 1615, there were only about 50 in these two ports. There were many fewer on the plateau. In the important plateau center of Masapa, there were a mere eight in 1628.[139] At Bvuma (Vumba) in 1631, another important market, there were 10 Portuguese and a church, but no priest.[140] Numbers continued to fluctuate through the seventeenth century, but after the invasion of Changamire in the 1690s few Portuguese remained on the plateau. In 1693, Sena and Tete together had only 8 substantial Portuguese residents.[141]

The Portuguese had much larger aims than did the Muslims. The state-directed (at least in theory) Portuguese goal was to control trade and expel

Muslims. However, the Portuguese failed in this. Perhaps one could say that they moved from being one of several torwa communities to, by the later seventeenth century, being *prazo*-holders and these institutions have been commonly described as thoroughly "Africanized." In other words, as the Portuguese became prazo-holders, they stopped being torwas. The prazo-holders were eclectic in most things: religion, progeny, language. The first prazos can be traced back to the late sixteenth century,[142] and in the way that they symbolize acculturation and mingling, they reflect Portuguese attitudes generally to Africa, and even to Muslims (see chapter 5). While the official Portuguese attitude to Muslims was vigorously hostile, in reality, there was always considerable intermingling, so that the Mutapa attitude that they were both really just torwa communities seems justified. Silveira's death must be seen as quite atypical: As a member of the thrusting new Jesuit order he was too pushy, too devoted to setting off Christians from others. His attitude led to his death, but most Portuguese got along well enough with others in a commendably pragmatic fashion.

The extension far inland of the ivory trade, and the existence there of Muslims, whoever they were in detail, and Portuguese, both official and private, all point to the southern Swahili coast having a very deep hinterland as compared with the north. The gold trade, which of course came from far inland but was able to reach the coast, is an excellent example.

The location of the gold fields of the Zimbabwe Plateau can be confirmed. The diggings and washings were very scattered indeed, as the Portuguese found out. In 1513, the Portuguese factor at Sofala told the king that he had received little gold in the last eight months, and nearly all of this came not from traders from the interior but from the local Muslim merchants of Sofala. One problem was that "although there is gold in all the land it is spread out throughout the land and there is none who has it in such quantity as to allow him to come so far to trade it, and also because they wait for the merchandise to be taken to them where each one may buy what he wants; and so they come to established fairs where are the sheikhs [xeques] here from Sofala, the factors of these merchants [of Sofala presumably], and where they buy the merchandise that is sent to them from here."[143] This account claims that agents of Swahili merchants provided the link between the coast and gold production areas, but other evidence claims that gold was in fact brought to the coast by Africans. The best early observer, Duarte Barbosa, claimed that from the capital of the Mutapa state "thence the traders carry the inland gold to Çofala and give it unweighed to the Moors for coloured cloths and beads, which are greatly esteemed among them; which beads come from Cambaya."[144]

In 1506, the Portuguese captain of Sofala gave presents to the first African who had come there from the Mutapa state to trade gold for goods.[145] Other accounts, however, describe gold being brought by Shona speakers to the littoral river ports of Sena and Tete, or to inland bazaars at Teve, and there exchanged for goods with Muslim or Portuguese traders.[146] Certainly, the hinterland of the southern port cities stretched far inland, for this was where their main exports of gold and ivory came from, but the actual traders involved could be Africans all the way to the coast, or, at the other extreme, coastal agents who dealt directly with the producers. Similarly with slaves. The east African slave trade expanded greatly only in the late eighteenth century. Before this time the trade was small, though it is true that Swahili settlements, Portuguese Goa, and many inland armies all had large numbers of slaves. For our purposes, the main point is that the slaves came from far inland even at this time.[147]

Getting access to gold was not just a trading matter because all would-be exporters, whether Swahili or Portuguese, had to take account of local political matters in order to get supplies. There are important differences between the north and south coasts. In the north, the Swahili port cities had political relations with their umland neighbors. This was also the case in the south, but the ports also had to take some account of far inland states, especially the Mutapa one. There were no inland states in the north. Additionally, in the south, these relations with inland states were changed once the Portuguese arrived. The following discussion explores political relations between port cities and their hinterlands.

Shireen Moosvi provides an excellent discussion of how political changes affected the trade of port cities in India. The Mughal conquest of Gujarat in 1572 extended Gujarat's hinterland and made its ports responsive to the needs of the inner core of the empire, that is, the Agra-Delhi *doab* region. These changes also led to a reorienting of the existing port city hierarchy in Gujarat. Cambay and its outer ports, Gogha and especially Gandhar, had been dominant. The route to the north went from Ahmadabad to Ajmer and Agra, but this passage was dangerous in Rajasthan, and it also crossed a difficult desert. After the conquest, the route went from Agra, south to Gwalior, Malwa, and Burhanpur, and then west to southern Gujarat. This route crossed fertile country as compared with the Rajasthan Desert, and the area was also directly administered, as compared with the semiautonomous Rajput states, and so was safer. The end result was that Surat rose, and Cambay and its outer ports fell.[148]

Similar changes in the interior affected the fates of the southern Swahili port cities. This reminds us of our discussion of the extent to which the land, the hinterland, determined their fates, as compared with the foreland. In other words, are the port cities oriented to the coast or the interior? Ricardo Teixeira Duarte has begun a preliminary investigation of Somaná Island, which was abandoned before the sixteenth century. The island is 100 km north of Mozambique Island. This small coral island measures only 80 meters by 40 meters, and is 500 meters from the mainland, where there also are some ruins. The island is extremely difficult to access, especially for large vessels. The land-facing part of the island was defended by a wall, as was the seaward-facing area. It seems clear that the umland was of most importance, or rather, it posed the greater threat. The island was a refuge, and could be used as such by the people on the mainland if they were attacked. They could leave their farms and cross over to safety.[149] It is hard to know how to evaluate this site. Perhaps it is rather atypical because it was on an island, while most Swahili settlements were not. The location and the difficult access from the sea may point to a very fearful community that felt threatened from both sides. Yet Duarte notes connections with the land, and these were found in other areas of northern Mozambique also. For example, there were extensive commercial relations between the inland Makua people and the Swahili on the coast, especially with Angoche. Some of these contacts went far inland, for example to a Makua chief who lived 30 to 40 km inland.[150]

Beach claims that the orientation of the port cities was north-south, that is coastal, rather than westward and to the land, yet he has often discussed relations with the interior. These relations were not completely symmetrical, for the coast needed the interior much more than the other way around. There was a market for cloth in the interior, but the demand for imported cloth was discretionary, for there were local substitutes: skins and locally made cloth. The port cities, however, needed the products of the interior for the huge profits they provided, yet they could not penetrate far inland to control the source of supply. The Swahili never tried to do this; the Portuguese did but failed.[151] The port cities needed to get access to the far interior, and to do this they had to establish relations with intervening chiefs who controlled the inland trade routes. This pattern describes Portugal's two main port cities on the southern coast: Mozambique and Sofala.

Because there is no reason to suspect that Portuguese relations with the immediate interior differed from those maintained by Swahili-ruled port cities, we may use the wealth of evidence from Portuguese sources to illuminate and reconstruct political connections between coast and interior. When the Portuguese arrived they were, despite being a notoriously sea-based empire, dependent on relations with the interior just like everyone else. The land provided not only prestige luxury goods but also the most basic necessities of water and food. The port cities needed their umland. J. H. van Linschoten described Mozambique Island. While many Indian plants grew there, the island was dependent on the mainland, half a mile away, for cattle and sheep; grain, corn, and rice came from far-away India. Water was imported from Cabaceira on the mainland, according to Linschoten, or from Quitangonha Island [?], 15 km north of Mozambique, according to Lancaster.[152] Zimba raids affected Mozambique from 1570, and threatened the farms the Portuguese had established on the mainland as well as the farms of Africans who supplied provisions to the island. The result was that Mozambique Island "was left in want of everything, as all its supplies came from the mainland on the other side."[153] Newitt describes the social aspect of Mozambique's umland: "Mozambique Island became a European city supported by a rural African hinterland with the Afro-Portuguese moradores the connecting link between them." The same situation prevailed in Sofala, where a rurban settlement made up the umland: "It was typical of so many towns of eastern Africa where the urban life and culture shaded imperceptibly into, and was intricately bound up with, the life of the rural agricultural communities."[154]

Sofala, regardless of who ruled it, was completely dependent for its trade on the neighboring power, the Kiteve, who ruled from the Manica Mountains to the sea. He could threaten the Portuguese fortress, negotiate from strength with them, and block their trade. Consequently, the Portuguese had to conciliate him, send embassies to him, and pay what was in effect tribute to ensure that traders could cross over the lands of the Kiteve.[155] As early as 1507, as the Portuguese completed their fort in Sofala, they had problems with the interior.[156] In 1519 and 1527, the Kiteve blocked the trade routes, causing major problems for Sofala.[157] Indeed, it was not only the Kiteve who could be a problem. In 1511, the puppet king of Sofala revolted, moved off inland, and blocked the trade of Sofala.[158]

The Kiteve and his peers were well aware of the vital intermediary role of their territory, and they strove to preserve it. Barreto's expedition faltered after his death at Sena in 1573. His successor, Vasco Fernandes Homen, decided to attack through Sofala in order to get to the mines of Manica. The territory of the Kiteve lay between, and he refused to allow passage to the Portuguese, for he feared that if the Portuguese controlled the actual gold production area, his levies on trade would end.[159]

Clearly the Kiteve and other inland rulers saw the Portuguese and other coastal residents as milch cows, to be exploited at will. This, however, could lead to competition between the various inland chiefs, and so a blockage of trade. In 1542, a writer said of Sofala that he:

> found this land greatly devastated by the war being waged between the Kaffirs which is such that they do not let anyone come to trade at the fortress and, since they have no reasoning or knowledge and are men who will never keep their word, it is very troublesome to await their leisure or make any bad or good deal with them, nor do they have any fault by which they can be led and all of them say they want the friendship of the said fortress, and the war is to prevent one another from coming to trade or take merchandise from the factory because, whosoever has it, will forthwith be more powerful than the other. . . . it is more than two years since they have allowed any trade to come to this fortress, although there is, so it is said, much gold inland and a great lack of merchandise, which is the thing they most desire and esteem.[160]

Even the Mutapa state was concerned at this blockage of their main trade route, and sent an ambassador to Sofala to see what could be done.

Thus the Portuguese had to conciliate the Kiteve and other local rulers. They also rewarded individual traders who came to Sofala with gold. When a man arrived claiming to be an envoy from the Mutapa state, he was given presents as a reward.[161] Later, they gave cloth to some Africans who had come to trade, "to do them honour, because they were new men who had never come here, so that, later, they might enjoy coming here to buy and sell in the fortress."[162]

In these attempts to secure trade and to keep open a passage to the distant hinterland, the Portuguese often relied on Muslims as intermediaries. In 1506, rewards were given to three Africans who had come "to establish peace and friendship" and also to the five Muslims who had conducted them to Sofala.[163] Once the Portuguese had established a treaty with the Kiteve in 1571, they were required to pay tribute each year. This payment was made through the Muslims. A delegation from the Kiteve came to Sofala to collect the *curua* (*curva*, that is, tribute). When they got near Sofala, they sent word to the Portuguese captain, and he ordered them to be received by the Muslim sheikh of Sofala and several of his retinue, and they and the people from the Kiteve came in together to the Portuguese fort.[164]

Although some Muslims fulfilled this vital role, others competed strenuously against the Portuguese in an attempt to counter the Portuguese attempt at a trade monopoly. The growth of Angoche as a counter to the Portuguese is described by Newitt.[165] Other Muslims from Malindi, in theory a Portuguese ally, and Kilwa also opposed the Portuguese.[166] In the interior, Muslim traders denigrated the Portuguese, telling the locals that in Sofala they would be charged high prices for imports, while the Muslims charged less and brought the merchandise right up-country to the customers. Even the Muslims of Sofala, so vital as intermediaries, were accused of undermining the Portuguese. Traders from Kilwa and Malindi traded to Angoche in small boats, sambuks, laden with cloth which then depressed the market in Sofala. These illegal traders were able to flourish because the Muslims of Sofala told them when it was safe to make their passages, that is, when there were no Portuguese ships in Sofala.[167]

The Portuguese built up Mozambique as their main center in southern east Africa. Here, too, their power was far from being untrammeled. Their own documents describe how they used Muslim residents in the town and neighborhood as intermediaries. They consulted them on important matters; in 1542, for example, the subject under discussion was whether to send an embassy to the Mutapa state.[168]

The Portuguese also had to deal with the neighboring chiefs on the mainland. For most of the sixteenth century, the main power in the interior was the ruler of Makuani. Late in that century, the area was taken over by an expansionist Maravi state, one of whose elements was the Zimbas. This state ended up controlling large parts of east central Africa, from the Shire Valley into and through Makuani. In particular, they controlled the overland trade from the Shire Valley to Mossuril, inland from Mozambique.[169] Dos Santos describes Portuguese relations with Maurusa, the new ruler of the Makuani area, in the 1580s. At first he was totally hostile to the Portuguese, and they attacked him, but were defeated. Later, however, Maurusa modified his behavior and encouraged trade between his people and the Portuguese.

Most of the time, the Portuguese had relatively pacific relations with the near interior of Mozambique. The Portuguese were able to trade through his territory to link with other traders who brought ivory from far inland. Increasingly, it was the Yao who performed this interior trade. Sometimes they came to Mozambique themselves, though their main outlet increasingly was Kilwa.[170] The Makua people then are to be seen as similar to groups we described in the north, acting as hinges between the coast and inland tribes, though we know much more about this structure in the south than in the north. Whether the Makua can be described as brokers is a bit more difficult; they seem to have been mere exchangers. They did not play the facilitative role in the actual production process that the Indian brokers did, nor did they provide the sort of expertise and credit facilities that brokers did in India.

Before the the arrival of the Portuguese, the coastal towns had placed agents in the Mutapa state, and in its predecessor Great Zimbabwe, south of the Zambezi River, but they never tried to exercise any political control, or even influence; nor did they interfere in the production process. The Portuguese had much larger ambitions, hoping to do both, and so dominate the whole of the hinterland of their ports of Sofala and Mozambique. In this, they were motivated by the desire to make converts, and, more important, to emulate the Spanish and find their own El Dorado or, a little more prosaically, Potosí. If they could control production, especially of gold, they would no longer have to negotiate with, and even be subject to, such people as the Makua rulers, the Yao, the Mutapa ruler, and others. Beach and Mudenge have described Portuguese relations with the disaggregated Mutapa state very well.[171] The scattered political structure and the gold-producing areas were impossible to control. Newitt notes that the actual Mutapa empire or state measured perhaps 230 km by 150 km, and was surrounded by partially loyal and/or subordinate various other Karanga chiefdoms and ministates. The power of the Mutapa ruler extended over fluctuating and dubiously defined areas.[172] Indeed, to call this a state or an empire may be to side-step an analysis of precisely how one should describe this sort of entity. The more neutral term "authority structure" may be more appropriate.

The vicissitudes of Portuguese activities on the plateau in the seventeenth century, and the coup de grâce administered by Changamire, meant that the Portuguese were unable to create a settlement colony on the plateau; instead, by the end of the seventeenth century, they were driven back to the Zambezi Valley, where the existing institution of the prazos expanded and became the dominant motif of the Portuguese presence in east Africa. But so loosely were the prazos tied into the official Portuguese presence in Mozambique that it is not correct to see their existence as extending Portuguese political control over the vast hinterland of the southern Swahili coast. Economic ties continued, especially for ivory, and then for slaves, but these were mediated by various African groups.

In sum, there are intimate political and economic relations between umland and port city. None of these cities can be described as an entrepôt in the way that Melaka or modern Singapore can be; all had relations with some hinterland extending beyond the umland. This assertion is still debatable in the north. Further research may help us describe more accurately the hinterlands of these cities. If the present claims of vast hinterlands are not backed up with more hard data, then we may be justified in seeing these northern port cities as entrepôt with connections only to their umland. The current trend stresses that there were hinterlands, and here my discussion of the origins of ivory makes a contribution. In the south, we can clearly see coastal people, that is, Muslims and Portuguese, connecting the port cities and the far interior, both in economic and political ways. A more precise use of port city terminology will enable us to use new empirical research findings more rigorously and to be more precise about coast-interior connections in this period.

Chapter 4

East Africa in the World-Economy

It is clear that the Indian economy was much more advanced than was that of either the coast or interior of east Africa during the sixteenth and seventeenth centuries. This applies in such areas as credit facilities, banking, an integrated and productive manufacturing sector, craft specialization, and even in the general penetration and efficiency of the state. A concrete illustration of this general proposition is the vast profits that Indians, and others, made when they traded with the Swahili coast. On the face of it, the exchange seems to have been unequal. However, the nature of this inequality, or whether it existed, are subjects of debate.[1]

Much of east Africa's trade was with western India. Sketching the economies of these two areas will lay the foundations for a discussion of the political economy of east Africa. I concentrate on the production of cotton cloths in India and gold and ivory in Africa. The areas under discussion are Gujarat, in northwest India, and the Mutapa state on the Zimbabwe Plateau, which was linked to the Swahili port cities of Sofala and Kilwa.

For centuries on either side of 1500, India was the world's great producer of cotton cloths in a vast array of styles, colors, and qualities.[2] The two main producing areas were Gujarat and Coromandel. One reason for the predominance of these two areas may be that wet-rice cultivation had reached a peak of efficiency, thus releasing labor for craft production. Cotton was grown in the black-soil belts of the river valleys of the Gujarat heartland, especially in the zone from Broach to Baroda. Broadly speaking, coarse cloth for local consumption was produced in the village itself, with the whole productive process taking place locally, and the basis being exchange rather than sale for money. Thus, the bulk of production never entered the market. Other cloths, both fine and coarse, were destined to be traded either within India, where there was a market of some 100 million people, or overseas. In this case the cotton was grown, harvested, cleaned, and spun by the peasants in the village. The work still took place in household units; the home served as the factory.

Full-time specialists did the later processing. One category of people wove the thread into cloth. A specific caste group bleached the finished cloth. After bleaching, the cloth was colored, either by printing, painting, or dyeing. The ingredients for the dyes came from local natural products, including the famous indigo. A large degree of specialization had developed, with different family groups doing the cotton-carding, spinning, unwinding and rewinding of the yarn, formation of the cloth on the loom, bleaching, dyeing, and printing and painting of designs. This was a highly integrated production process. In Gujarat, for example, the towns of Broach and Navsari were major weaving centers, drawing in thread from far-flung rural areas. Similarly, one variety of cloth was produced near Agra, but it was dyed near Ahmadabad.

How did this cloth enter the market? The answer is that some cloth really was in the market even before it was produced. Some peasant producers were specialists who grew no food, others alternated according to season between food and cotton (really thread) production. In either case, the raw materials for the cloth had to be bought before the arduous process of manufacture could begin. It was merchants, or more likely their agents, in these rural or urban areas, who provided capital to buy the dyes, the raw cotton, the "machinery," and food for subsistence. This was still a remote relationship, in the sense that the owner of capital, the merchant, did not control the means of production: The producer did. Most often the merchant and producer were separated by the ubiquitous figure of the broker, the essential go-between and facilitator. The merchant could specify what patterns and quality he wanted, but the process of production was outside his control. At first glance, this looks something like the well-known European putting-out system, where an owner of capital advanced money against the finished product. In the Indian system, however, producers were less rigorously bound to the financier than was the case in Europe. For example, producers had the option of accepting a better offer for their output, and returning the advance to the original financier.

It is unclear how extensive this system was. Much cloth entered the market only when it was finished. The various producers doing their variegated processing retained ownership until the product was finished; only then was it sold. Thus, much merchant capital did not get near to production, even in the remote-controlled putting-out form, but rather was restricted to commerce. One way to look at this is to see substantial merchants, who sent off ships each year, using advance payments, while petty traders and visitors would buy a finished product for export in the port itself.

Much of the process was regulated by the seasons. Weaving was usually done during the monsoon months, June to September, when the air was moister. During the dry season, November to February, the final stages of production—dyeing, painting, and printing—were at their peak. Goods had to be ready to send to east Africa, and to the more important great market of the Red Sea, by April. The finished product was collected, loaded on bullock carts or pack animals, or taken by river (or for short distances portered by men) and taken to a central town. The great ports and their outlying villages were major weaving centers as well; thus their transportation costs were minimized. The whole productive process was very complicated. Merchants interacted with moneylenders, though often the two were the same. Others provided facilities for transferring money within India, and even beyond. Shipowners were usually also merchants. Brokers played a large role in facilitating collection and payment, and they were the essential mediators between producer and buyer. Rich merchants had their own brokers; others acted on behalf of various merchant groups. This was a highly sophisticated and differentiated precapitalist system.

Cloth destined for trade was distributed over a vast area—not just within India but all over the littoral of the Indian Ocean. Different markets required different cloths. The finest went to elite customers; cheaper, more common, stuffs went for general consumption wherever there was a market. By the time the cloth reached a port, it may have changed hands several times, but it ended up with a merchant who specialized in exports, often to areas where he had kin or caste fellows resident. The cloths were bundled into bales that contained twenty pieces of cloth. Then they were loaded on board ship. Taxes here were minimal, probably reflecting the land-oriented ethos of the Muslim rulers of Gujarat. On board ship were a range of travelers. Some were peddlers, petty traders with a bundle of cloth that they hoped to hawk in some distant port. They would receive a local product in exchange, and hope to make a small profit on the transaction. Then they would go on to another port, and repeat this same process of exchange and minimal profit. Other people on board ship were much more substantial; they were big merchants or their agents. Crew and master also took goods along, free of freight, to sell on their own account.

The situation in east Africa, and especially in its only large "state," the Mutapa entity, was very different. Gold was mined, and washed from rivers, in many scattered locations all over the Zimbabwe Plateau. Well over 1 ton was exported each year. Gold collecting was a part-time occupation for the Shona-speaking peoples of the region within the Mutapa state and its neighbors. The economy was self-sufficient, based on cattle and agriculture. Gold had no intrinsic value, for this area had no coined money. Rather, at slack times in the agricultural cycle, peasants would wash and mine for gold. The product was exchanged for more useful items, particularly cloth and beads from India. The former was something of a necessity, for it can be cold on the plateau, and local cloth was scarce and expensive. Both cloth and beads were also widely used in exchange. It seemed strange, to covetous Indians and Europeans, that gold production was a discretionary activity, undertaken only when there was a need for an imported item that could only be paid for with gold.

Ivory was highly prized in India. It was widely used for ornamentation, and especially to make bangles for women. The demand was extremely elastic, for Hindu women traditionally broke their bangles on the death of the husband. For Africans, gold, just like ivory, had a very different meaning. It was not valued as it was in India. Africans of the area had evolved efficient, albeit hazardous, methods for hunting elephants, including pits, traps, and the use of spears. However, the object of the hunt was to acquire meat. One elephant could yield up to 5 tons of meat, and hence invaluable protein. The tusks, which could weigh up to 40 kg, were a by-product, and accordingly had little value. In some areas, they were stuck in the ground as fences or palings. In this almost noncommercial world, Muslim merchants or their agents often had to press cloths onto the locals, and trust that they would produce gold or ivory in return; this trust was usually well placed.

The Mutapa state, from which these products originated, took little part in this trade. The concerns of the rulers and chiefs lay in land and cattle and women. Certainly gold production was heavily taxed, even to 50 percent; similarly, when an elephant was killed the tusk that lay nearest the ground was sent off to the ruler. This was not, however, a state that had much concern with, or derived much revenue from, trade. The success and failure of these Shona states was governed by internal factors, not by levies on goods produced for export.

To reach the market, gold and ivory had to travel some hundreds of kilometers to one of several port cities on the coast, of which Kilwa and Sofala were the most important. The gold and ivory were loaded onto the heads of porters, or shipped down rivers, to another world and to a market in the Swahili port cities.

Around 1500, the great exit for gold was Sofala, in the extreme south of the Swahili-speaking area of the east African coast. However, Sofala was too far south for ships from India, or the Middle East, to make a direct passage on one monsoon. Instead, local Swahili craft took goods north in various kinds of dhows to the great center of Kilwa, where they entered the international trade of the Afrasian (or Arabian) Sea, or indeed entered the world economy. This may explain why Kilwa dominated Sofala. Merchants from all over the shores of the Afrasian Sea were found in Kilwa. It was in these Janus-faced Swahili port cities that cloths and beads were landed, and gold and ivory exported. In other words, highly skilled manufactures with a very large value-added component were exchanged for unprocessed primary products. The profits for the foreign merchants, or the local Swahili middlemen, could be enormous, reflecting the lack of use value of the primary products from the interior, and the high use value of the imports.

The Swahili port cities functioned as hinges, collecting goods from the interior and bringing them to the coast, and exchanging them for goods brought from Gujarat and other places. Unlike Gujarat, the economies of these Swahili port cities were not yet fully monetized; gold was almost never minted at Kilwa. Rather, gold was treated as a commodity, and it was exchanged unminted for Indian goods. The ports were classic mediators, or compradors. The dominant clans in the town, or the ruler, took full advantage of their position, levying enormous taxes on this trade. This is in marked contrast to India. In the Mutapa state, the rulers levied tribute on the production of certain goods destined to be exported, notably ivory and gold. In India, the state taxed cultivation, that is, demanded land revenue be paid on all cultivated land. A relatively sophisticated administration ensured that actual collections were much closer to the ideal norm than was the case in Africa. The Swahili city-states were autonomous, and so could demand high customs duties. The governors of Gujarat's port cities were dependent on their inland masters, and so took only low duties. Even these were not retained in the ports, but rather made up part of the inland-oriented state's total revenues.

The ivory and gold were transported from east Africa to India, where it was turned into fine works of art and minted or used for ornamentation. The better cloths stayed in the ports of east Africa; a small amount was traded to the elite up-country, or were used as presents to conciliate the rulers of the territories from whence the gold and ivory came. Coarser cloths, and beads, went in to the interior and were traded to those common people who needed them and who were prepared to produce gold and ivory to buy them.

Obviously these two economies were closely connected, yet vastly different. How can we conceptualize these connections? East Africa has been subjected to a range of political economy analyses, most of them inspired at least to an extent by Marx. In the following section, I sketch dependency analyses, discussions of the African mode of production, and world-system models.

In the 1970s, much work was produced on the nature of impacts on east

Africa before colonialism, or before capitalism. Some of these works claimed an unbroken process of underdevelopment affecting Africa for many centuries before the capitalism appeared; others tried to elaborate on the nature of this earlier impact and its precise effects on Africa.[3]

The first to apply dependency notions to Africa was the radical scholar and political activist Walter Rodney. In the preface to his seminal, albeit flawed, book of 1972, he made his stance clear by writing he does not say "'all mistakes and shortcomings are entirely my own responsibility.' That is sheer bourgeois subjectivism. Responsibility in matters of these sorts is always collective, especially with regard to the remedying of short-comings. The purpose has been to try and reach Africans who wish to explore further the nature of their exploitation, rather than to satisfy the 'standards' set by our oppressors and their spokesmen in the academic world." While he writes of Africa's "freedom of choice, which had clearly been seriously undermined by the pre-colonial trade," the analysis of the earlier period concentrates on the west African slave trade. He seems to equate the real impact with colonial conquest, which he dates at 1885. This, in a Leninist way, he sees as capitalist imperialism. No doubt there were African and Indian collaborators, but it was Europeans who were the main agents, and their impact was massive only from the late nineteenth century. But while capitalism and imperialism were to blame, the final responsibility, he says, must rest with Africans themselves.[4]

There have been two more recent major empirically based dependency analyses of east Africa, by Abdul Sheriff and E. A. Alpers. Sheriff put forward his basic ideas in an article published in 1976.[5] His key theme is that when two areas that are not at the same level of socioeconomic and technological development engage in trade, the weaker party suffers. Thus, east Africa before 1500 was already a classic example of underdevelopment, even though the situation was greatly exacerbated once industrial capitalism appeared in the nineteenth century. His thesis found fuller, but not noticeably different, expression in his book.[6]

A powerful trend in African historiography in the 1960s and 1970s was an attempt to show the autonomy of Africa, to avoid depicting it as merely a passive recipient of influences, some benign, most detrimental, from more advanced societies.[7] The English empiricist A. G. Hopkins noted that if the trend is to stress the autonomy of Africans and their history, then there is a problem in saying that all African history is the history of dependency.[8]

There is a lack of fit between two most desirable trends in African history, one concerned to stress African autonomy, the other to write from a dependency standpoint. Alpers presents the dilemma very clearly. In an article published two years before his major book, he claimed that the trading activities of Europeans or foreigners over five hundred years led finally to political subjugation in the nineteenth century.[9] His views had changed by the time *Ivory and Slaves* was published. In a most refreshing self-analysis, he wrote that his thesis, written for the School of Oriental and African Studies in 1966, took part in the then-current attempt to show the autonomy of African history. "The present book no longer shares these assumptions. The basic argument of this study is that the changing patterns of international trade in East Central Africa during these centuries [c. 1400 to the late nineteenth century], including the initiatives taken by Africans themselves, must be set within the context of the historical roots of underdevelopment in Africa."[10] Dependency writers conclude that while things definitely got worse from the late eighteenth century as capitalism impacted fully on the area, this was only an exacerbation of a long-standing exploitative situation. My task is to identify the nature of this exploitation before capitalism, and to ask whether it existed at all.

A second area of scholarly discussion was the matter of modes of production in Africa. The first person to investigate this was Catherine Coquery-Vidrovitch. Influenced by Marx's notion of an Asiatic mode of production, she wrote that "In Asia . . . it is a question of despotism and direct exploitation through generalized slavery, whereas in Africa . . . there is a superimposed bureaucracy which interferes only indirectly with the community."[11] In a later elaboration, she found a dual economy in Africa: There was subsistence agriculture and parallel with this "war and trade activities creating prosperity for vast political ensembles." This is what she calls "an African mode of production characterized precisely by the apparently contradictory co-existence of the subsistence village and long-distance, even transcontinental, trade." In Africa, the elites never interfered directly in production. Rulers did not levy taxes on the peasants, as African agriculture could not produce a surplus, nor did any ruler need to take large quantities of food from the villages. What tributes were taken were not used to pay for services or to provide finance but rather were hoarded, immediately consumed, or even destroyed.

African despots did not exploit their own people, but rather their neighbors, by means of long-distance trade. Much of their surplus came from this activity, and some from war. In short, this is a tributary mode of production, but an unusual one in that "it was based upon the combination of a patriarchal agrarian economy with a low internal surplus and the exclusive ascendancy of one group over long-distance trade." However, "No African regime, nor matter how despotic, felt the need to eliminate communal village structures within its borders, for the village scarcely interfered with the process of exploitation. As long as the village transmitted its tribute to the chief of the district or of the province, it ran the life of the collectivity as it pleased."[12]

Coquery-Vidrovitch asserts that this contrasts with what she calls the Asiatic mode, but she claims that this mode has despots and generalized slavery below, which produces huge irrigation works, or the Pyramids, or the Great Wall of China. My understanding of the Asiatic mode is similar to her account of the African mode, where, contrary to her (and Marx), the state's writ in fact ran rather lightly over the land, and certainly there was no generalized slavery.[13] There may be theoretical and empirical problems with a mode of production based on a dual economy, for surely the very essence of a mode of production is that there is at least some integration.

A useful, though now dated, overview was provided by Robin Law. He stressed the unresolved divisions among the protagonists, and doubted the utility of Marxism for an analysis of precolonial Africa.[14] The debate was extended in a collaborative work in 1981, while a more recent synopsis of the whole modes of production debate in Africa appeared in a Canadian journal in 1985.[15] Coquery-Vidrovitch provided a defense of her past work, though she was noticeably vaguer than she was in her original and seminal analysis. Most of the contributors claimed that the notion of a mode of production has very little utility for African studies at all. The third part of the symposium was meant to be about "initiating new approaches" but there is very little discussion of neo-Marxist alternatives, such as dependency theory or the world-systems model.

This is not the place to sketch the basic outlines of Immanuel Wallerstein's great work.[16] Although his influence has waned over the last few years, I believe that his model deserves to be taken seriously, and that elaborations and rebuttals of it can still produce excellent work.[17] I discuss how a world-systems approach may be helpful when we look at east Africa in this period before capitalism. However, the empirical data I present below leads me to wonder if indeed the world-system model is most useful; it could be that more attention to production and less to exchange will provide a more convincing way to understand relations between India and east Africa at this time.

I do not treat Wallerstein's main concern, namely, the modern world-system that emerged in Europe during the sixteenth century, but rather the contributions of Wallerstein and others that attempt to apply world-system notions to the period before capitalism. In areas outside Europe that were external to the modern world-system, this of course extends until they were incorporated; in some areas, this occurred only in the nineteenth century.

The main trend in research on the period before capitalism is towards uniformitarianism, that is, that there were several or many centers in the world that had exchange relations both within their own areas and with other areas. Being precapitalist, these were mostly benign exchanges. There were weaker and stronger areas to be sure, but in none of these areas did capital control production, and this meant that exchange usually was beneficial to both sides, even though production methods or modes varied greatly.

Wallerstein's contribution to the study of precapitalist world-systems is important. He found two sorts of earlier world-systems, namely world-empires and world-economies. Both were inherently unstable. Sooner or later world-empires collapsed, as their rulers lacked the capacity to enforce their will over their vast territories and also because, as rulers, they had to defend their whole domain. World-economies were destined to be taken over by world-empires. World-economies are more or less a residual category; he noted early on that there are world-empires, and then "For convenience and want of a better term," there are world-economies. "Prior to the modern era [and the modern world-system], world-economies tended either to be converted into empires or to disintegrate."[18] Wallerstein recognized that this was unsatisfactory. In 1990, he wrote that the new challenge for world-system theorists is the "elaboration of world-systems other than that of the capitalist world-economy."[19] Earlier, he said that "We shall have to rework our knowledge of world historical data (as well as expand it) in order to analyze coherently how precapitalist economies functioned, which will—I believe—open many doors for us."[20]

Wallerstein and Ravi Arvind Palat wrote on India as a precapitalist core.[21] They sketch the growth of trade all around the Indian Ocean area and the subsequent accumulation of riches in the two most commercialized areas: Coromandel and Gujarat. These flows "represented a transfer of the products of lowly-remunerated laborers located elsewhere along the Indian Ocean littoral to South Asia." This was especially to be seen in the huge rise of coarse cotton cloth production in Gujarat and Coromandel, and the consequent "deindustrialization" of other regions in the Middle East and southeast Asia. Indeed, in this precapitalist world-economy, there are semiperipheries too. Bengal exported rice to Coromandel and raw silk to Gujarat, but at the same time, it sent cloths to Indonesia, and thus has the Janus-faced character of a semiperiphery. The emerging core zones of Gujarat and Coromandel "progressively drew upon sources of subsistence and raw materials for artisanal manufacture from increasingly distant regions—leading to the incorporation and subsequent peripheralization of the latter zones within an emerging world-economy centered around, and integrated by, transport across the Indian Ocean." Thus, there was "from the eastern coasts of Africa through the Arabian peninsula and the Indian subcontinent to the Malay archipelago . . . an evolving world-economy." This did not lead to capitalism in the area, especially because there was no ruthless drive to accumulate, and also because the basis lay in the nature of wet-rice cultivation.

Janet Abu-Lughod's book identified a world-system in the century from 1250 to 1350 whose heartland was the Middle East, but which included Europe, China, and the Indian Ocean.[22] The linkage of these areas, based on long-distance trade, resulted in an economic upturn in them all. This was a world system that linked a number of world-systems, each of which had cores, semiperipheries, and peripheries making up an integrated production system. None of these world-systems were dominant; rather, there was existence and mutual tolerance and profit within the larger world system. In short, she finds a benign interacting group of world-systems, or world economies. One core was the "Arabo-Persian imperial centers" another "the towns of developing western Europe."[23]

André Gunder Frank claims that there has been a world-system in existence for at least the last five thousand years. I believe this sort of analysis obscures change, yet this should be the prime concern of any historian. Frank finds that there were shifts within this world economy over this long period, and especially that "the 'Rise of the West' represents a shift from East to West within the same world economic system." He explicitly denies the significance of the emergence of capitalism, something that I still find to be an absolutely seminal event in world history. His attack on European exceptionalism is well taken, though hardly novel in this day and age.[24]

Christopher Chase-Dunn and Thomas D. Hall have produced a much more satisfactory and challenging contribution. In the opening chapter of their edited collection, they assert that there have been world-systems long before capitalism.[25] Some of these are stateless, but most are state-based. However, it is incorrect to assume that in these systems one must find the sort of core/periphery (this is their usage) relations that one finds in the capitalist system. Rather than assuming this, they ask that scholars look in a fresh way at "the existence and nature of intersocietal inequalities." Even though one may find, in state-based world-systems, a core that accumulates resources by exploiting peripheries, intersocietal hierarchies could also be quite different from those that developed under capitalism.

Chase-Dunn and Hall also confront Wallerstein's perceived economism by noting that there are all sorts of exchanges: trade, information, presumably, along Voll's lines, even religion.[26] Even if one only looks at material exchanges, these can be gifts, tribute, commodity trade, and so on. Here they agree with Jane Schneider and say that exchange of prestige goods is not epiphenomenal at all. They can be very important because elites can use them to get or maintain power. Thus, at least by implication, they find that luxuries as well as necessities can create systemic relations, as can political and military power.

For Chase-Dunn and Hall, all exchange is not unequal exchange. There are broadly two types of core-periphery relations in precapitalist world-systems. First is core/periphery differentiation, where there is interaction between societies in a world-system, as compared with core/periphery hierarchies, where there is domination that can include political domination, extraction of resources, and unequal exchange. One task is to measure degrees of intersocietal exploitation, and this is very difficult, especially when the kinds of resources that are socially valued differ.

Finally, Chase-Dunn and Hall produce a list of world-system types. They follow Eric Wolf's three modes of production, and find the Indian Ocean to be an example of "commercializing state-based world-systems in which important aspects of commodification have developed but the system is still dominated by the logic of the tributary modes." In the core of these commercializing world-systems, in which the core seems to be an empire, there is more use of money, of credit and interest, of wage labor, and of price-setting markets. In the core-empires, the rulers use sophisticated means to tax merchants, "and outside the bounds of empires, in interstitial semiperipheral regions, autonomous city-states controlled by merchant and production capitalists created and sustained market relations between empires and peripheral regions." They say these centralized empires will be more exploitative toward peripheries than earlier empires because they are better at concentrating resources at the center.

Turning now to Africa, Wallerstein has very little to say about Africa in general, and even less about east Africa in his main work, *The Modern World-System*. However, in two shorter pieces, he locates east Africa firmly within his wider framework. In an essay published in 1973, Wallerstein left a few doors open. He noted, in familiar fashion, that "Prior to that [that is, incorporation around 1750], African world-systems were non-capitalist systems. They related as external arenas to specific other world-systems, including in one case the European capitalist world-economy. To understand this earlier period is in many ways far more difficult than to understand the present, for we shall have to sharpen our understanding of social systems to do it."[27]

By 1976, he had become less hesitant. He noted that "The contemporary economy and polity of Africa, while its antecedents are indigenous, must be analyzed in the context of the specifics of an evolving world system of economic and political relations starting in the sixteenth century, leading at first to the gradual involvement of Africa with worldwide exchange relations and later, by the middle of the nineteenth century, into more direct incorporation and finally, by the early twentieth century, to the subordination of the continent to the economic and political needs and objectives of the major Western powers."[28] Before this time, contact consisted only of a trade in luxuries. The trade of the Portuguese was

> essentially of the same nature, and involved essentially the same products, as the trans-Saharan trade that dates back at least to the tenth century A.D. and the Indian Ocean trade that goes back further still.
>
> All of this trade prior to 1750 which involved various African states with partners outside of themselves was "long-distance trade" whose quantity varied on a market determined less by demand than by effective supply, that is, of products successfully transported from the point of production to the mart. As a consequence, production was not determined by variations in this demand but by the politico-technological ability of the long-distance traders to transport the material. The resulting trade involved no transfer of surplus, but could in fact be considered a mutual windfall. Because this was so, this trade had very limited consequences for the social organization of the trading societies, except perhaps to strengthen somewhat the political machineries that guaranteed it. A stoppage in the trade, which occurred frequently over the centuries, had relatively few repercussions other than on the lives of the state officials and merchants directly living off the trade.[29]

Wallerstein's and Palat's article, mentioned above, raises several questions about the place of Africa in the early modern world. Remember that they claimed that the cores in Gujarat and Coromandel fed on lowly remunerated laborers in other areas, and even caused deindustrialization in the Middle East and southeast Asia. However, they include "the eastern coasts of Africa" as part of "an evolving world-economy" centered on Gujarat and Coromandel. This leaves the position of the African interior obscure, but we must assume that it is not to be included.

This point must be made clear. In his own major work and in smaller pieces devoted to Africa, Wallerstein finds no exploitation while an area is external to the modern world-system and when the exchange is only in luxuries. Later, Palat and Wallerstein write more fully about the situation before the modern world-system, and they find that in this India-centered world-economy there can, even though there is no capitalism, still be inequality and unequal trade. The coast of east Africa is included here as part of this precapitalist world-economy. The interior is implicitly to be seen as external to this world-economy, just as both it and the coast were to the evolving modern world-system until the nineteenth century. The key questions are the precise position of the east African coast in this world-economy, and then the coast's relations with the interior. Palat and Wallerstein, at least implicitly, leave out the interior, which then must be external, while Chase-Dunn and Hall imply that it is included.

In the following section, I provide some data that will specify more clearly the position of the interior of east Africa in this world-economy. I look at profits first, which raises the matter of use values and how export goods were produced in the African interior. We will find that in the interior the traders from the coast had to try and create a market de novo. I look at the role of the state. Finally, a case study of cloth will test the notion of deindustrialization.

The European sources are full of accounts of the vast profits to be made by foreign traders in east Africa. On the face of it, this looks like economically advanced foreigners shamefully exploiting naive Africans, and this both when trade was backed by force, as the Portuguese did, or when it was done on a basis of peaceful competition, as everyone else did. In 1653, an English merchant, Nicholas Buckeridge, found that goods that cost 8,000 *mahmudis* (a Gujarati coin) in India could be traded for ivory on the Swahili coast that would sell for 80,000 mahmudis in India.[30] A Portuguese memorandum of 1525 said that a quantity of small yellow and blue beads that cost 1.05 maticals in Cambay would sell for 21.28 maticals in Sofala; in the same markets, cloth sold for five times its cost price.[31] In virgin markets, even greater profits could be made. In the extreme south, at Delagoa Bay, João de Castro told the king in 1545 that for a few beads worth 3 *vintems* one could buy a bahar of ivory that would sell for more than 100 cruzados in India. A vintem is 20 *reis*, a cruzado 400, so 60 reis worth of beads bought ivory worth 40,000 reis.[32]

Alexandre Lobato and Manuel Lobato have produced useful data that summarizes much information on this matter, and shows the effect of the cost of transportation.[33] For example, prices increased enormously between Malindi and Sofala. In 1530, cloth bought for 100 in Gujarat sold for 220 in Malindi and 780 in Sofala. Large beads went from 100 in Gujarat to 200 in Malindi and a staggering 1,300 to 2,600 in Sofala. In 1611, a particular sort of cloth cost 100 in Gujarat, 200 in Goa, and 620 in the Mutapa state.

Luckily we have two estimates of net profits, which presumably take into account transportation costs, taxes, and other charges. In the 1630s, even though prices had fallen in the Zambezi Valley, the Portuguese figured that they could buy cloth for 264,000 xerafins in Goa and sell it for 1,270,000, leaving a net profit of about 500,000 xerafins.[34] Costs then seem to be about 500,000 xerafins, or almost two times the original investment. In 1570, Monclaro claimed that one could buy 100 cruzados worth of beads in Chaul, string them in Sena, and sell them on the other side of the river, producing a profit after all expenses of 3,000 cruzados.[35]

In an early modern context, these profits seem to be high, but not far beyond normal returns of the time. We must remember that sea trade was extremely hazardous, subject as it was to shipwreck; the losing of a monsoon; spoilage on board ship; and sometimes also extortion from local land powers, port city controllers, and pirates, including the Portuguese. On the Red Sea route, Indian merchants made a return of at least 50 percent on their investment.[36] As a rule of thumb, the English East India Company said that the sale price in England must be three times the prime cost in India in order for a profit to be made.[37]

Nevertheless, these are huge profits, and this of course rings a bell with dependency theorists: Surely the Indians and Arabs and Portuguese who are making these profits are exploiting someone? Consider that the exports are primary products—gold and ivory—while the imports are manufactures—cloths and beads—and we seem to have a classic first world–third world situation, as noted by authors such as Rodney, Sheriff, and Alpers. The reality is rather different. If we study the three main products traded, and introduce the notion of relative values or use values, we may then find a very different result, a rather Panglossian one where it seems everyone did well. This conclusion would confirm Abu-Lughod's view.

In terms of quantity, internal trade was much more important than was long-distance trade to the coast. It dealt in such local products as iron, salt, and foodstuffs, and was handled by Africans from the inland. When we investigate this, as the proponents of the autonomy of African history have urged us to do, we find no state interference. It was taxed, to be sure, but at nothing like the rate levied on export goods.

Where did the export goods come from? Gold came from very scattered areas of the Zimbabwe Plateau. It was produced both from mines, using relatively sophisticated techniques, and from alluvial deposits. Regardless of method used, this was a part-time, and a seasonal, activity. António Bocarro noted that people in the Mutapa state "will not exert themselves to seek gold unless they are constrained by necessity for want of clothes or provisions." This activity was unusual because food, and cattle, were readily available.[38] The producers dug and washed gold when the agricultural cycle gave them free time, and they did this only to satisfy an immediate need. In this economy, if winter was coming on, one would get some gold and exchange it for cloths; there was apparently no notion of producing extra amounts to be hoarded and sold later.

In part this was because this was an economy where commodities were exchanged but coins were not used.[39] There have been many studies of coins in the east African interior and on the coast. In the later sixteenth century, Dos Santos described various weights of uncoined gold, and small copper bars, but he noted that small earthenware beads, glazed and colored, and any sort of cloth were also used just like money.[40] Kilwa minted copper coins, but their circulation was very restricted. Recently, Helen Brown has found three gold coins from this port city from the early fourteenth century. Silver coins were produced in Pemba in the eleventh century, and in Mombasa in the sixteenth.[41]

Gold was a commodity, and it was exchanged by weight like any other product. Presumably, coined gold should be seen as a universal commodity, even if at this time it was not a token but rather had an intrinsic value, so that the amount of gold in a coin reflected not some notional value but a real one. The point is that coins can be used to buy anything, but in this economy one could exchange a piece of gold for some other product only if the other partner wanted gold.

There were other factors that militated against gold being produced, and accumulated, routinely. The state took a heavy tax on production, and this must have been a disincentive. In this nonmonetized economy, purchasers were not easy to find. Dos Santos wrote that in one area "the natives of the country do not trouble to seek it or dig for it, as they are at a distance from the Portuguese who might buy it; but they are much occupied with the breeding of cattles, of which there are great numbers in these lands."[42] On the other hand, the presence of Portuguese could also act as a disincentive, for the Africans knew how covetous these torwa (foreigner) people were. In Maramuca, "the Kaffirs who possess these lands will not allow more gold to be extracted than is necessary, that the Portuguese may not covet and obtain possession of their lands."[43]

Indeed, even the Portuguese had to reorient their thinking on this matter. Like other Europeans, they were conditioned to think of gold as providing immediate riches. The model they had in mind was the fabulous silver production of Potosí. The reality on the Zimbabwe Plateau was quite different. Around 1570, some inland Portuguese had already been offered mines to work, "but they would not accept inasmuch as there is greater expenditure in extracting the gold, and but little is taken in a day; business and trade are more profitable."[44] When the Portuguese got to Manica at this same time they "expected to find it [gold] in the streets and woods." They soon found out that it was extracted only with great difficulty, so they went back to Sofala.[45] In short, gold was "the product of the secondary activities of an agricultural economy."[46] As Hall says, it was "mined as a marginal activity in the interstices of the annual agro-pastoral cycle."[47]

Comparative advantage or comparative costs, the sort of thing David Ricardo wrote about, is not the key defining characteristic of this trade; rather it was use or relative values. The general notion is that a society can export products which it does not value, but which are valued in other areas. Goods, then, have a cultural as well as a material value. This would seem to account for the massive profits that the traders, nearly all foreigners, made. In the case of gold, it was of little use in a nonmonetized society, but in one like India, which in the early modern period was monetizing rapidly, it had an obvious demand. The same holds true regarding the slave trade from late in the eighteenth century. Slaves were essential for Brazilian plantations, but they were not in great demand in Africa except for some domestic and minor agricultural work. And so also for beads, produced in massive quantities in India for little cost, but highly prized in Africa.

The concept of relative values applies most clearly to the trade in ivory. From an Indian point of view, when an African killed an elephant, he was gaining a tusk that could be sold. But from the African point of view, it was much more than this. A dead elephant provided an important source of protein. Killing an elephant got rid of a pest that damaged crops. And, a dead elephant produced two tusks. One went to the local ruler, but the other could be exchanged for some other product of more use or prestige value than ivory, such as cloths or beads. Jean-Baptiste Tavernier, basing his account on a Portuguese who had just returned from the northern Swahili coast, noted an even more extreme disregard for the value of ivory. On this coast, there were "many enclosures fenced with elephants' tusks only, and that some of them are more than a league in circuit."[48]

Our sources are clear that the African hunters wanted elephants for food; the tusks were a by-product. Dos Santos relates: "The principal reason why they hunt the elephants and kill them is to obtain the flesh for food, and secondly to sell the tusks."[49] J. H. van Linschoten confirms this: "Their chiefest living is by hunting, and by flesh of Elephants, which is the cause that so many Elephantes teeth are brought from thence."[50] An account from 1560 elaborates on the food value of elephants. Up to 150 Africans went into bush, each with a small hatchet, found elephants, and drove them into the bush, "and once they are in the bush they attack them whilst some of them run ahead and others stay behind without being able to leave the path, and the Kaffirs fall upon them and hit them at will with their little hatchets on the legs when they can, or only on one leg and, though these wounds they make are small, the weight of their bodies quickly breaks their legs. And it takes only a few of them to eat a whole one and the trunk, which is the best, they send to the king and they say that, after the trunk, the feet are the best. The meat has a strong smell but seems to be edible."[51]

These findings are directly contrary to those put forward by E. A. Alpers.[52] His thesis is that both the gold and the ivory trades were quite central in the economies of east Africa, and that these trades produced underdevelopment in the area because they extracted labor from agricultural production. More recent research makes an overwhelming case for this being a misguided analysis; in particular, the ivory trade in this period, though not later, did not have any detrimental affects on the economies of east Africa. It is a matter of scale. At this time, the trade was not so large as to cause detrimental results in east Africa either ecologically or economically. Indeed, Alpers himself really knows this. Contrary to Africa, in India ivory was highly valued, especially because of the Hindu requirement that a woman's bracelets be broken when she was widowed, thus ensuring a constant demand. Hence the massive profits, and also the lack of "exploitation." As Alpers noted, "the precolonial trade of east Africa was governed by the congruence of different economic systems with different sets of perceptions."[53]

Overall, the advantage lay with Africa. Most of the products they received were discretionary rather than necessities in their agricultural and hunting lives, except for cloth on the plateau, though even for this there were local substitutes. For the trader, however, a sale or exchange was obviously essential, for this was his raison d'être. Thus, Africans could work as much or as little as they wanted. A Portuguese account of 1513 sums up the matter well: "Although there is gold in all the land it is spread out throughout the land and there is none who has it in such quantity as to allow him to come so far to trade it, and also because they wait for the merchandise to be taken to them where each one may buy what he wants."[54] Similarly, Couto noted that "when they have found sufficient to buy two pieces of cloth to clothe themselves, they will not work any more."[55]

Faced with this situation, the traders tried to create a market, or force one, on the African producers. In a manner reminiscent of unscrupulous hire-purchase arrangements today, the Muslim merchants foisted off their goods and forced the Africans to consume, and so also produce. João de Barros's account is something of a classic:

> As the land is rich in gold, if the people were covetous a great quantity would be obtained, but they are so lazy in seeking it, or rather covet it so little, that one of these negroes must be very hungry before he will dig for it. To get the gold from them, the Moors who carry on the trade among them make use of artifice to arouse their cupidity, for they cover them and their wives with clothes, beads, and trinkets, with which they are delighted, and after they have thus pleased them, they give them all these things on credit, telling them to go and dig for gold and if they return in a certain time they can pay them for all; and by thus trusting them they oblige them to dig, and they are so trustworthy that they keep their word.[56]

A century and a half later, another Portuguese reflected on this matter, and estimated the vast profits to be made if only the natives could be forced to consume. Again, there are amusing modern echoes in this account, for this time the Portuguese sound like the many Europeans who for centuries have speculated on the profits to be made if only the Chinese could be persuaded to buy their products. If Portugal ruled all of Zambezia, "they could oblige every negro to wear cloth, instead of hides and the bark of trees, as many do even in our lands, when the whole of the cloth which India can produce would be but little to provide for the whole of Kaffaria. By this means the natives would search for gold to pay for the cloth, a large quantity would be forthcoming, and there would be a demand for many ships laden with cloth and other merchandise which these people value highly."[57]

Sometimes an Adam Smith–like propensity to traffic and trade emerged spontaneously. It is significant that the following account deals with an African ruler who had moved to the coast, and so presumably, unlike say the inland gold producers, was in close touch with the active mercantile society of the coast. A ruler called Maurusa took over the area inland from Mozambique Island. For a time, his relations with the Portuguese were hostile, and he attacked them and stopped trade through his new territories. However, "when he had settled in the lands and had commenced their cultivation he saw that he would require to carry on commerce and have dealings with the Portuguese residents of Mozambique, because of the advantages he would gain therefrom, whereupon he made peace with them, and in ratification thereof he commanded that no Macua should offer any further violence to the Portuguese or commit any thefts of their property, or eat human flesh, but that all of them should cultivate the land and carry on commerce with the people of Mozambique, buying and selling merchandise in a friendly and trustworthy manner."[58]

It seems, then, that this trade was, from the African point of view, a benign one. Differing use values and the autonomy of the African hunter or peasant faced with mercantile capitalism meant that the notion of exploitation or any more general detrimental impact is hard to sustain.

It also seems that there was a pronounced gender differentiation here, which meant that men accessed goods destined for trade, while women performed basic production. Men received privileged access to prestige goods such as beads and cloths. Products from the interior were acquired using discretionary and surplus labor, often done by men who, for cultural reasons, declined to engage in cultivation. As a Jesuit noted in 1560, "No man, whatsoever his condition, sets his hand to tilling the fields. The women are the farmers and supply the needs of the household."[59] Herding and guarding the fields was mostly done by men, while both men and women did heavy agricultural work. Tending, weeding, and gathering was women's work; they were the main cultivators, and also the main weavers.[60]

Many scholars have studied the role of the state. Wallerstein found world-empires collapsing due to the increasing cost of defending their territories, something world-economies did not have to do. Eric Wolf pointed to degrees of effectiveness of the political elite in his tributary empires,[61] while Chase-Dunn and Hall found in their commercializing, state-based world-systems a comparatively strong and effective central/core state. This perception is reinforced if we look briefly at the role of the state in one such area: Gujarat. Most of the state's revenue came from the land; indeed, power was control over land and its inhabitants. The great mosques and tombs of the Muslim rulers, their palaces, and especially their wars, were financed overwhelmingly from a tax on the produce of the land, the justification being a rather nebulous belief that ultimately the land was the ruler's. Peasants paid for the right to use it, and in return, the ruler provided protection from internal disorder and external attack. The theoretical rate of taxation was high, up to one-third or even one-half. Yet this massive demand was ameliorated by the incapacity of this tributary state to impose routinely and completely effectively its demands over all the land. Those fortunate enough to live in remote, turbulent, or unproductive areas paid much less than did the wealthy cotton producers in the lowlands of Gujarat. Yet even here, where royal attention was most concentrated, the extraction was mediated through local people, and was subject to negotiation. Village heads, generically referred to as minor *zamindars*, collected taxes from their fellow villagers. They were personally aware of the productivity of different areas of land, and of exceptional matters including: a partial failure of the crop due to poor rains, a bad year for a peasant who had lost a family member, or exigencies caused by the marriage of a daughter. Similarly, weavers had their own heads who acted in the same connective way between the state and themselves.

The state's demands were mediated on the ground. Revenue collection was a balancing act, for the frontier was still open, and a grossly exploited village could simply pack up and move to an area controlled by a less extortionate zamindar. The state, therefore, interfered little in such areas as the complex cloth manufacturing process described above. It levied a tax on rural production, and minor transit duties, but otherwise played no role either in facilitating or hindering this vast industry. Yet, in one area the state had a decisive indirect effect. Most land revenue was collected in cash. This was done for the benefit of the state, but the result was a thoroughly monetized rural economy in which market relations penetrated right down to peasant level.

When we look at states in east Africa, we find two distinct types: territorial empires, tributary if you like, and coastal city-states whose role was to connect the Indian Ocean with the territorial empires. Of the territorial states on the Zimbabwe Plateau, the two that have attracted most attention are Great Zimbabwe, and its successor, the Mutapa state, also referred to as Monomotapa, or Munhumutapa. These two states, and indeed others that have been less studied, such as the Torwa state (fifteenth to seventeenth centuries in the southwest) and the one ruled by Changamire and his successors (in the same area from the late seventeenth to the nineteenth centuries) are best analyzed if they are located within a tributary mode of production. Within this mode, as Wolf notes, there are important variations in the power and effectiveness of the state, with, for example, European feudalism being a weak version. The literature on these African states emphasizes the lack of control of the central rulers (inappropriately called "emperors" by the Portuguese) over the edges of their domains, and constant fissiparous tendencies. These were disaggregated and attenuated states. While they taxed trade, they made no effort to interfere in production or the conduct of trade.

The role of the state in trade, and conversely the effects of trade on the fates of these two states, is complex. Certainly some items of production, and trade, were heavily taxed. Ivory production was taxed at a high 50 percent, that is, one tusk was taken for the chief or king from each elephant killed.

Similarly with gold, where again the ruler took one half. Apart from this levy on production, long-distance trade was taxed at rates of between 5 and 15 percent. However, this is not to say that trade was important in the total revenues or control of the state. For both peasant and ruler, the items of long-distance trade, namely, gold and ivory, were peripheral, part-time, and optional.[62] As S.I.G. Mudenge says, "It is accepted that the proceeds of external trade had a role to play in the Mutapa state, but this was a supportive role, reinforcing, modifying perhaps, but never ultimately determining the political system of the state."[63] This being the case, the rise and fall of these states were not connected very much with the rise or decline of external trade; internal, autonomous, factors have to be given more weight. While both internal and external trade were widespread both north and south of the Zambezi, this does not seem to correlate with state formation or decline.

After a long exposure to the area, the Portuguese also recognized this. In 1608, the king told the viceroy that he was keen to proceed with the conquest of the mines of Monomotapa. To soften up the ruler, he was to be told "that this does not imply that we are taking his land from him, nor his government, nor are we fighting for possession of his pastures and cultivated lands, which are his means of subsistence and which he values above all. Our only interest is in the metals, which are not important to him and do not constitute his wealth."[64] Recent archaeological work provides further confirmation of the slight significance of long-distance trade in the interior, for site catchment analysis in the area of Great Zimbabwe and the Mutapa state suggests results that are "significantly different from the classic theories of location being chosen in the context of gold-mining, external trade or transhumance. Instead, site catchment analysis suggests that proximity to suitable agricultural land, as well as grazing, was important. Two other variables, proximity to sources of permanent water and granite for building, presumably must also have been important factors. The overall scenario is of settled and self-sufficient communities."[65]

Cloth imports merit a more extended discussion, for it has been claimed that African production was undercut by imports from India based on more advanced productive techniques. If so, we have a clear reinforcement of Palat's and Wallerstein's finding of deindustrialization, or more general claims that foreign trade exploited Africa. There were vast imports of cloths from India to east Africa; indeed, the Portuguese quickly discovered that it was only these which would find a market and allow them to participate in the trade of the coast. Alexandre Lobato's tables give some idea of the huge dimensions of this trade.[66] Almeida's account of his voyage along the coast in 1505 provide a more qualitative confirmation. He notes that, in Mombasa, there were "quantities of cotton cloth from Cambay because all this coast dresses in these cloths and has no others."[67]

The question is whether these imports undercut an existing textile industry in the area, that is, deindustrialized it. The evidence is a little confusing; blanket claims that either Indian competition or the activities of the Portuguese destroyed an indigenous industry seem to be wide of the mark. At the time of the first Portuguese voyages, Kilwa apparently grew much cotton, and presumably turned it into cloth.[68] Soon after, when António Fernandes traveled far inland to the Mutapa state, he found cotton cloth being made in several places.[69] Around 1570, we have another account of interior production. Monclaro noted that all the inhabitants of the Mutapa state "commonly wear loosely-woven cotton cloth made on the other side of the river in low looms but very slowly, which cloth, called machiras, I saw being woven near Sena. These machiras may measure two rods and a half in length and a rod and a half across."[70]

Monclaro implies that productive techniques in the interior were not advanced, and this may be confirmed by another much-quoted account of Sofala earlier in the sixteenth century. The passage in question, from the informed observer Duarte Barbosa, runs as follows: In Sofala "now [c. 1515] of late they make great store of cotton and weave it, and from it they make much white cloth, and as they know not how to dye it, or have not the needful dyes, they take the Cambaya cloths, blue or otherwise coloured, and unravel them and make them up again, so that it becomes a new thing. With this thread and their own white they make much coloured cloth, and from it they gain much gold."[71] This text suggests that the Portuguese blockade had hindered Muslim trade with the traditional supplier, India, and so they encouraged local production. However, there are problems with this interpretation, which in effect would make the Portuguese responsible for an increase in local cloth production. We will demonstrate later that the Portuguese system was far from being so effective as to force traders to promote local production. Further, the passage in question is rather dubious, as it is probably a later addition to Barbosa's text.

Barbosa implies that cloth production in the south was not very advanced, especially as they did not know how to dye cloth. However, the mention of blue dyes is significant, for this was produced using indigo, which was grown in Gujarat. It could be that indigo was unavailable in east Africa, and so the method just described was resorted to. Another account from around 1570 seems to point to the same sort of technique, and to an inability to make strong thread locally. Monclaro noted a large trade in Indian cloth, and commented that "They want this cloth for unthreading, and by a subtle artifice the thread being stringed with beads, they make rich pieces after their fashion and cloth for wearing with sundry workmanship according to the various colours of the beads, and with them they make strings like twisted hatstrings which they carry about their necks instead of necklaces." Monclaro further notes that Indian cloths (*bretangis*) were worth twice as much as the locally made *machiras*.[72] In the light of this evidence, António Gomes's claim from 1648 seems quite incredible: The elite in Mutapa "wear cloths of rich silk, damask, satin, gold and silk cloth . . . the whole well made by the Kaffirs themselves."[73]

D. N. Beach provides an excellent explanation of this matter, which again has to do with use values, and the very nature of the African economy. Remember that clothing was a necessity on the Zimbabwe Plateau. Freezing temperature are rare, but there are occasional frosts. Given that local clothing was produced with slow and primitive techniques, imports were needed.[74] Beach says that Africans had learned to spin and weave by copying the techniques used in imported Indian cloth; by the sixteenth century, the growing of cotton and weaving of cotton cloth was well established. However, their methods were slow as compared with their Indian competitors, and weaving interfered with the dominant crop cycle. Thus, it made economic sense to import cloth, given the nature of Shona society. This was a stratified society, and when it was possible, they collected gold and ivory to get beads and cloth which in turn could "buy" grain or cattle.[75]

The situation in the north was rather different. In 1331, Ibn Battuta found excellent, indeed unequaled, cloth being made in Mogadishu and exported to Egypt and elsewhere.[76] W. Howard Brown claims there was a flourishing cloth industry in the northern Swahili area from the ninth century, especially at Siyu, and also embroidered cloths and fine silks from Pate Island in the sixteenth and seventeenth centuries. He thinks that foreign competition from India undermined this.[77] Pate seems to have been unique in its production, for Monclaro noted that "In it, trade is different because there are many rich silk fabrics of great profit to the Portuguese, there being none in other Moorish towns because only in this town of Pate do they make them, spreading them from here to the others. The Portuguese trade these fabrics against iron, beads and cotton cloth which they have not. Naos from India resort to this town, which is a kingdom in itself."[78] Late in the sixteenth century, Dos Santos wrote that Pate Island manufactured excellent cotton and silk cloths, which were worn by the elite of the coast and also by the women of some of the Portuguese.[79]

Recent anthropological studies have shown that cloth can have many meanings, and is far from being merely a utilitarian product. In our area, it was not just cost, or even quality, that determined demand. This locally made cloth from Pate was often bought by the Portuguese and presented to the rulers of the Zambezi area, including the Mutapa ruler, as presents and as part of the curva, or tribute, the Portuguese had to pay them.[80] The reason for this preference was that many African rulers wanted to wear locally made cloth. Barros noted that while the wives of the Mutapa ruler wore very fine and expensive foreign cloth, the emperor himself wore only indigenous materials, "through fear that any coming from the hands of strangers might be infected with some evil quality to do him harm." For the ruler, "the greatest ornaments in his house are cotton cloths made in the country with much labour, each of which is about the size of one of our sumpter-cloths and is worth from twenty to fifty cruzados."[81] On other occasions, however, we are told that fine and symbolically significant animal skins were preferred by the elite on the Zimbabwe Plateau.[82]

Peter Garlake makes similar observations about Great Zimbabwe and the later Mutapa state: The king wore locally produced cotton cloth, but the nobles wore imported silk. Cotton production was really an elite activity, and was used to pay tribute, as an offering at funerals, and as bride price. Ordinary people wore small skin aprons, or cheaper imported cloth if they could afford it.[83] On the other hand, António da Silva's study of the same area, based on missionary sources, notes a mixture of local and Indian cloth. Nobles wore fine cloths of cotton and silk as well as coarse cotton from local producers.[84] This sort of social differentiation was also practiced by the Yao. Before coast cloth was available, only the elite could wear lion and leopard skins, while others wore barkcloth and common animal hides. Once cloth came in from the coast, the nobles continued to set themselves off by restricting some cloths, especially a bright-red quality cloth called *ndeule*, to themselves.[85]

The reverse could also be true, that is, rulers might exhibit a preference for the exotic and foreign. One cultural role of cloth was its ability to signify the power and authority of ruling groups."Possession of an exclusive form of wealth (a condition that livestock could not easily fulfil) was a corollary of class formation and therefore of the tributary mode of production."[86] The Thornton debate in *African Economic History* drew mostly on central and west African data, but seems to hold true for east Africa also. He claimed productivity in fact was high, despite technological gaps. How then can we explain large cloth imports? The answer has to do with style and fashion and the attraction of foreign goods *qua* foreign. At least one can accept, as Patrick

Manning points out, that cloth imports did not enter a vacuum, but rather supplemented existing local supplies.[87]

If long-distance trade, especially that to the coast, was peripheral for both producers and rulers in the interior states, though for different reasons, it seems that a benign situation existed where trade produced no exploitation. Valuable goods were taken from Africa, but these were valued in the receiving areas around the Indian Ocean but not in the producing areas, where their production, from the peasant point of view, and their taxation, from the view point of the state, were marginal to more central concerns to do with food production and animal husbandry for the peasant, and politico-military matters for the elite. The labor to produce export goods was surplus labor, not labor extracted from, say, food production. Nor was it labor that otherwise would have been used to "develop" Africa, claims by Sheriff and Alpers to the contrary. On the other hand, Indian products—beads and cloths especially—found an extra market, though probably not one of very great comparative size, for east Africa was a minor outlet for Gujarat's total production.

Hall summarizes the matter well:

> But the trading relationship between Islam [that is, the coastal Swahili states] and the Zimbabwe state was not one in which a primitive economy and naive rulers were exploited by more sophisticated merchants, for when the system is viewed from the African end a certain symmetry is apparent. Just as Indian glass beads were mass-produced at little cost, and shiploads of porcelain were exported by order of the Ming dynasty in place of ordinary coinage, so gold was probably acquired by the rulers in their *madzimbahwe* [regional and central locations of power] as tribute, mined as a marginal activity in the interstices of the annual agro-pastoral cycle. Thus Kilwa and Great Zimbabwe emerge as partners in a mutually beneficial relationship, both exchanging trinkets of little value in their own economies for exotica that were important because of their rarity.[88]

We have already discussed the Swahili port cities in some detail in the two previous chapters; now we must locate them within world-system theory. These cities played a vital connective role, a compradorial one no doubt, but one that needs to be seen not as exploitative but rather as facilitative in their relations with the interior. Unlike the interior, these city-states were closely linked to the world-economy. As classic semiperipheries they suffered from this. Their fates often were determined by forces beyond their control, not the activities of the Portuguese in the sixteenth and seventeenth centuries but rather far-distant forces that affected them within the world-economy. In general terms, producers and consumers at either end of the far-flung network determined kinds, quantities, and values, and the Swahili had to adapt to this.[89] For example, levels of gold production in the Zimbabwe Plateau determined Sofala's gold exports and hence Kilwa's prosperity.[90] But consumption at the other end of the network also affected Kilwa, that is, competition from new gold supplies from the Americas and Japan, and the varying demand for gold in the various consuming countries. As India monetized, its demand for gold rose.

As one would expect in a semiperipheral area, things were not entirely one way. In certain areas, such as niche cloth production, the Swahili cities could play a productive, rather than merely compradorial, role. Other local products included: lime burning, stone carving and building, mat making, the production of perfume, and food. Gold was worked, iron smelted.[91] As one other example, the city-states did well in another sort of niche market, that is, a trade in a necessity where their own coastal areas produced the product, and they were faced with no competition. The best example is the vast lumber trade to the wood-deficit area of the Red Sea, a trade that historians have tended to neglect in favor of the more glamorous products, gold and ivory.[92]

The coast played a very different role in the world-economy as compared with the interior. It seems that these ports were semiperipheries, but they did not help to exploit an interior that was a periphery. Thus, if unequal exchange is essential in a world-economy, then the African interior must be seen as external rather than being an exploited periphery. Palat and Wallerstein are much nearer the mark, again assuming that systems always have unequal exchange, even before capitalism. It is not clear if their notion of deindustrialization in the Middle East and southeast Asia as a result of more advanced techniques in Gujarat and Coromandel is meant to apply to east Africa also, but, in fact, this may have been the case on the coast for some products and some areas. In this world-economy where the core was parts of India, we can clearly locate the Swahili coast in a semiperipheral position and follow them in their implicit exclusion of the interior from the system. In terms of world-system theory, trade between a world-economy and an external area is by definition equal trade, and in luxuries only. Thus, we have a precapitalist world-economy where a core is connected by a semiperipheral area to an external area. However, if we follow Abu-Lughod and Chase-Dunn and Hall and accept that systemic trade does not necessarily have to be unequal, then we can include the African interior, which was involved in a trade where all did well.

Ostensibly, these findings reinforce doubts about the utility of the standard world-system distinction between luxuries and necessities. Here, and in many other areas, the notion seems to be of little use in determining when relations between two areas move from being external to systemic. There may be a terminological problem here. As I understand Wallerstein, he is not using "luxury" in the modern sense. Rather, he is merely trying to connote the idea of a luxury item as one that is valued by the purchaser and not by the seller. As he once wrote: "Each side tends to have different cultural definitions of value."[93] Thus the problem evaporates, and presumably he would not disagree with my claim that the key to understanding the nature of exchange between India and east Africa is the concept of differing use values in these two very different economies.

Is this laborious exegesis useful? My findings may add something to the large body of world-system writing, but maybe fitting east Africa into a particular box is not particularly rewarding, except in a completely academic way. One could sketch a different analysis, one that concentrates on production rather than exchange, and that ignores the world-system terminology of cores and peripheries, the existence or otherwise of coerced labor (this of course being important in defining which areas belong in which category of core, periphery, and semiperiphery), and whether the trade was in luxuries or necessities. If we follow Wolf's analysis, we can see both India and the interior east African states as being tributary modes of production, though the African ones were much more disaggregated than were the Indian states, to the extent indeed that "state" may not be the best term to use for the Mutapa "authority structure." In both areas, merchants provided the crucial linkages to keep exchange and production going and to connect the state and the producer. In both, labor was coerced. In Africa, it had to pay tribute; in India, it paid taxes in the form of land revenue. In neither area, however, was labor subsumed by capital. To use the world-system model is simply to say that goods were being exchanged across the Afrasian Sea. This is a very familiar statement. There was exchange, and, due to differing use values, this involved no exploitation or asymmetrical extraction of resources from the less developed, primary producing African side. We have two sorts of systems of production that intersect rather nicely, with benefit to all involved. Furthermore, there are significant problems with using the level of remuneration of labor to explain unequal exchange, especially before capitalism. More concretely, we can say nothing definite about the levels of remuneration of laborers in Africa as compared with India. No doubt producers in India profited from the sale of their manufactures to less developed areas, of which east Africa was a minor part, yet this does not automatically set up a relationship of exploitation.

Perhaps we need more empirical studies before we engage in model building and theorizing. In this regard, Stephen Dale's new book may be an example of what is needed. His study of Indian trade with Iran, Central Asia, and Russia in the seventeenth and eighteenth centuries shows how dominant Indian traders were in these areas. For him, these traders represented part of the hegemonic trade diaspora of the Indian world-economy. Mughal India is described as a regionally dominant economic power, and Indians in these areas had an asymmetrical economic relationship with their local interlocutors.[94] A similar effort is James D. Tracy's two-volume collection of articles on merchant empires, which he describes as "a group effort at intermediate-level syntheses."[95] Maybe this level of analysis is all we need at present. It is precisely this sort of detailed empirical work that can provide building blocks for those who would try to write world history, or even the history of precapitalist world-economies.

Chapter 5

The Portuguese on the Coast

This chapter sketches the impact of the Portuguese on east Africa. It is a comparative effort, and draws on themes and controversies having to do with the Portuguese presence in other parts of Asia. It looks at the Portuguese in east Africa both in a context of their wider imperial effort in the Indian Ocean and in a context where they can be seen operating in an African or indigenous context. It sees the Portuguese not as all-powerful, all-successful people of a quite different genus from what had gone before, but rather as people who were constrained in a great variety of ways by the milieu in which they operated.

I do not provide a chronology of Portuguese activities on the Swahili coast; there will be no lists of captains, or discussions of the various changes in official policy. These topics have already been covered in several standard books. Alexandre Lobato's massive compilation of material on the Portuguese in Mozambique from 1498 to 1530 provides a detailed survey of Portuguese activities and policies on the southern coast. It is sober, comprehensive, and has very little, except in passing, on the locale or the actions of Africans or Muslims. A large number of his sources are now published in the valuable *Documents on the Portuguese in Mozambique* series. His third volume, a vast compilation of figures on trade, is especially useful.[1] In essence, it is a vast compilation of figures, every number he ever saw, thus handily making it unnecessary for later historians to do this exercise themselves. Eric Axelson's various publications cover two centuries, and are invaluable as a sober, unanalytical narrative, useful for "facts" and chronology. These works focus primarily on the role of the Portuguese in southeast Africa even though he identifies the need for research on Portuguese relations with "African peoples."[2]

In his recent book on Mozambique, M.D.D. Newitt says that Lobato's and Axelson's works "have left little more to be said about the sixteenth and seventeenth centuries" though he is being unnecessarily modest, for his book is quite invaluable as a source of reference and analysis.[3] He provides a detailed history from 1498 to the present. He has little interest in "theory" or in generalization, but his work will certainly remain the standard for many years. The Portuguese political relations with the Mutapa state are covered in S.I.G. Mudenge's fine book,[4] while David Beach's numerous publications not only provide an outstanding analysis of the history of the Shona people, including Great Zimbabwe and the Mutapa state, but also are excellent in locating the Portuguese in this context.[5] A collective work from historians at the Universidade Eduardo Mondlane provides an interesting and intelligent overview of the history of Mozambique as seen from Maputo and in the light of Mozambique's freedom struggle and later disastrous developments.[6] Two other publications begin to provide a context in which we can see the whole Portuguese empire, namely, A.J.R. Russell-Wood's overview of recent research, and Sanjay Subrahmanyam's enthusiastic, rather idiosyncratic, survey volume.[7]

Attempts to "indigenize" the early Europeans have made some progress in India. In particular, there have been provocative attempts to evaluate quantitatively the precise impact of European trade on the host economy. Om Prakash has been the pioneer here. His several studies of Bengal, and of India as a whole, have set a standard for getting beyond grand statements of large or minimal European impacts on the economy of India in the early modern period.[8] But when we look at the current state of research on European influence in east Africa we find too many bald and often unbacked statements; some are attempts to impose preexisting theory or prejudice onto Africa without much supporting evidence.[9]

Portuguese aims in east Africa were nicely set out as early as 1506, when Pero Ferreira Fogaça wrote to the king from Kilwa that he had been visited by the rulers of four (unspecified) islands north of Kilwa, who had made peace and become vassals of the Portugal:

> Each one engaging himself and the residents of their islands to pay yearly to Your Highness in acknowledgement certain oxen and sheep and bales of maize and chickens and coconuts and also to sell to all the Portuguese both in this fortress and on the naos all the supplies available in the said islands for the price that they sell them to one another without raising the price in any way and so, Sire, I had their safe-conducts formally given to them signed by me and sealed with Your Highness's royal seal and on condition that they shall not trade with the mines of Sofala nor do anything against your service; I gave them assurance that in all the other islands and lands of the Moors they may trade in the supplies that Your Highness has not forbidden and bring the supplies to this city and come and go in safety if they follow your given orders.[10]

Another contemporary account extends this depiction of Portuguese aims. In 1595, the king was worried at the large trade of banians and non-Christians from India to Portugal, Mozambique, the coast of Malindi, and to the south of Goa, to the detriment of Portuguese traders. In a grandiose gesture, the king decreed that, henceforward, none of these people could trade to any of these places, except in nonprohibited goods to Hurmuz, Sind, Malabar, and Cambay. No other places were allowed.[11] In 1653, Nicholas Buckeridge wrote about the area around Mozambique, Pemba, and Zanzibar: "Nor doe the Portugalls suffer any they can hinder to trade to any of these places espetialie ye Arabians & Indeans whom they doe punish with Confiscacion of Vesaile & goods (if not captivitie of their persons) if they are taken tradeing there."[12]

One final example again gives the flavor of Portuguese aims; in this case, even a loosely vassal king was expected to conform to Portuguese aspirations. This is from a letter from Gaspar de S. Bernadino in 1606:

> When we reached Pate we were informed that some Moors from Arabia had arrived in a small vessel for the purpose of bartering for African boys whom they then carried off to their country. There the boys were made to follow the Moorish religion and treated as slaves for the rest of their lives. Six of them had already been purchased. My companions and I . . . went at once to the king and expressed our surprise at his giving his consent to the sale, more especially because it was the desire of the King of Spain [at this time ruling Portugal]—whose vassal he was—to save souls and to snatch them from the clutches of the enemy of our salvation.

The ruler of Pate, himself a Muslim, agreed that this could not be allowed. The boys were found, and all said they wanted to be Christian. "The Portuguese thereupon bought them, and had them baptised, and I have since seen two of them here in Lisbon."[13]

In essence, Portugal wanted to force the allegiance of local Swahili rulers and make them pay tribute. They and the merchants in their area were then to be allowed to continue to trade in items specified by the Portuguese, but not in others in which they claimed a monopoly. In the wider context, this meant spices; in the case of east Africa, gold and ivory. Further, "legal" trade was to be done in ships licensed by the Portuguese, and such ships had to carry a pass, or *cartaz*, from a Portuguese captain. This pass required that the ship concerned must call in at a Portuguese fort and pay customs duties on its cargo; it also stated that the ship was not allowed to trade with enemies of the Portuguese. To enforce this system, the Portuguese conquered or sacked most of the port cities of the coast, and built forts at Sofala (1505) and Mozambique (1507). They established factories in many other coastal sites. Some of them were fortified, for example on Zanzibar, Pate, and the appropriately named Ilha dos Portugueses off Inhaca Island. Mozambique became the center of activity on the southern Swahili coast during the sixteenth century. Late in the century, the threat of attack from the Ottomans led them to raid extensively on the northern coast, and to build the great Fort Jesus in Mombasa (begun in 1593), which was ruled through a puppet sultan.

By the middle of the seventeenth century, east Africa had become a vital part of the wider Portuguese empire. They had lost or were about to lose their access to spices. A string of their possessions had fallen to the Dutch. Angola produced only slaves. Gold was yet to be discovered in Brazil, though the sugar trade was vast and profitable. Mozambique thus enjoyed a greatly enhanced reputation as a vital possession. However, Fort Jesus fell to the Omanis after an epic siege in 1698, and this may mark a convenient end to our time frame, for this was a time of troubles for the Portuguese. It was also in the 1690s that they were expelled from the Zimbabwe Plateau by Changamire and his Rozvi troops. From that time, Portuguese activities in the southern interior were restricted to the Zambezi Valley and the area to its north, where they established fairs or trading posts.

The Portuguese were quick to take advantage of the endemic rivalry between the various Swahili port cities, just as they did in Malabar, where Cochin invited them in to counter its much stronger neighbor, Calicut. Tristão da Cunha's fleet arrived in Malindi in 1506, and the sultan told them that his biggest enemies were the rulers of Mombasa and Angoche, and "he begged that, before the chief captain left those parts, he would take vengeance upon them, that they might know he enjoyed the friendship of the King of Portugal." The Portuguese obligingly sacked Angoche. Then at Braboa, up the coast from Angoche, da Cunha told the king that "if he was willing to be his vassal [of the King of Portugal], he would serve him with that fleet against his enemies, just as he had done for the King of Melinde."[14] In effect, when Mombasa harbored a Turkish fleet in the 1580s, they were doing precisely what Malindi had done earlier, that is, using a foreign naval power to suppress a rival neighbor. The Portuguese were not prepared to tolerate this, so they first sacked and then conquered Mombasa.

The Portuguese had a relatively coherent underlying strategy. First, they identified the main choke points and strategic sites around the Indian Ocean littoral. The early correspondence, histories, and other accounts devote much effort to this sort of identification. Goa, Colombo, Melaka, Hurmuz, Diu, and Aden were seen as most strategically located to serve Portuguese ends, and all except the last were taken. In the case of east Africa, Mozambique had several advantages. It was conveniently located to control trade on the southern coast, and to block trade from the hostile Muslim world down to the gold available in Sofala. Mozambique was also well located to ensure communication with the capital of Goa, for it was only one monsoon from one to the other. The Portuguese hoped that the gold from the interior would come to Mozambique rather than to the previous centers further south, so that it would serve as the outlet for this valuable trade. Finally, and here Mozambique was unusual when compared with the other ports the Portuguese conquered, it was to be the vital way station for the *carreira* (voyage) from the colonial capital of Goa to the metropolitan capital of Lisbon, thus fulfilling the same function that the Cape of Good Hope later provided for the Dutch. In theory this voyage was to be done without lengthy stops along the way, but, in practice, the great ships often needed to call in on the African coast to heal their sick, to get supplies, to collect cargo for India on the outward voyage, or to await the next monsoon. Mozambique became the vital link in the chain between Goa and Lisbon. In the north, once the threat from the Turks appeared, Mombasa was identified as vital; it was captured and a great fort was built in the 1590s.

These strategic sites were acquired with several ends in view. Their conquest helped the Portuguese to undermine the Muslims who had previously dominated Indian Ocean trade, especially the trade in spices. They functioned as nodes in the vast seaborne network of the Portuguese maritime empire. They provided facilities for the vital armadas, and the carreira to Portugal. They were beachheads from which conversion drives were launched. They provided places where the Portuguese elite could give themselves fancy titles and indulge in an anachronistically feudal lifestyle, and from which they made vast private profits during their terms of office, a system of out-door, in fact foreign, relief for the Portuguese ruling classes. In a more general sense, the Portuguese were trying to create or impose a hierarchy de novo in the Indian Ocean. From a situation of autonomous port cities and free trade in which competition was economic but not military,[15] they now wanted to establish an articulated structure where Lisbon controlled Goa, and Goa controlled all the conquered port cities, including Mozambique, Sofala, and Mombasa. The Portuguese effort was unsuccessful, yet both the nature and the extent of the aspiration were revolutionary. It is important to note that the Portuguese merely took over existing port cities. Their much more thorough-going successors, the Dutch and the English, not only created networks but increasingly based them in port cities they founded: Batavia, Bombay, and Calcutta are examples.

The case of east African represents an additional, and little-discussed economic imperative. At least in material terms, the Portuguese were in Asia to buy spices cheap and sell them dear in Europe, thus undercutting the traditional Mediterranean route. To forbid this trade to all others was one thing, and, in any case, this effort met with little success. But the Portuguese had to be able to buy the spices themselves, for they monopolized, partially, sea trade only, and not land trade let alone production. Nor did they have the domestic resources to be able to send large amounts of money out from Portugal. This requirement, to find money to pay for the spices, meant that the Portuguese were soon intricately linked into the country trade of Asia, a matter that has been much discussed in the case of the English and Dutch, and rather less so for the Portuguese.

East Africa provides an excellent case study of this matter. The Portuguese quickly discovered that gold from the Zimbabwe Plateau could be used to pay for the spices. If they could secure supplies of gold, or better still a monopoly, then payment for spices would be no problem. It soon became apparent that gold had to be paid for, too, at least until that happy time when the "mines" could be conquered and the Portuguese could get it for nothing. Gold could be acquired only in exchange for goods, and not Portuguese goods either.

East Africa's other prized export, ivory, presented a similar dilemma. The Portuguese had no hope of controlling supply, for elephants were hunted in very far flung areas. However, they could try to block its export. Once again, they still had to be able to pay for it. The only items in demand on the plateau and elsewhere were beads and cloths from Gujarat, the traditional trade items the producers of gold and ivory wanted. Here, as in so many other areas, the Portuguese then had to fit into existing patterns. A continuing supply of Gujarati cloths to east Africa was essential in their wider designs, and this was recognized early on by all the correspondents based in Kilwa, Sofala, and Mozambique. The Portuguese were immersed in an intricate web of country trade in the Afrasian Sea: cloths from Gujarat to exchange for gold and ivory, which then could pay for spices, which then could be extracted from the Indian Ocean network and sent outside it to European markets.

The rationale and nature of the official Portuguese system in east Africa provides the groundwork for a look at the problems they encountered and for a discussion of their tactics.[16] First, it is appropriate to note that the Portuguese did have some success on the east African coast. Many of them, both officials and private traders, made large profits. One Portuguese captain claimed that he had been robbed of goods worth 4,000 cruzados, gold worth 24,000 *pardaos*, and no less than 80,000 bares of ivory, which would be worth 12,000,000 xerafins.[17] Even if we accept that people claiming compensation often exaggerate their losses, these are still very large sums. The post of captain of Mozambique sold for 40,000 cruzados, sometimes much more. The holder expected to make a large profit after he had paid this sum. The markups were often huge. In 1545, João de Castro wrote the king about the virgin market at Delagoa Bay. He said that, for a few beads worth 60 reis, one could buy ivory that would sell for more than 40,000 reis in India.[18] The Portuguese exported large quantities of gold. Vitorino Magalhães Godinho quotes the following figures for kilograms of gold being exported to Goa: 1585, 573 kg; 1591, 716 kg; 1610, 850 kg; 1667, 1487 kg.[19] So also with ivory. The Portuguese sent many thousands of kilograms of this valuable product to India each year; in some years, more than 100,000 kg were sent.[20]

The Portuguese never came close to enforcing their total system. African realities and Portuguese inefficiencies intertwined to make the official system a creaky, spavined, affair. While the official system has been described several times, its problems are less well known. Inefficiencies and lapses in official conduct were ubiquitous. Fort Jesus was to be a cornerstone of Portuguese policy on the northern coast, a bulwark against the Ottomans. The eminent Italian military architect João Batista Cairato designed the fort, and construction began in 1593. In 1614, the viceroy noted that there was still much work to be done, and allocated more funds.[21] At the same time, the king also was appraised of the problem. He noted resignedly that some 30,000 xerafins had already been spent, "without anyone knowing where the money has gone," but even so allocated another grant.[22] The fort was finally completed in the 1630s.

Many other examples of inefficiency could be quoted. The trade between Diu and Mozambique was vital for the residents of both port cities and for the health of the state generally. In 1653, however, litigation over who was to be the new captain of Diu meant this voyage was lost.[23] In another example, in 1617, the king wrote to the viceroy that he had been told that the person sent to be judge in Mozambique was in fact illiterate. Not surprisingly, the king thought this rendered the incumbent unsuitable.[24] As for military prowess, one could read the chronicles and letters and many modern histories and get an impression of marvelous Portuguese efficiency and valor. The reality, both on the east African coast and elsewhere, was often different.[25]

Portuguese officials often behaved inappropriately, causing many problems. Peculation was rife in the state; every officeholder expected to make large profits from his three-year term. Whether we call this corruption is another question. Ideal standards of official conduct today are hardly appropriate to condemn the standards of the Portuguese, or anyone else, in this early modern period. However, there is no doubt that Portuguese officials often engaged in conduct that was highly detrimental to the interests of the state. While an underlying cause may have something to do with premodern notions of appropriate official behavior, another cause was a result of the fact that the Portuguese system was not monolithic. It was comprised of various layers and interests, many of them in competition with official policy. In fact, officials themselves often dealt with competing interests. Officials had to serve the king and his trade, but they had to think of their own trade as well, for most of the time they had paid for a post that included extensive trade privileges. In 1604, an official *alvará* noted that the captains of Mozambique too often ignored their obligations to guard the fortress and instead spent their time up the Zambezi River looking after their own trading interests.[26] In addition, the captains competed with householders in the forts, who all traded, and with the transfrontiersmen who were right outside the system.

Complaints start almost as soon as the Portuguese arrived. As early as 1514, a complaint to the king said that the captain of Mozambique and Sofala was oppressive and that he stole slaves from the local Muslims.[27] A few years later, the king of Malindi complained that although he was very loyal to the Portuguese, the local Portuguese treated him and his merchants very badly, capturing ships and seizing goods on land and sea.[28]

These tensions were exemplified in the practice whereby Portuguese captains issued passes to local ships that allowed them to trade outside the bounds of the official system; one must assume they charged for this. For example, officials allowed ships to trade between Portuguese forts north of Goa and Muslim areas in east Africa without making them call in to pay duties at Mombasa, as they were meant to do.[29] These complaints date from 1617. In 1635, Mombasa was still being bypassed and so its customshouse was losing revenue. The solution was to make every ship leaving India for east Africa provide a security of 2,000 cruzados to guarantee that they would call at Mombasa.[30] The same situation existed with trade to the Red Sea. In theory, this was totally prohibited, but the captains of Mombasa allowed the trade anyway, no doubt for a price. The king was particularly upset as the main trade item was lumber, which would be used to build warships that then could attack the Portuguese.[31]

Smuggling was also rife; sometimes it was the result of bribing the relevant Portuguese official. Other officials knew this was happening, but they were powerless to prevent it. In 1510, the king received no gold from Sofala, but others were able to get more than 30,000 maticals (some 128 kg) of it, all of which was taken to India.[32]

Officials engaged in illegal trade. In 1610, the governor of Mozambique sent a ship laden with ivory and other goods to Cambay, and it did not pay duties in his own fort of Mozambique before it left. Nor did it pay duties in Goa en route to Cambay, as it was obliged to do.[33] Only six years later, the situation was even worse in Mozambique. The captain, Ruy de Melo de Sampaio, had many debts and so could not afford to buy cloths to take with him to use in trade. In order to get money, he was very tyrannical in Mozambique, confiscating goods and taking forced loans. As a result, the householders became very upset, and refused to trade, and thus the customs revenues declined precipitously. The viceroy sent an official to investigate.[34] Unfortunately, the official, Francisco da Fonseca Pinto, took cloths to Mozambique to sell illegally; an investigation of Fonseca ensued.[35] The illegal profits could be very substantial. In 1548, the factor in Sofala reported that the king's factory had almost no ivory, but the captain had shipped off 40,000 *arrobas* of ivory on his own account.[36] Late in the sixteenth century, the king complained that the Portuguese captains of Chaul had for some time been publicly, and illegally, sending off large quantities of iron and steel to east Africa for sale to enemies of the state.[37]

The consequences of these activities were serious, apart from the obvious fact that it made the whole official system less than efficient and effective. So substantial was this peculation that one priest claimed that the bad example set by the Portuguese made the natives much less likely to convert to the religion of such evil people.[38] On the other hand, the king claimed that the Dominicans spent more time trading than preaching.[39] More generally, corruption and oppression helped those opposed politically to the Portuguese, for example, the Ottoman Turks in the north and Changamire in the south.[40]

More important than this official misbehavior, however, were African realities. The Portuguese were trying to disrupt, and take over, a well-integrated trading system, one they did not always understand. Not surprisingly, they met resistance from those they were trying to replace.

The Portuguese lacked the numbers to get anywhere near enforcing their aims. They consistently had to take account of facts on the ground which constrained them very severely. For example, the king of Malindi was not always as loyal as they hoped, but he had to be allowed to continue his own trade with Gujarat, although this undermined Portuguese control in the south. In 1593, this same king was made king of Mombasa after the Portuguese had taken this port. The Portuguese thought they had a very docile puppet in place. The Augustinians had been able to convert a member of the royal house, Yusuf, who then was known as Jeronimo Chingulia. In 1614, the Portuguese murdered his father, the sultan, and put Dom Jeronimo in his place. Alas, in 1631, he reconverted to Islam, and revolted.[41] Other puppet rulers, such as those of Sofala, also proved intractable at times. As we noted in chapter 2, the Portuguese always had to be concerned to conciliate local rulers, whether they were those in the immediate hinterland, or the far-distant ruler of the Mutapa state, to whom the Portuguese paid the curva, in order to trade in his territories.

Once Portuguese intentions became clear, the existing Muslim traders sometimes worked in cooperation with the Portuguese, but many of them refused, and instead continued their trade in locations outside Portuguese control. Given the length of the coast and difficulties in navigation, especially in the vast and complex Zambezi Delta, the Portuguese found it very difficult to do much about this. At different times, Angoche, Mombasa, and Pate fostered a trade that flouted the Portuguese and in effect continued the preceding system of open and free trade. In the first decades of the sixteenth century, the Portuguese became aware that Angoche had become a major center of trade from the ports further north, and was underselling the Portuguese in Mozambique and Sofala very substantially.[42] To counter this, the Portuguese established themselves on the Zambezi River, at Sena and Tete, and also on the coast at Quilemane. Mombasa continued to send ships south, laden with Gujarati goods, until this flouting of Portuguese aims together with their fear of the Turks led them to conquer Mombasa in 1593. No sooner was one gap closed than another opened, for now Pate and other ports in the Lamu area became centers of opposition and "illegal" trade, despite several Portuguese attacks in the seventeenth century.[43]

Another method used to circumvent the Portuguese was to substitute local production for imports, thus avoiding the advantage the Portuguese had at sea. Cloth production expanded greatly in Pate, for example. The clothes were of such high quality that the Portuguese used it as presents to local kings. Even early in the sixteenth century, Duarte Barbosa claimed that Sofala had a flourishing cloth manufacture industry, this being a substitute for imports, which the Portuguese were blocking.[44]

The Portuguese were hampered by their lack of knowledge, specifically about the matter of gold in Africa. The Portuguese thought that gold on the plateau must come from great mines, just as silver came from Potosí. If they could find the mines, they would be able to control them and monopolize gold exports. João dos Santos described their disappointment once they realized the true situation: "When the Portuguese found themselves in the land of gold they thought that they would immediately be able to fill sacks with it, and carry off as much as they chose; but when they had spent a few days near the mines, and saw the difficulty and labor of the Kaffirs, and with what risk and peril of their lives they extracted it from the bowels of the earth and from the stones, they found their hopes frustrated."[45] The Shona mined and washed gold as a part-time occupation, and only when they needed cloth. The activity was very dispersed; there was no central mine that could be controlled, nor could the producers be forced to mine full-time and provide large quantities. In 1614, the treasury council in Lisbon noted the situation: "All the gold that has over the years been traded in the Rivers does not come from one verifiable seam, but is drawn from the sands of rivers, panned by the Blacks in various places."[46]

New, and perilous, conditions affected the Portuguese. While they adapted to some parts of this new environment, such as the monsoon pattern, they found it difficult to cope in other areas. Disease laid a heavy toll on Portuguese manpower. This was made worse by Portuguese clothing and diet. Mozambique Island, in particular, was notoriously unhealthy; hundreds died in its hospital. The building of this hospital was considered necessary even as the fort was being built in 1507, yet the mortality rate was very high.[47] Other areas were not much better. In 1528, Nuno da Cunha's fleet traveled up the east coast. He was on his way to India to be viceroy. He left 200 sick Portuguese in Zanzibar to recover. Then he wintered in Mombasa with a force of 800 men. Of them, 370 died during the "winter" months.[48] In 1570, the nao *Saint Catherine* arrived in Mozambique with 300 men, and not even 15 were healthy.[49] Ironically, it seems that the Portuguese suffered more from African diseases than did Africans from European ones. Certainly the arrival of the Portuguese did not unleash the devastating epidemics that resulted from the arrival of Europeans in Oceania and the Americas. Most east Africans seem to have had some immunity to Eurasian endemic strains. This may have been a result of the movement south of Bantu people, or the penetration of immunity from the coast to the interior. It seems that east Africa was more closely connected to Eurasian, or perhaps in this context Afrasian, disease pools than were the Portuguese.

Given these difficulties and failures, we can question whether the whole basis of Portuguese policy was fatally flawed. The argument is counterfactual, and not accepted by some authorities, but one could argue that they would have done better to trade on the east African coast, and indeed the whole Indian Ocean, on a basis of equality with all the other traders there. Cost advantages, and the efficiencies of the Cape route as compared with that up the Red Sea, would have given them a very lucrative trade; and peaceful competition would have meant no vast expenses on fleets, soldiers, and forts.

There is some evidence that trade in east Africa was in something like a state of nature when the Portuguese arrived. The Pate chronicle says the notion of levying customs duties was, at least in this area, a Portuguese one, and the Swahili word used for a customshouse there is derived from the Portuguese term *alfandega.*[50] However, we also know that the rulers of Mombasa and Kilwa levied very high duties. The important point, however, is that there certainly was no state-controlled trade, and no compulsion in trade, before the Portuguese arrived. João de Barros claimed that when da Gama reached Mozambique, he was greeted by a native of Fez, who said the custom of the sultan "was when strange ships arrived to send and enquire what they sought; and if they were merchants they might trade in that country, and if navigators bound to other parts he provided them with whatever was to be had there."[51] Four years later, in Sofala, the Portuguese claimed that they wanted peace and friendship and to be treated like all other merchants in this port. The ruler replied that this was quite acceptable. All merchants were welcome, as he derived much profit from them. The Portuguese were welcome to trade on the same terms as everyone else.[52]

The parallels with other areas are obvious. In Calicut and Diu, the rulers welcomed the Portuguese as traders, but resisted them once their monopolistic aims became clear. In 1502, the Portuguese tried to get the ruler of Calicut to expel his "foreign" Muslim traders, but he responded that he could not do this, "for it was unthinkable that he expel 4,000 households of them, who lived in Calicut as natives, not foreigners, and who had contributed great profits to his Kingdom." A century later, the Dutch had the same response. The ruler of Surabaya, in eastern Java, was asked by the Dutch not to trade with the Portuguese as they were enemies, and he replied "that he could not help it that we were in enmity with the Portuguese and that he did not wish to be in enmity with anyone; also that he could not forbid his people to trade, as they had to support themselves by it." Later in this century, the port of Macassar greatly increased its trade, and the Dutch noted that local merchants flocked there because the ruler "treats those same foreigners very civilly" and allowed all to trade "freely and openly, with good treatment, and small demands of tolls." Unimpressed, the Dutch conquered the port city in 1669.[53]

Godinho has discussed this matter in his magisterial work. He says that in

1501 and 1502 the Portuguese got access to the gold trade of Sofala without using violence. Beginning in 1505, with the arrival of Almeida with his very militant instructions, everything changed for the worse, and the policy became one of loot-and-plunder, compulsion, and forced monopoly.[54] The reasons are various, but one problem in east Africa was the serious opposition to the Portuguese from Kilwa and Mombasa. In Kilwa, for example, the ruler had been influenced by Muslims from Calicut, who had told him of the barbarities the Portuguese had inflicted on this Indian port city.[55]

The Portuguese attempted a reign of terror; Almeida sacked Sofala, Kilwa, and Mombasa. In Mombasa, according to the locals, he killed 1,500 people and got booty of 20,000 cruzados.[56] The town was sacked three times in the sixteenth century, in 1505, 1528, and 1589, before it was finally conquered.[57] The Portuguese launched invasions of the Mutapa state in the 1570s and again after 1620, the aim being to drive out the Muslims (the ruler was required to sign treaties which in theory obligated him to do this) and take control of the gold.[58] As Beach points out, this was completely unnecessary. As we noted, there were no mines to control, so that whoever controlled the trade routes would control gold as well. Control of production based on military force was both impossible and unnecessary.[59]

Portuguese policy was gravely flawed and misdirected in the matter of cloth prices, too. Cloth was the vital import to the area, and the essential carrot to get production of gold and ivory. Yet the Portuguese, imbued as they were with dreams of monopoly, foolishly tried to impose a huge markup on Cambay cloth. In 1530, there was a markup of forty times the initial value between Cambay and Sofala. Yet the nonofficial markup was only between eight and eleven times cost price. The result was a vast "illegal" trade. But the important point is that a mark up of about ten times would have been adequate: The Portuguese could have achieved this without any forts or fleets at all.[60]

These problems of adaptation and local opposition meant that Portuguese policy shifted throughout the two centuries under discussion. As an example, at the end of the sixteenth century, they turned to the north coast and tried to control it also. After they failed to control the gold export trade, they ventured inland, up the Zambezi River to Sena and Tete in the 1530s, and later right up to the plateau. After the massive losses all over the Indian Ocean around the middle of the seventeenth century, east Africa became comparatively much more important for the Portuguese. The area where policy seems to have changed most often is in Mozambique, where there were a series of confusing changes having to do with the rights of the captain, and whether trade should be controlled or open. These changes were necessitated by the difficulties the Portuguese faced in getting control over the trade of the southern coast. They make up a tedious story that has been described in detail elsewhere.[61] So confused were these changes that they seem to constitute not a remedy for Portuguese problems but rather part of the problem itself, for they are quite bewildering at times. For example, in 1591, the king opened up the gold trade to all, and four years later closed it again.[62] The shifts are fundamental, confusing, and apparently poorly thought out. At different times, there was free trade, a monopoly for the captain of Mozambique (who paid a large sum for the privilege), a crown monopoly, a company of Diu banians, a junta of commerce, and various settlement schemes.[63] The various official accounts of Mozambique that record expenses and revenues are of little use, for they reflect only part of the total picture.[64] The essential point, however, is that the essential element of Portuguese policy was always the use of force to get a monopoly.

One could argue that underpinning these Portuguese policies was a pronounced racism, which meant that the Portuguese considered themselves justified in taking over trade, destroying towns, and so on. Race relations in the Portuguese empire have been much discussed.[65] On the one hand, the Portuguese despised Africans and Asians, yet, on the other, they intermingled with both. This contempt included the Canarins, the converted local inhabitants of Goa. For example, in 1696, when the Portuguese were trying to foster colonization of the Rios area, it was recommended that various forts be rebuilt. This was to be done by engineers, stonemasons, and master carpenters from Portugal, but for the more lowly tasks Indians should be used, "as it is not fitting in this Conquista that the natives see Portuguese doing manual work."[66]

Racism was more pronounced when the Portuguese looked at Africans. As late as 1950, a report on the Mozambique census of that year noted a rise in the number of Africans included in the "civilized" population, these now numbering 4,316 as compared with 45,599 Europeans, 861 east Asians (*amarelos*), 8,538 Indians, and 24,892 *mestiços*. These few Africans were included in this prestigious civilized category because they had "finally attained the status of being assimilated."[67]

Sometimes this racism was reciprocated. In the early 1630s, a group of Bantu were watching a Portuguese *fidalgo* strum his guitar, and one said to his companion "You see, these savages have musical instruments just like we do."[68] This is a benign form of racial misunderstanding, but often relations were very hostile indeed. The chronicle of the Muslim port city of Kilwa looked back on early Portuguese-Kilwa relations with great bitterness.

When da Gama got to Mafia Island in 1498, "The lords of Mafia rejoiced, for they thought they were good and honest men. But those who knew the truth confirmed that they were corrupt and dishonest persons who had only come to spy out the land in order to seize it." Da Gama then sailed on to Malindi. "When the people of Malindi saw them, they knew they were bringers of war and corruption, and were troubled with very great fear. They gave them all they asked, water, food, firewood and everything else. And the Franks asked for a pilot to guide them to India, and after that back to their own land—God curse it!"[69]

This pronounced antipathy to the Portuguese was widespread among the Muslims of the east coast. The Muslim view of the converted sultan of Mombasa, Dom Jeronimo Chingulia, was that he "had been brought up among the Portuguese. He ate pork like them, and, in general, ate the food they use . . . when he had obtained power, he governed in a most tyrannical manner; he compelled the people to eat pork, and was wicked and an infidel."[70] Later, of course, he reconverted to Islam and revolted against the Portuguese. A common Swahili saying went "Go away Manoel, you have made us hate you, go, and carry your cross with you."[71] This hatred was most openly shown in the widespread support for the Turks when they sent fleets down the coast in the 1580s.

This hatred was fully reciprocated by the Portuguese, as an incident in 1651 showed. While visiting Mozambique, Nicholas Buckeridge was told of a Portuguese vessel bound for Chaul in which the Indian sailors had mutinied and massacred the thirty-five Portuguese on board, the reason being the behavior of the Portuguese, who had "put Swines flesh into their water." It was thought the mutineers had headed for the Red Sea.[72] This incident seems to show innate anti-Muslim feeling from the Portuguese. One possible explanation of Portuguese policy may be their visceral anti-Muslim feeling, derived long before their voyages to the Indian Ocean from the experience of driving Muslim rulers out of their homeland, which was reinforced by bitter battles against Muslims in north Africa. The Portuguese brought with them hatred of Muslims.[73] When Almeida followed his instructions and attacked Muslims wherever he found them, he was also told to differentiate between Muslims and others. He was ordered to seize all Muslim merchants in Sofala and take all their goods, but treat natives of the land well, "and you shall tell them that in ordering those Moors to be made captive and their property taken, we do so by reason of their being enemies of our holy catholic faith and because we wage war continually upon them, whilst to themselves it will ever be our pleasure to bestow every bounty and grace."[74] In 1569, Portuguese "men of learning" opined that an invasion of the Mutapa state would be a just war, in part because its ruler had sheltered Muslims.[75]

This pattern was found all over the Indian Ocean area. However, the south coast of east Africa was unique in the wider Portuguese empire in two ways: the fruitless search for El Dorado and official colonization schemes.

The fabled mines of the Zimbabwe Plateau assumed an almost mythical importance for the Portuguese. They ranked with such other chimeras as the search for the mighty Christian potentate Prester John, who would help the Portuguese smite the Muslims, and Albuquerque's scheme to block the Nile or to capture Mecca and hold the Prophet's body for ransom. What is interesting about the gold mines is that the Portuguese persevered for so long with their hope that one day they would find their own El Dorado, or more prosaically Potosí, which began full production in the mid sixteenth century. They hoped to be able to emulate, or even surpass, their Iberian neighbors.

From the time of their arrival, the Portuguese were aware of the substantial gold trade from the interior to the coast. For them, gold meant mines that could be controlled. The first large expedition got to the gold mining area of Manica in the 1570s. They "expected to find it [gold] in the streets and woods," but they soon found out it was extracted only with great difficulty.[76] Numerous subsequent accounts reinforced this finding,[77] yet they continued to hope. Couto, normally a careful chronicler, wrote of a nugget that yielded 4,000 cruzados (14.8 kg) and another which in its rough state weighed 12,000 cruzados (44.4 kg).[78] In 1608, the king told the viceroy that "I have been informed of the importance and richness of the gold and silver mines of the Kingdoms of Monomotapa"; and now that the Muslims had been expelled from the plateau, it was time to exploit them fully.[79] The negative opinion of the treasury council in 1614 was countered by an optimistic report of the same year.[80] As late as 1635, Viceroy Linhares reported "news of the greatest mines of all metals which have yet been discovered in the world."[81]

So great were these hopes that the Portuguese were tempted into the interior in a way they avoided everywhere else, except briefly in Sri Lanka. This was a fatal move, for the essence of their strength was their cannon mounted on ships. They had no particular advantage on land, not even when confronted by poorly armed Shona warriors, let alone when facing the formidable Mughal army in India. The various Portuguese expeditions have been covered elsewhere.[82] Their aims were large, but they were in pursuit of a myth. In any case, the Portuguese were unable to maintain a strong presence on the plateau for longer than the seventeenth century. What success they had was dependent on the weakness of the Mutapa state at several times during the century. Even before Changamire, the Rozvi leader, drove them out in 1693, their position had deteriorated greatly.[83] This vainglorious effort produced nothing except the ironically much more Africanized institution of the prazos along the lower Zambezi Valley. The Portuguese succeeded when they acculturated, rather than when they tried to dominate.

The second unusual feature of the Portuguese presence in the south was the official attempt to establish settlements of colonists far into the interior. This effort has no counterpart anywhere in their Asian empire. What they wanted to do was to turn a *conquista* into a *colonia*. Such efforts to get people to move to the area began very early. In 1507, the king informed the captain of Kilwa that he was sending him 30 *degradados* (exiled criminals) and they were to be put to work. "And see if you can endeavour to make Christians of the people of the land, especially the women, and that you endeavour to marry them to the said felons who would have them for wives that may be the cause of making the land more peaceful and have better service out of them."[84]

Over the years, many Portuguese did move inland, some with the cognizance of the state, others on their own. In the late 1580s, Dos Santos found 800 Christians in Sena, 50 of them Portuguese, and in Tete 600, with 40 Portuguese. These were still greatly outnumbered by those on the coast: There were 600 Christians in Sofala, some Portuguese, some mestiços, and some natives, and a total of 2,000 Christians in Mozambique.[85] By the second decade of the seventeenth century, numbers in the inland had fallen,[86] and a census of 1722 shows that this trend continued into the next century.[87]

Nevertheless, the officials were always keen to establish large, controlled colonies. In 1635, the king said he was going to send not only 200 soldiers to Mozambique but also 200 *casados* (married men), these being skilled tradesmen and farmers.[88] Such Wakefieldian schemes were put forward from time to time, but never succeeded; settlement was ad hoc and very loosely controlled. The prazos are merely the best-known example of this. In this same year, Viceroy Linhares, claiming that a vast gold mine had been found, asked the king to send 2,000 Portuguese settlers, and also married Canarins to grow food.[89] The notion of settling Canarins was often actively mooted. Padre António Gomes said they would be better settlers than people from Portugal, as they were poor in India and so would be grateful, and also they were more accustomed to the ways of these areas.[90] Others saw the Canarins as a threat. They flooded into the Zambezi Valley in the last quarter of the seventeenth century, and there engaged in all sorts of crooked conduct, or so the Portuguese claimed.[91] The real problem, we may suspect, was that these diligent Indian settlers outtraded the Portuguese. Nevertheless, in 1682, 40 soldiers and 50 Canarin settlers, 8 of them married, were sent to Rios from Goa.[92]

Earlier, the Portuguese had made a large effort to get a substantial number of Portuguese to migrate and settle. In 1678, the king announced that he had sent off from Lisbon five ships with 600 soldiers and 50 married settlers, who were to settle in the Zambezi Valley.[93] Alas, by June 1680, of the 68 who arrived in Rios (26 married couples and 16 children) 5 men, 9 women, and 6 children had died.[94] Yet even this was a substantial addition to the total Portuguese population inland.[95] By 1696, Father Conceição was recommending that only very young Portuguese women be sent, as older ones never had issue. Failing them, married Indian couples should be sent, especially ones who were good at trade.[96] The qualification was redundant, for many of those who went under their own steam were formidable merchants and petty traders. By the turn of the century, the prazo system was well established—its origins go back well into the sixteenth century—and this apparently had produced a surplus of Portuguese females, both widows and younger unmarried women. The viceroy asked the king to send out 50 soldiers each year so these women could find partners.[97] Canarins certainly came in, and became dominant in trade, arm in arm with banians on the coast. And the Canarins also were important holders of prazos, along with people of pure or more likely mixed Portuguese blood. Neither of these groups were colonists in the state-controlled sense that the Portuguese had attempted to establish in the Rios in the seventeenth century.

It would be a travesty to write only of official policy, and its successes and failures. There was another layer of Portuguese action in east Africa that included cooperation, acculturation, and dependence. In real life, the Portuguese, whether officials or not, lived lives and mixed with Africans in ways that had little to do with the hard-nosed official pronouncements.

This was even to be seen in relations with Muslims, in theory so hated and seen to be so threatening. Especially in the early days, the Portuguese relied heavily on existing Muslim trade networks in the south to get their goods. To ensure their cooperation, the Portuguese treated them well, gave them presents, and tried to work with them on matters such as choosing a new sultan for those ports in the south where puppet sultans ruled.[98] In 1507, two Muslim merchants of Sofala had some of their goods confiscated, even though they had a Portuguese pass. The Portuguese captain ordered that the goods be returned, in order that this example of fair play might "bring people to this city that is presently wholly lacking in people that they may see how favourably His Highness looks upon the Moors."[99] In 1514, the captain of Mozambique and Sofala was condemned for ill-treating Muslims in these towns.[100] Some years later, a new viceroy arrived in Mozambique and found that an overly zealous Franciscan had been allowed to tear down a mosque in the Muslim village. He had to spend a lot of time and effort to calm the resulting upheaval.[101] In 1570, a cleric noted good relations all along the coast between Muslims and Portuguese.[102] At Sena before 1570 rich and honored Muslims mingled with the local Portuguese, and traded happily with them.[103] Couto noted that they were "our friends. . . . Through intercourse with the Portuguese, with whom they were brought up, they spoke and understood our language, and wrote with our characters."[104] But in 1572, Barreto's expeditioners accused them of treachery and massacred them all.

Sometimes Muslims cooperated actively with the Portuguese. In 1509, a Portuguese gunner fled from Malindi and became a renegade. A local Muslim provided the Portuguese with information on his whereabouts, and then a mixed party of Portuguese and Muslims went off and captured him.[105] A century later, in 1616, four English ships attacked and sank a Portuguese ship coming from Portugal. The crew finally got ashore in the Comoro Islands, where they were mistreated by the natives. They were rescued by a ship owned by a leading Muslim of Pate Island, who happened to be in the vicinity, and he took the Portuguese back to safety in Mombasa.[106]

These stories point to considerable mutual dependence between Muslims and Portuguese, and even official recognition of this at times. This theme becomes very clear when we remember that the Portuguese moved in on an existing, intricate, and sophisticated trading network, and tried to control and tax it for their own benefit. They did not open important new trade routes, nor did they interfere in any way in the productive process. This was most clearly to be seen in the case of cloth, the vital trade item not only in east Africa but all over the littoral of the Indian Ocean; for example, cloths were often used as currency both inland from the Swahili coast and also in parts of southeast Asia. The earliest correspondence from east Africa stresses the centrality of cloths from Gujarat in any attempt to trade. Cambay cloth was often described as the lifeblood or the sustenance of the whole trade. With cloths one could buy gold, with gold one could buy spices.

This sort of dependence was also seen in the matter of labor. Even before the prazo system was fully established, the Portuguese often had some hundreds of slaves each, who were used for porterage, as militia, and often as concubines. One of the five companies of troops that Barreto took with him to chastise the Mutapa for having let Father Silveira be killed was composed of 60 Canarins and 80 Africans. Around 1600, the Portuguese at Sena and Tete raised a force of 75 Portuguese and 2,000 Africans to help the Mutapa ruler defeat a rebel.[107] At the end of the century, a priest noted that African troops were quite splendid, because they needed to be paid only one-fifteenth or one-twentieth of what a European required.[108] On board a ship seized by the English early in the seventeenth century were 250 people, 70 Portuguese, the rest mestiços and slaves.[109] Many examples confirm the truism that a small country like Portugal must find labor and soldiers where it could.

This sort of dependence was also evident in relations with African rulers. We have noted how the Portuguese depended on hinterland rulers to allow the passage of goods to the coast. Further inland, every time a new Portuguese took office in Mozambique, he paid the curva, or tribute, to the ruler of the Mutapa state. If it were not paid there was a threat of an *empata*, or uprising, that would block trade and imperil the lives of Portuguese living inland. After the 1530s, preexisting Muslim-dominated bazaars, sites where imports and exports were exchanged, often came under Portuguese control. Sena and Tete are two large-scale examples of bazaars that became *feiras*, or fairs. However, these two places were also important way stations for passage up the Zambezi River. Portuguese guarded the Mutapa ruler; yet they also paid tribute to him. It is this sort of dense, intertwined, reciprocal relationship that characterized the sixteenth century.

During the seventeenth century, the Portuguese tried to break out of this dependent situation and assert themselves as rulers or at least controllers. The Mutapa ruler was made, at least in theory, to cede the gold mines to the Portuguese, expel his Muslims, and become Christian. Yet even here the Portuguese knew it would be politic to define their aims quite clearly: they wanted the gold, but were realistic enough to know that a vast inland empire was not achievable. In 1608, at the start of this process of increasing control, the king, demonstrating how much the Portuguese had learned about African society and economy over the last century, told the viceroy that he was to tell the Mutapa ruler that the Portuguese wanted to control his gold and silver mines, but "that this does not imply that we are taking his land from him, nor his government, nor are we fighting for possession of his pastures and cultivated lands, which are his means of subsistence and which he values above all. Our only interest is in the metals, which are not important to him and do not constitute his wealth."[110] Portuguese control did increase, and the net effect was to weaken further the control of the Mutapa ruler over the numerous *fumos*, or Karanga chiefs, in his loosely articulated state, not least because a Christian king was cut off from local society and the influence of spirit mediums. Representatives of the Portuguese state imposed these treaties, but the people who took advantage of them were the backwoodsmen, outside the official Portuguese structure, who moved in on the ruins of the Mutapa state. From quite early in the sixteenth century, some of these men tried to control men and trade and they also began to acquire land.

The prazos are prime examples of interaction between Africans and Portuguese, or so at least the recent influential studies of Newitt and Allen Isaacman have claimed.[111] Prazos were different from the feiras because they involved ownership of land. They were found even late in the sixteenth century along parts of the Zambezi Valley. After 1693, when Changamire drove the Portuguese from the plateau, they became the dominant Portuguese institution in the interior of Mozambique, all across the Zambezi basin. Some were vast expanses of land, several days' march from one end to the other. The owners, really conquerors, claimed control over both the land and the people on it; from late in the eighteenth century, they so vigorously sent their people into slavery in Brazil that many prazos became depopulated. While the prazo-holders did acquire Portuguese title to their vast lands, they really were African institutions acquired by conquest. Frontiersmen straddle a frontier, but Africanists have coined the term *transfrontiersmen* to describe Europeans who cross the frontier and acculturate to dominant local cultures. The prazo-holders are an example.[112] A Portuguese description of 1667 captures the essential fact that these were not new, different, "European" institutions, but rather had their roots deep in African society. The report noted that a small quit rent was payable to the Portuguese king, but "the holders of these lands have the same power and jurisdiction as the Kaffir fumos from whom they were conquered, for the deeds of lease were passed in that form; and therefore they are like the potentates of Germany, and can pronounce sentence in all causes, put to death, declare war, and impose tribute, in which great barbarities may be committed, but they would not be duly respected by their vassals if they did not hold the same powers as the fumos whom they succeeded."[113]

These prazos make up one, but not the only, example of interaction and intermingling between the Portuguese and the societies in which they operated. A small example is the way the Portuguese gave "deserving girls" dowries so they could be married; the dowry might include an entitlement to a particular office, and the successful suitor thus acquired a position along with his bride.[114] Around 1589, many Portuguese, both soldiers and married men, lived on Pemba Island. They behaved in a most tyrannous fashion, and finally the Muslim inhabitants revolted, killed many of the Portuguese, and drove out the king of the island. He fled to Mombasa, and converted to

Christianity. Early in the next century, his brother also converted, becoming Dom Felipe. He was married off to one of the orphans sent out from Portugal. As his brides's dowry he was given back the island of Pemba. However, the islanders refused to accept him. Nor did the sultan of Mombasa help him, even though he was meant to be a puppet of the Portuguese, because he wanted to take over Pemba for himself. This story illustrates both interaction and also the limits of Portuguese power in the face of local realities.[115] Dowries could go to the most unlikely people. In 1614, Doña Maria, a niece of the Muslim ruler of Ampaza, in the Lamu archipelago, converted to Christianity and was given as a dowry for her successful suitor the post of factor at Mombasa.[116]

Other examples of very human interaction are numerous. The best examples include copious intermarriage, or interbreeding, between Portuguese and local inhabitants, and the eclectic practices of Christianity and even Islam in the area. C. R. Boxer notes an "amicable mixture of Christian, Muslim and pagan practices," and these syncretic practices were followed not only by newly converted Bantus but by whites, mulattoes, and Goans as well, despite the opposition of the clergy.[117] Such happy mixing and intermingling was also found at Sena in 1633, where the church school was attended by the children of Portuguese, and also people of Chinese, Javanese, Malabari, Sinhalese, and various African backgrounds. This school is reminiscent of the College of St. Paul in Goa, where the Jesuits trained a similarly diverse group of students.[118]

This sort of low-level intermixing was seen in a variety of other contexts. In 1606, Gaspar de S. Bernadino arrived at Siyu. There were no Portuguese, or indeed Christians, in the area, so the status of priest was unknown to the locals. However, two Hindu merchants from Diu did know what they were. They spoke good Portuguese and acted as interpreters for the cleric and told the local king all about how Christian fathers behave.[119] In the same area, at Takwa on Manda Island, there is another example of mixing and mingling. The ruined mosque at this settlement has an ablution trough outside it. Set into the base of this trough is a blue-and-white Portuguese dish.[120]

Thus the Portuguese cannot be seen as representing the arrival of a new and more advanced European civilization. Nor can they really be seen as harbingers of later European control. The notion of uniformitarianism, of a broad commonality in the world before the industrial revolution, seems to apply very aptly to this time and place and to these people. Two final examples reinforce this depiction of the Portuguese. First, outside of the small areas ruled by the state, the Portuguese fitted in, being in no way different from their African interlocutors. Second, the Portuguese, at least initially, showed a quite touching need to find things they understood in order to break down the culture shock they experienced when faced with unknown peoples and religions.

There have been many studies of the Portuguese all over the Indian Ocean area "going native," assimilating to the intricate, long-standing networks of trade, especially in the Bay of Bengal area and many parts of southeast Asia. These people operated outside official Portuguese channels, spoke various Asian languages, and very seldom had the opportunity to be counseled by a priest.[121] They were in a position no different from Armenians, Jews, Shirazis, Turks, and the host of other people trading and living and marrying in this polyglot and heterogeneous maritime world.

Such people are to be found in east Africa also. Some were stigmatized by the state officials for having fled from their duties, and for having taken military techniques and expertise with them. Others were humble traders of whom the state took little or no notice. As early as 1511, it was claimed that Portuguese deserters were setting themselves up in the interior of Mozambique, and one had even married a daughter of a local king, thus behaving very much like the later prazo-holders.[122] In the mid 1520s, it was claimed that there were hundreds of Portuguese roaming around in the south: some were deserters from ships and forts, some were degradados who had fled inland, and others were attracted to the mirage of a new El Dorado.[123] No doubt some derived from the thirty degradados the king had sent out in 1507, who in theory were to marry local women, convert them, and settle down.[124] Such escapees were also to be found in the north. As early as 1500, a Portuguese renegade went from Malindi in a Gujarati ship, and ended up with many of his fellow deserters in Bijapur.[125] As we noted, in 1509, a gunner fled from Malindi, but he was recaptured.[126] Not surprisingly, the state was actively opposed to these people taking their military skills to be used by Muslim enemies, yet in 1528, some were doing just this, especially in Mombasa.[127]

Most Portuguese outside the official structure were simply men who had served in the forts, and then by getting married had become casados. Many of these people found better trading opportunities outside the forts and strips of the coast controlled by the state. They went to other areas and traded alongside all the others found there, whether Swahili, foreign Muslims, or Indian Hindus. Many of these people can be seen as transfrontiersmen, the appropriate term for people who do not straddle a frontier, but rather move right over to the other side and acculturate more or less fully. These men were scattered all up and down the coast, from Inhaca Island, off modern Maputo, all the way up to the Lamu archipelago. Axelson thinks there may have been, by 1600, a maximum of 400 of them all along this 3,360 km coast. Boxer found at most 200 adult males on the northern coast.[128] In the south, these men penetrated far inland. An early example was António Fernandes, who traveled 300 miles inland and produced a most valuable report.[129] He was succeeded by many others. In the late 1580s, Dos Santos found 50 Portuguese in Sena, and 40 in Tete.[130] This Africanist concept of transfrontiersmen usefully illuminate studies of similar people in other parts of the Portuguese area, such as in the Bay of Bengal, or the "renegades" who worked for Muslim Indian states.

In the north, late in the sixteenth century, the observant cleric Dos Santos found Portuguese scattered all up and down the coast. Many lived on the island of Pemba. He claimed these men were greatly disliked by the locals, so that when the Turk Mir Ali Bey raided in 1585, the local Muslims joined him and handed over Portuguese to him.[131] At Pate, Mir Ali Bey captured several Portuguese ships along with the Portuguese on board, and considerable booty.[132]

The largest concentration of Portuguese on the north coast was in Mombasa. Even before the Portuguese took over the port city in the 1590s, it was preferred by private Portuguese and all other traders as being a much better market than its rival, Malindi.[133] This was despite the fact that the port city was considered by official Portugal to be an enemy, responsible for flouting Portuguese trade control policies, and consequently sacked three times during the century. The fort was begun in 1593, and the military party was accompanied by two Jesuits. They confessed everyone on the fleet from Goa; many Portuguese came into Mombasa from their scattered locations along the coast to confess, for many had not been able to do this for four, five, or even more years.[134] By 1606, there was a street of the Portuguese, called Rapazeira, of some seventy houses.[135] At the end of the street was the gate of the Fort Jesus, still some twenty years away from completion.

In the seventeenth century, the other two preferred settlements were at Pate and Ampaza, in the Lamu archipelago. In Pate there was a Portuguese factory under the authority of the captain of Mombasa; there was also a customshouse for a time. Pate was the more important trading center, being visited by numerous Portuguese and other ships from Gujarat and elsewhere. However, Ampaza had a church and resident friar, and so was often visited by the more pious of the Portuguese from the coast. In 1624, during Holy Week, there were four religious at Ampaza, and four ships with a total of seventy Christians, some Portuguese and some Indian. They had an excellent Easter, with lots of scourging, an all-night vigil, and confessions, sermons, and a procession.[136]

Both in east Africa and in India, the Portuguese searched for the familiar. They tried desperately to come to terms with, even appropriate, unknown people and religions, and understand them in terms familiar to themselves. In both cases, they met Hindus, followers of a religion at that time unknown to nearly all Europeans, and thought their religion was a form of Christianity. They were also predisposed to find Christians because they hoped to find Prester John, the Christian emperor who would ally with them and smite the Muslims from the south. When da Gama arrived in Mombasa, in April 1498, four "Christians" came on board his ship. Later, in the town, two "Christian" merchants showed them a paper to which they showed reverence. On the paper was a sketch of the Holy Ghost. The fleet then sailed on to Malindi.

> We found here four vessels belonging to Indian Christians. When they came for the first time on board Paulo da Gama's ship, the captain-major being there at the time, they were shown an altar-piece representing Our Lady at the foot of the cross, with Jesus Christ in her arms and the apostles around her. When the Indians saw this picture they prostrated themselves, and as long as we were there they came to say their prayers in front of it, bringing offerings of cloves, pepper and other things. These Indians are tawny men; they wear little clothing and have long beards and long hair, which they braid. They told us they ate no beef. Their language differs from that of the Arabs, but some of them know a little of it, as they hold much intercourse with them.[137]

When he got to Calicut, da Gama repeated these mistakes, and he reported back to the king that he had found Christians, schismatic to be sure, but definitely Christians.[138]

It is not surprising that retrospective accounts by Portuguese later in the sixteenth century do not make this mistake. The Portuguese soon became relatively well informed about Hinduism, and recognized it was quite different from their religion. Possibly the dogmatism and certainty of the Counter Reformation also helped them to set off other religions from their own. In any case, Barros noted that what da Gama found in Malindi were not Christians but banians from Cambay, "such devout followers of the teaching of Pythagoras that they will not even kill the insects by which they may be infested, and eat nothing which has life." In fact, da Gama may have crossed paths with Jains, the prominent community who are well known for their extreme reverence for all forms of life. Barros then goes on to say more about these people, and, with the benefit of hindsight, notes the mistaken identification the first visitors had made:

> These people [the banians] coming on board Vasco da Gama's ship, and seeing a picture of our Lady in his cabin, to which our people did reverence, they also offered their adoration with still greater respect, and as men who delighted in the sight of the said picture, they returned next day, offering before it cloves, pepper, and other samples of the spice they had come thither to sell, and they departed well pleased with our people and the manner of their worship, and our people were also well satisfied with them, supposing that they must be evidence of some Christian mission existing in India at the time of St. Thomas.[139]

To modern eyes and susceptibilities the official claims and actions of the Portuguese in the Indian Ocean in the sixteenth and seventeenth centuries seem reprehensible, not in any way to be condoned or justified. They found a peaceful, open trading system, and tried forcefully to monopolize some parts of it and control and tax the rest. They found a relatively tolerant religious situation, and introduced bigotry and forced conversions. They destroyed several flourishing open port cities on the east African coast, and they sacked many others. They showed a lamentable degree of racist antipathy to many of the people they met: the Muslims on the coast were to be opposed in every way possible, while the native Africans were merely barbarous, so much so that it was hardly worthwhile to try and convert them even. It looks like a completely unacceptable picture.

Yet when we look beyond the bombastic pronouncements and chronicles, and even beyond the atrocities, we find a very different picture. Fortunately, most of the grandiose aims of the state were not achieved. As the best example, the main Portuguese effort was devoted to monopolizing the trade in spices to Europe, and they failed here. In Africa, control of the mines of the plateau was the main objective, and here also they failed. It could be argued, then, that the whole thrust of their policy was misdirected; that they would have done much better to forget about chimeras of dominance, and instead do very well by trading along with everyone else in the area. In fact, this is what many Portuguese did. At this level, we find a much more human, and humane, dimension to the Portuguese presence, one which cooperated, and merged. Portuguese assimilated to Asian trade regimes, incorporated aspects of other religions into their own, married local women, and ended up, once the Dutch had defeated the official Portuguese presence, as one among many strands in a very rich and heterogeneous Indian Ocean maritime society.

Chapter 6

Conclusion

This study ends around 1700, but a brief account of later developments reinforces and makes more explicit the themes with which I have been concerned. The broadest theme in this book revolves around writing "world history," that is, a history that at a minimum goes beyond frontiers. Writing world history facilitates comparative study of major themes and trends. One result of this approach is that it can help the historian avoid analyses that privilege the activities of Europeans. While most of the empirical data is drawn from east Africa, I have found it useful to draw on other materials. My analysis has benefited from comparable and contrasting data from elsewhere and from broad middle-level theory. An example of the latter is my attempt to look at east Africa through the prism of world-system analysis. I paid homage to the power of this important model, but I modified it significantly with regard to notions of "value."

In other parts of the book, I have drawn on descriptive work from other areas. The discussion of the Swahili port cities, and their ties with the interior, was enriched by my familiarity with other studies of such cities in other places and times. Similarly, the analysis of the Afrasian Sea drew silently or otherwise on a host of other efforts in maritime history covering all the oceans of the world. Like anyone who has worked in, studied, and loved India, I have been appalled by the recent rise of communalism, more correctly called racism *tout court*. My awareness of recent lamentable events in India, and the role of historians both in fostering and opposing the growth of antipathy between India's two major religions, led me to sound a note of caution when one looks at comparable events in east Africa, and at the role of historians there. While historians are creatures and creations of their own times and places, they have a duty to transcend this, to write history that opposes, rather than causes, divisiveness and conflict.

I have drawn heavily on the works of others, and have tried to acknowledge the main influences that have affected my work, hence, the rather copious footnotes. More important, the themes I have sketched in this book need to be filled in. If my book has reflected certainty about anything, then this is a false impression for me to have given. There is so much to be done. Looking first at maritime history, we can explore further the notion of a certain commonality between communities located all around the littoral of the Indian Ocean, or just the Afrasian Sea. The idea of a distinctive littoral society needs more attention. We need to analyze folk customs; religious activities specific to coastal and maritime people; and styles in song, dance, architecture, and food. The notion of the Pacific Rim, and by extension an Indian Ocean Rim, has recently had some currency. A rim may be the same as a littoral, but in any case we could extend our analysis into quite new areas. For example, does the Indian Ocean Rim, or the ocean itself, have an environmental history that can be analyzed as a category?[1] Where does Madagascar fit in to the Afrasian Sea, and how is it connected to or different from the world of the Swahili? What about the other islands scattered all around the ocean? Their role as links, or way stations, is important to study. Is there something distinctive about insular societies? What affect does distance from a continent make? Can we analyze fluvial islands in the same way as oceanic ones? The list is endless. Some years ago, James Warren put forward the notion of the "Sulu zone."[2] He shows that the concept of a maritime zone has considerable utility in his work on the southern Philippines. Perhaps we could transfer this broad idea to the Afrasian Sea.

Work will continue on other themes touched on in this book. World-system theory will continue to provoke controversy and arguments, both internecine and with opponents of the whole notion. Certainly the world-systems list on the Internet is vigorous. When Immanuel Wallerstein publishes his fourth and last volume of the *Modern World-System*, world-systems analysis will return to the front of the scholarly agenda, even if he has already told us the whole story, and now ventures into prediction. As for studies of the Swahili and the coast, archaeologists will continue to dig, producing artefacts and analyses that will require historians to rethink their work. Anthropologists, historians, and other social scientists will continue to reinterpret the role of the Swahili people both on the coast and their relations with their fellow Bantus in the interior. Let us hope this can be done in an atmosphere unaffected by the ethnic policies of some governments in the area. It seems unlikely, however, that many new written sources will be found to provide us with more "facts." It seems doubtful that new Swahili chronicles will be found, though no doubt the interpretation of these difficult sources will continue to promote discussion and controversy. So also for Arabic sources, especially from Oman. Any new materials from this area will presumably deal with the eighteenth century, a period beyond the bounds of this study. For written sources in the early modern period, we have to rely heavily, and regrettably, on European documentation, and especially that from the Portuguese. Luís Frederico Dias Antunes has recently shown how much is available for Mozambique.[3] However, Portuguese materials for the northern coast seem to be very scanty. We can only hope that further investigation in Portugal's rich archives will reveal more material.[4] In short, there are gaps in our knowledge still to be filled, and many new concepts and theories can enrich our studies of east Africa and the coast.

Historians have had a difficult time coming to terms with the eighteenth century. Nineteenth-century, Protestant, northern European writers, reflecting the prevailing imperial certainty, dismissed their Catholic, southern predecessors. They condemned the Portuguese as unbusiness-like, inefficient, and far too prone to interbreed. Richard Burton put into blunt words what many thought. His view of intermarriage was that "experience and stern facts condemn the measure as a most delusive and treacherous political day dream" while the unfortunate results are called "Mestici—in plain English, mongrels."[5]

By the eighteenth century, the Portuguese were out of the game in the Indian Ocean. The main players now were the Dutch and the British, and it was all too easy to see this century as merely a prologue to western expansion. Indigenous regimes in both India and east Africa were stigmatized by the northern Europeans as being corrupt, ruthless, or tyrannical. Western colonialism rescued both areas from these times of troubles. Colonialism was *au fond* a positive force, for it brought these areas into modernity. Among the imperial writers who held this as an act of faith Karl Marx must be included, albeit for rather different reasons.

Recent efforts have looked at India in more autonomous terms. This brief account of changes in India in the eighteenth and early nineteenth centuries makes clear the contrast with east Africa. The eighteenth century should not be seen as an unsatisfactory prelude to imperialism, but rather as a time when important developments took place. Fruitful though these may have been, they were cut short by the advance of the west, and so denied the chance to come to fruition.

The historiography is much clearer for India than for east Africa. The imperial umbrella of the Mughals folded early in the century, maybe following the death of the emperor Aurangzeb in 1707, maybe after Muhammad Shah in 1717. This gave existing political networks the chance to develop. Regional modifications of the imperial Mughal system appeared in many of the successor provinces. This was a time when local land-controllers, acting in smaller states, became more prominent, as did the rulers of these states, who essentially moved from being high functionaries within the imperial system to being de facto independent rulers of smaller states. The history of the rulers of Bengal and Hyderabad demonstrate this pattern. This was also a time of considerable regional cultural creativity in poetry, building, and history writing. In more structural terms, we can see the emergence (or maybe we can see more clearly what was always there) of gentry farmers, tax farmers, and a business-noble nexus.[6] Much of this was not so much innovative as merely a reinforcement on a smaller scale of relationships that existed during the Mughal hegemony. Indeed, if we see Mughal rule as relatively disarticulated, with local powerful figures playing an important role, then the collapse of central authority merely removed an impediment to a correct depiction of the real locus of power in India, which was always rooted in the land and the local people who controlled it.

Similarly, financiers always had a connection with political controllers in Mughal India. They lent money for the trading ventures of the nobility; they functioned in the entrails of the revenue-collecting system as vital intermediaries between the state and the peasant revenue provider; they moved funds within the empire. These men became more visible as the scale of operations moved from imperial to provincial, and certainly their influence increased in these smaller arenas. The Jagat Seths in Bengal are but one example. In all this we see the resilience of commercial, social, political, kin, and manufacturing networks in Indian society. Much remains familiar in the first half of the eighteenth century: India continued to be a major manufacturer, especially of cotton cloth. So effective were Indian productive techniques that, at the end of the seventeenth century, the English legislated to block their importation, hoping to protect their long-standing woollen trade. The unexpected result, however, was to encourage cotton manufacture in England, signaling the beginning of modern industry.

Most port cities continued to function as before. Some, of course, came under British control, Others, such as Bombay and Madras, were created by the British. And European trade extended greatly the forelands of all of them, as trade with Europe in European ships expanded through the seventeenth and early eighteenth centuries. Many port cities competed successfully with European enclaves well into the eighteenth century. Bombay and Surat provide the clearest example. Writers who trace the present dominance of Bombay to its acquisition by the English East India Company in the 1660s are wide of the mark. Surat, despite being bedeviled by unrest in its hinterland, remained far superior to Bombay until the 1730s.

All this changed in the later eighteenth century as the British first gained ascendancy over their European rivals and then began to defeat these regional powers. In India, the East India Company changed from being a trading entity that used force only in self-defense, or to increase their profits, to a power that aimed for territorial control in India. They were helped in this by their advanced military technology and techniques, which can be seen as a result of the early process of industrialization in England. Once they conquered, they began to impose radically new notions of property and revenue collection. The clearest example is Cornwallis's "Permanent Settlement" of Bengal late in the eighteenth century. The novel view of land as a commodity that could be bought, sold, and mortgaged is an element in the seismic change that in total is called the industrial revolution.

The following figures show starkly what happened in India. In 1750, India had 24.5 percent of the world's manufacturing output, and the whole of what is now called the developed world had 27 percent. By 1830, the percentages were 17.6 and 39.5; by 1900, 1.7 and 89. Per capita levels of industrialization tell the same story. In 1750, India's index was 7, and the developed countries 8. By 1830, the indexes were 6 and 11; and by 1900, 1 and 35.[7]

East Africa had a rather different eighteenth century. While India was well on the way to being subordinated by 1800, east Africa was entering the anachronistic blind alley of Omani dominance. A brief chronology will be helpful. Portugal dominated the coast of Oman until 1650, when they lost their last stronghold of Muscat. This successful Omani dynasty, the Ya'rubi, is conventionally described as being more interested in religious matters than in sea trade. Yet, during the seventeenth century, Oman became a feared enemy of the Portuguese and other Europeans; it may have learned lessons in warfare by sea from the period when Oman was ruled by the Portuguese. Portuguese settlements were attacked frequently, though not it seems with any clear plan in view. The great center of Diu, in Gujarat, was sacked in 1668. In east Africa, the Omanis sacked Mombasa in 1661, raided Mozambique in 1670, and destroyed the Portuguese settlement at Pate in 1689. Their greatest seventeenth century success was their epic siege, begun in March 1696, and capture, in December 1698, of Mombasa. This signaled the end of Portuguese influence on the northern Swahili coast.

During the first half of the eighteenth century, Oman was distracted by a long civil war, which finally ended in 1749 with the victory of the more sea-oriented and commercially minded Busaidi dynasty. During this time, Mombasa became de facto independent under Mazrui rulers. Once Oman had solved its internal problems, east Africa quickly became the focus of their attention, as any political or military role in India was made difficult by the rising power of the British. The Omanis established themselves in Zanzibar in the mid eighteenth century. In the early nineteenth century, they established dominance over most of the Swahili coast; in 1837, they reestablished control over Mombasa. Zanzibar soon became their main center, and the ruler of Oman moved there in 1840.[8]

Superficially, this trading empire looks very similar to the Portuguese one it in part displaced. The Omanis were most interested in exporting dates to east Africa and importing slaves. Their control lay lightly over most areas. Their main beachhead on the mainland was Kilwa. Customs duties of 5 percent were imposed, and trade was allowed to continue, albeit compulsorily centralized at Zanzibar. However, the increased demand for slaves and for ivory led to much more dense and articulated connections between coast and interior. Over time, the Omanis and the Swahili displaced some interior traders, due to their better weaponry. Thus, the Yao, who had moved their trade from Mozambique to Kilwa, were slowly put under Omani control. Indians played a large financial role here. As we noted, during the eighteenth century, Portuguese Mozambique and the Zambezi Valley became dominated by Indians. Canarins, Christians from Portuguese India, became the rulers of many of the prazos, while trade and commerce was dominated by banians from Gujarat. A similar situation existed for the Omani state. Gujaratis farmed the customs for the Omanis, and continued their traditional trades in cloths and ivory. Indian capital and commercial expertise were the backbone of the Portuguese empire, even in the sixteenth century; so also with the Omani state in the late eighteenth and nineteenth centuries; and even the British colonies in Kenya and Uganda from the late nineteenth century.

On the surface, one aspirant to thalassocracy, the Portuguese, were replaced by another, the Omanis. But this is to neglect the world historical context as it impinged on east Africa. The century from 1750 to 1850 saw the rise of England as the dominant industrial, commercial, and military power in the world, in our area symbolized by their conquest of India and their moves to exercise a controlling influence over the Indian Ocean. This was manifested in their attacks on people they arbitrarily defined as "pirates," and, from the early nineteenth century, by their efforts to control, and then end, the trade in slaves. Much of what the Omanis did in east Africa was courtesy of, or influenced by, the interests of western powers, and especially of Britain. In effect, they put themselves under the wing of the rising British power so that they could continue to trade to India. Thus the cloth trade from India was slowly strangled as machine made goods from Lancashire outcompeted Indian production and took over traditional Indian markets in east Africa and elsewhere. The trade in ivory was powerfully affected by rising prosperity based on industrialization in the west, for this raised demand to such a level that it could be met only by a greatly increased exploitation of this resource. In consequence, vast herds of elephants far into the interior of east Africa were wiped out. Yet this large demand, so destructive for east Africa, was in western terms a very minor one, for the ivory was used only for trivialities: billiard balls, piano keys, combs.

The slave trade also shows increased exploitation by Europeans. This is not the place for a detailed analysis of this difficult and controversial topic. There had been a major slave trade from east Africa to Abbasid Iraq in the seventh to ninth centuries. Many of these apparently came from the far north coast, that is Somalia and Ethiopia. They were used as labor to reclaim the marshlands of southern Iraq. As the Abbasid empire declined, so did the slave trade. Subsequently there was an hiatus of some thousand years in the trade. It continued, but in much reduced numbers. Slaves from Ethiopia were taken to Muslim states in India and the Middle East and used for military purposes: Their role was not dissimilar to that of the Janissaries in Ottoman Turkey. In India, they were known as Habashis, while the small number who came from further south were called Zangis.[9] There also was extensive internal slavery in Africa, both inland and on the coast. It could be argued, however, that this was a comparatively benign form of slavery, first, because they were not uprooted and taken far across the sea, and, second, because over time they often merged into the kin groups of their owners. M.D.D. Newitt prefers the term "clientage" to "slavery" in these circumstances.[10]

The Portuguese may have increased the trade slightly, for they took some hundreds each year to India, where they were used for domestic purposes in Portuguese cities.[11] They also used slaves extensively in Africa, with the residents of Sena and Tete having up to one thousand each.[12] These slaves were kept more separate from their owners than was the case with African slave owners. However, the major export trade both at this time, and earlier, was north and east to the Muslim world. Ralph Austen estimates a large number for this trade.[13] Whatever its dimensions, it was only late in the eighteenth century that the export trade in slaves became a major one, and one that had demonstrably detrimental effects on Africa. This was the trade to South America, especially Brazil. For the first time, the trade extended far south, and far inland, as Dr. Livingstone and Richard Burton noted. As the trade across the Atlantic to Brazil and Cuba was blocked after about 1860, an apparently new trade opened up, to Madagascar.[14]

The huge rise in the slave trade was a direct consequence of a demand based on western prosperity and policies. The trade began to flourish from around 1780, resulting from the need of French plantation owners in Bourbon (now Réunion) and Ile-de-France (now Mauritius) for slaves to grow sugar to meet the demand in Europe. Subsequently, the main trade was to Brazil, once the trade from west Africa had been blocked by the British. Again, the impetus came from European demand for Brazilian sugar. Similarly, once the trade in the Afrasian Sea was declared illegal, slaves continued to be used in plantations on Zanzibar, to grow cloves, again for the European market, and on the Swahili coast, to produce foodstuffs. Other slaves were used in Oman, and in other areas of Africa, especially on the prazos on the Zambezi.

The Omani regime, then, was quite different from the Portuguese, not because it was "Asian" instead of "European," and not because its basic aims were very different, but because it operated in a very different world historical context, that of rising western affluence and dominance.[15] Increasingly, the Omanis operated a merchant-capital empire in a time when merchant capital was being replaced by modern, industrial, capital. The latter, dominant, form allowed the older, and increasingly anachronistic, form to continue for a time. During this period, there was a strong commonality between the Omanis and the Portuguese. They both operated inside the British system. In the first decades of the nineteenth century in India, the Portuguese were able to circumvent British control of the lucrative opium trade to China; they made huge profits. So also with the Omanis. Yet through the nineteenth century the exemplar of the west, Britain, asserted more and more control over Zanzibar, culminating in the treaty of 1890 that made Zanzibar a protectorate. So also Portuguese participation in the opium trade was finally blocked in the 1830s.

Many areas of life, both on the coast and islands and in the interior, had been profoundly affected long before east Africa was formally colonized. While the maritime areas were affected most, this process occurred in the interior as well. For example, long before colonization, the vastly increased demand for slaves and ivory, both these being a product essentially of western needs even if indirectly, had produced major effects far inland. Both trades led to a rise in violence in the interior as African leaders competed to exchange slaves for advanced western weapons. Vast areas were depopulated as Africans enslaved each other.

The consequences of the rise in demand for ivory and for slaves were significant. In the early modern period, ivory and gold production impacted little on the internal economy, for this was discretionary, part-time, effort. Now, however, African peasants and tribals far into the interior were taken from subsistence production by these increased demands. On the coast, the

Swahili escaped Portuguese control only to be subjected to the more ruthless Omanis. There may have been a minor florescence in the north during the first half of the eighteenth century, but essentially the Swahili, before 1500 members of a vibrant and wealthy civilization, were reduced to a compradorial role. This role increased as the slave trade grew and they began for the first time to penetrate the interior in numbers.

Formal colonialism had vast effects, for this symbolized the complete incorporation of east Africa, both coast and interior, into a world-economy dominated from Europe. The various political economists whom we discussed in chapter 4 are quite correct: Something dramatic happened to east Africa, and to India, once a capitalist-based industrialized western Europe turned its attention to these two areas and asserted not merely influence but control. In world-system terms, both areas moved from a status of being external to the system to one where they were incorporated and became peripheries. Whether or not we accept Wallerstein's model, there is no doubt that something cataclysmic happened in both these areas, though at different times in different places. India was politically and economically peripheralized during the century from 1750 to 1850; that happened in east Africa in the late nineteenth century. Yet the process was the same. Western capital penetrated deeply, and it produced major, and extremely detrimental, changes in such basic areas as access to land, craft production, indigenous political autonomy, and social and physic independence.

In Kenya, tribespeople and peasants were forced to pay taxes, and consequently to enter the market and sell their labor or produce. This, and the appropriation of large areas of land for white farmers, was a result of the formal colonization of Kenya. The new attitude to land—the insistence that it was private property that could be bought and sold—produced in Kenya in the twentieth century precisely the same upheavals and dispossession that had occurred first in Bengal late in the eighteenth century when the same standards and preconceptions first impacted on India. The arrival of Europeans in some areas, such as Oceania, Australia, and the Americas, produced devastating "virgin soil epidemics." Africa seems to have shared a disease pool with Eurasia, so new diseases impacted little. However, colonialism could still produce epidemics. It has been claimed that the tsetse virus became a major problem only after colonization, and as a result of changes enforced by the western powers.[16]

In both India and east Africa, distance was broken down. Western capital insisted on better access to distant inland areas that were to serve as suppliers of raw materials. From the materials, manufactured goods were produced in the west; those goods were then transported back to inland markets in the peripheries. The whole process is visually encapsulated by the railroads built by the colonial powers. These were vast networks. The British created an expansive network in India; Mombasa was linked with the imperial creation of Nairobi, and further inland to Kampala. Railroads provided markets for heavy industry in the metropolises, for the engines, the rails, and the rolling stock were all manufactured in Europe. Financing also came from the imperial centers, and returns to British investors were guaranteed against the revenues of the colonies. Their routes were precisely planned to serve two imperial aims: rapid movement of troops to frontier areas and within the colony, and to provide links between markets and areas producing raw materials and the ports that funneled these materials out and the goods back. Mombasa and Bombay are type studies. Routes that would integrate the internal economies of the colonies were not built: These had to be provided after independence. Rather, rail links between coast and interior were constructed, thus definitively breaking down whatever barriers may have existed in the past between these two zones. In Mombasa, we can see that the railroads linked this port city much more tightly to a far-distant hinterland. Similarly, steam navigation, nearly all of it owned by colonial interests, provided a vastly expanded foreland for Mombasa and all the other port cities. One consequence was the decline, and today the end, of the two-thousand-year-old dhow trade.

East Africa paid a high, yet inevitable, price as it was subsumed in the modern world-system. The effects can be seen even today, long after formal colonialism has gone. Indeed, the situation has worsened. Once Africa had products that the world needed: gold, ivory, slaves, and cloves. By and large, this is no longer the case; the world has many other sources for the tropical crops Africa produces. Africa is even faring much worse than the rest of the developing world. In 1980, Africa had a 15 percent share of the total trade of developing countries; by 1995, the share was only 6.4 percent.[17] This step backwards may be seen in most areas discussed in this book. The events and processes of the last two centuries have radically altered them all. A vibrant, autonomous littoral society and maritime trading network was subsumed and controlled from distant western centers. The coast and the interior became more closely linked, yet, this was first achieved as a result of the demands of the slave trade. A relatively benign trading connection across the Afrasian Sea was replaced by one based on force, dominance, and unequal exchange. An ineffective Portuguese structure was replaced by a more far reaching Omani regime, which had consequences, especially from the slave trade, far inland. The Omanis, however, should be seen as controlled and increasingly dominated by the British, a much more hegemonic power in the

Afrasian Sea than had ever been achieved before. Even history writing was increasingly perverted to serve the dubious ends of the new masters. These reflections do not represent nostalgia for a past age, or even pessimism about the present plight of Africa. Rather, it is a matter of seeing things in the round, of identifying long-term change in the Indian Ocean in world historical terms. If we accept that modern industry, and its various new variants today, has been the great force in world history over the last two hundred years, then the effects of this in a range of areas of historical concern can be clearly seen in east Africa.

Notes

List of Abbreviations

Barros
João de Barros, *Da Asia* (Lisbon, 1778–88). In referencing the chronicles of Barros, I cite the *década* number in uppercase Roman numerals, the book number in lowercase Roman numerals, and the chapter number in Arabic numbers.

Bragança Pereira
Arquivo Português Oriental, ed. A. B. de Bragança Pereira (Bastorá, Goa, 1937–40). In referencing the collections of Bragança Pereira, I cite the volume number in uppercase Roman numerals, the book number in lowercase Roman numerals, and the chapter number in Arabic numbers.

Bulhão Pato
Documentos remettidos da India, ou Livros das Monções, ed. R. A. de Bulhão Pato, 5 vols. (Lisbon, 1880–1935).

Castanheda
Fernão Lopes de Castanheda, *História do descobrimento e conquista da India pelos Portugueses*, 3d ed., 9 vols. (Coímbra, 1924–33).

Correa
Gaspar Correa, *Lendas de India*, 4 vols. (Coímbra, 1921–31; Lisbon, 1969).

Couto
Diogo do Couto, *Da Asia* (Lisbon, 1778–88). In referencing the chronicles of Couto, I cite the *década* number in uppercase Roman numerals, the book number in lowercase Roman numerals, and the chapter number in Arabic numbers.

Cunha Rivara
J. H. da Cunha Rivara, ed., *Archivo Português Oriental*, 9 vols. (Nova Goa, 1857–88).

DM
António da Silva Rego, et al., eds., *Documentos sobre os Portugueses em Moçambique e na Africa Central, 1497–1840*, 9 vols. (Lisbon, 1962–89).

IJAHS
International Journal of African Historical Studies.

JAH
Journal of African History.

Santos
João dos Santos, *Ethiopia Oriental*, 2 vols. (Lisbon, 1891). In referencing the material in Santos, I cite volume numbers in uppercase Roman numerals, book numbers in lowercase Roman numerals, and chapter numbers in Arabic numbers.

Theal
G. M. Theal, *Records of South-Eastern Africa*, 9 vols. (London, 1898–1903).

Chapter 1. Introduction

1. Immanuel Wallerstein, *The Modern World-System*, 3 vols. (New York, 1974–89), 1: 15.

2. *Journal of World History* 1, no. 1 (1990), iii–v. See other articles in this excellent new journal that discuss the nature of world history. The senior "world historian," William H. McNeill, ruminates on the whole matter in a somewhat opaque article, "The Changing Shape of World History," *History and Theory* 34 (1995), 8–26.

3. Philip D. Curtin, *Cross-Cultural Trade in World History* (Cambridge, 1984), ix.

4. See J. C. Van Leur, *Indonesian Trade and Society* (The Hague, 1955).

5. See, as one example of a vast literature, Ignacio Olabarri, "'New' New History: A *longue durée* Structure," *History and Theory* 34, no. 1 (1995), 1–29. The quotations are from p. 29.

6. Preface to Stephen K. Sanderson, ed., *Civilizations and World Systems: Studying World-Historical Change* (Walnut Creek, Calif., 1995), 9. This valuable book consists of various contributions that debate the utility of "civilizationist" as compared with "world-system" theories. I must pay tribute to the enormously challenging notion of "big history" as practiced by David Christian, which covers a very long time frame. For his approach, which deals with the globe from the origins of the universe to today, see Christian, "The Case for 'Big History,'" *Journal of World History* 2, no. 2 (1991), 223–38; and Christian, "Adopting a Global Perspective," in Deryck M. Schreuder, ed., *The Humanities and the Creative Nation* (Canberra, 1995), 249–62.

7. I use the term *India* throughout this book. It refers to the area now correctly known as South Asia.

8. A.J.R. Russell-Wood, "Ports of Colonial Brazil," in Franklin W. Knight and Peggy K. Liss, eds., *Atlantic Port Cities: Economy, Culture, and Society in the Atlantic World, 1650–1850* (Knoxville, 1991), 197.

9. K. N. Chaudhuri, *Asia before Europe: Economy and Civilisation of the Indian Ocean from the Rise of Islam to 1750* (Cambridge, 1990); Janet Abu-Lughod, *Before European Hegemony: The World System A.D. 1250–1350* (Oxford, 1989).

10. For a recent discussion of some of these matters, see D. N. Beach, *The Shona and Their Neighbours* (Oxford, 1994), 1–14.

11. J. C. Wilkinson, "Oman and East Africa: New Light on Early Kilwan History from the Omani Sources," *IJAHS* 14 (1981), 272–305.

12. G.S.P. Freeman-Grenville, *The East African Coast: Select Documents from the First to the Earlier Nineteenth Century* (London, 1962).

13. Neville Chittick, "A New Look at the History of Pate," *JAH* 10, no. 3 (1969), 375–91; Marina Tolmacheva, *The Pate Chronicle* (East Lansing, 1993); Randall L. Pouwels, "Reflections on Historiography and Pre-Nineteenth-Century History from the Pate 'Chronicles,'" *History in Africa* 20 (1993), 263–96.

14. George Hourani, *Arab Seafaring in the Indian Ocean in Ancient and Early Medieval Times*, rev. and exp. ed. (Princeton, 1995); G. R. Tibbetts, *Arab Navigation in the Indian Ocean before the Coming of the Portuguese* (London, 1971).

15. Ibrahim Khoury, *As-Sufaliyya, "The Poem of Sofala," by Ahmed ibn Magid translated and explained* (Coímbra, 1983); Beach, *Shona and Their Neighbours*, 9.

16. B. G. Martin, "Arab Migration to East Africa in Medieval Times," *IJAHS* 7, no. 3 (1975), 367–90.

17. D. N. Beach, *A Zimbabwean Past* (Gweru, 1994). See also several surveys of the sources by Beach: "Africana in the Goa Archives," in *History in Africa* 3 (1976), 171–3; "Documents and African Society on the Zimbabwean Plateau before 1890," in Beatrix Heintze and Adam Jones, eds., *European Sources for Sub-Saharan Africa before 1900: Use and Abuse* (Stuttgart, 1987); "Publishing the Past: Progress in the 'Documents on the Portuguese' Series," *Zambezia* 17, no. 2 (1990), 175–83.

18. Beach, *Shona and Their Neighbours*, 100.

19. *DM*, 9 vols. to date. This series has the original Portuguese on each left-hand page, and a generally accurate English translation facing it. There are occasional slips however. In 1: 531, the word *tres*, "three," is omitted in the translation. In 1: 393, four thousand cows become only four. In 2: 253, the Portuguese phrase "some Christians, there as in India" becomes "any Christians among them in India." On 8: 423, *fisico* is translated as "leech," while "healer" would be more appropriate, and in 9: 352, "he can get from Patte the cloth" is translated as "he may send to Patte the cloth." See also D. N. Beach, "Publishing the Past," for a review of vol. 9. There has been considerable duplication of effort. Many documents are printed in both Theal and in the *DM* series; when this is the case, I have usually quoted from the *DM* version. Much of the contents of *DM* vols. 7

and 8 deal with missionaries, notably Fr. Silveira. These are often printed, though not translated, in J. Wicki et al., eds. *Documenta Indica*, 20 vols. to date (Rome, 1948–). Some are also printed in António da Silva Rego, ed. *Documentação para a história das Missões do padroado Português do Oriente: India*, 12 vols. (Lisbon, 1947–58).

20. For recent overviews of developments in the discipline, see J. Malina and Z. Vasicek, *Archaeology Yesterday and Today: The Development of Archaeology in the Sciences and Humanities* (Cambridge, 1990); Norman Yoffee and Andrew Sheratt, eds., *Archaeological Theory: Who Sets the Agenda?* (Cambridge, 1993).

21. Matthew Johnson, *An Archaeology of Capitalism* (Oxford, 1995).

22. A. Bernard Knapp, ed., *Archaeology,* Annales, *and Ethnohistory* (Cambridge, 1992); for the same approach, see also Steven Lubar and W. David Kingery, *History from Things: Essays on Material Culture* (Washington, D.C., 1993).

23. Peter Garlake, *Life at Great Zimbabwe* (Gweru, 1982); Garlake, *Great Zimbabwe: Described and Explained* (Harare, 1992).

24. Graham Connah, *African Civilizations: Precolonial Cities and States in Tropical Africa, An Archaeological Perspective* (Cambridge, 1987), 184; Paul Sinclair, "Archeology in East Africa: An Overview of Current Chronological Issues," *JAH* 32 (1991), 210–1.

25. Paul Sinclair et al., "Urban Trajectories on the Zimbabwean Plateau," in Thurstan Shaw et al., eds., *The Archeology of Africa: Food, Metals, and Towns* (London, 1993), 718; see this article for archaeological evidence of links between Great Zimbabwe and the Mutapa state.

26. George H. O. Abungu and Henry Mutoro, "Coast-Interior Settlements and Social Relations in the Kenya Coastal Hinterland," in Thurston Shaw et al., eds., *The Archeology of Africa: Food, Metals, and Towns* (London, 1993), 694.

27. Ibid., 694–704; George H. O. Abungu, "Islam on the Kenyan Coast: An Overview of Kenyan Coastal Sacred Sites," in David Carmichael et al., eds., *Sacred Sites, Sacred Places* (London, 1994), 152–62; Henry Mutoro, "The Mijikenda *Kaya* as a Sacred Site," in David Carmichael et al., eds., *Sacred Sites, Sacred Places* (London, 1994), 132–9. See two articles in the special issue of *Azania*, "The Growth of Farming Communities in Africa from the Equator Southwards," edited by J.E.G. Sutton: George H. O. Abungu, "Agriculture and Settlement Formation along the East African Coast," *Azania* 29–30 (1994–95), 248–56; Henry Mutoro, "Tana Ware and the *Kaya* Settlements of the Coastal Hinterland of Kenya," *Azania* 29–30 (1994–95), 257–60. See also W. Howard Brown, "History of Siyu: The Development and Decline of a Swahili Town on the Northern Kenya Coast" (Ph.D. diss., Indiana University, 1985).

28. Abungu and Mutoro, "Coast-Interior Settlements," 704.

29. Ricardo Teixeira Duarte, *Northern Mozambique in the Swahili World* (Stockholm, 1993), 61–8.

30. Sinclair, "Archeology in East Africa," 210–1.

31. Connah, *African Civilizations*; Richard Wilding, *Swahili Bibliography of the East African Coast* (Lamu, 1990). For a valuable, and skeptical, overview of the uses of archaeology for African historians, see Jan Vansina, "Historians, Are Archeologists Your Siblings?" *History in Africa* 32 (1995), 369–408. This article is copiously documented with references to the most recent work in the field.

32. J. Devisse and S. Labib, "Africa in Intercontinental Relations," in *General History of Africa*, vol. 4, *Africa from the Twelfth to the Sixteenth Century* (Paris, 1984), 656.

33. *Encyclopedia of Islam*, 2d ed., s.v. "Kenya."

34. M. C. Horton, "Early Muslim Trading Settlements on the East African Coast: New Evidence from Shanga," *Antiquities Journal* 67 (1987), 290–323; Sinclair, "Archeology in East Africa," 185.

35. Reported in the *Independent* (London), 16 March 1992.

36. Henrik Ellert, *Rivers of Gold* (Gweru, 1993), 87–117.

37. See Norman Hammond, ed., *South Asian Archaeology* (London, 1973), and F. R. Allchin, "Seven Problems in South Asian Archaeology," in ibid., 1–13; see also a more recent survey of the field, D. K. Chakrabarti, "The Development of Archaeology in the Indian Subcontinent," *World Archaeology* 13, no. 2 (1982), 326–44.

38. Cambridge, 1995.

39. Stanley Wolpert, *A New History of India* (Oxford, various editions since 1977).

40. A. L. Basham, *The Wonder That Was India* (London and New York, various editions since 1954).

41. Gavin Hambly, *Cities of Mughul India* (London, 1968); Stephen P. Blake, *Shajahanabad: The Sovereign City in Mughal India, 1639–1739* (Cambridge, 1991).

42. C. Jarrige, ed., *South Asian Archaeology, 1989* (Madison, 1992).

43. See four volumes to date of *Vijayanagara: Progress of Research* (Mysore, 1983–). For an excellent example of combining history and archaeology, unfortunately still rare in India, see Kathleen D. Morrison and Carla M. Sinopoli, "Economic Diversity and Integration in a Pre-Colonial Indian Empire [Vijayanagara]," *World Archaeology* 23, no. 3 (1992), 333–52.

44. David Dorward, reported in the *Australian National University Reporter*, 14 June 1995.

45. For an example of this, which contrasts differing contemporary perceptions of a particular port city, see Richard M. Eaton, "Multiple Lenses: Differing Perspectives of Fifteenth-Century Calicut," in Laurie Sears, ed., *Autonomous Histories, Particular Truths* (Madison, 1993), 71–86.

46. Letter to Creighton, Cannes, 5 April 1887 in J. Rufus Fears, ed., *Selected Writings of Lord Acton*, 3 vols. (Indianapolis, 1985–88), 2: 383–4.

47. David Sperling, "The Growth of Islam among the Mijikenda of the Kenya Coast, 1826–1933" (Ph.D. diss., School of Oriental and African Studies, University of London, 1988), 15–20.

48. *Times Literary Supplement*, 2 July 1993; for another recent review article, see Martin Walsh, "Becoming Swahili and Mijikenda," *Azania* 28 (1994).

49. H. T. Wright, "Trade and Politics on the Eastern Littoral of Africa, A.D. 800–1300," in Thurston Shaw et al., eds., *The Archeology of Africa: Food, Metals, and Towns* (London, 1993), 660.

50. John Middleton, *The World of the Swahili: An African Mercantile Civilization* (New Haven, 1992), viii.

51. A. I. Salim, "East Africa: The Coast," in *General History of Africa*, vol. 5, *Africa from the Sixteenth to the Eighteenth Century* (Paris, 1992), 753; T. H. Wilson, "Settlement Patterns of the Coast of Southern Somalia and Kenya" (paper presented at the First International Congress of Somali Studies, Mogadishu, July 1980).

52. See Philip D. Curtin, Steven Feierman, Leonard Thompson, and Jan Vansina, *African History*, 2d ed. (London, 1995), chap. 4.

53. *Encyclopedia of Islam*, 2d ed., s.v. "Kilwa."

54. See, among others, Devisse and Labib, "Africa in Inter-continental relations," 4: 656; J. de V. Allen, "The 'Shirazi' Problem in East African Coastal History," in J. de V. Allen and T. Wilson, eds., *From Zinj to Zanzibar: Studies in History, Trade, and Society on the Eastern Coast of Africa [in honour of James Kirkman]* (Wiesbaden, 1982), 9–27; and especially Thomas Spear and D. Nurse, *The Swahili: Reconstructing the History and Language of an African Society, A.D. 500–1500* (Philadelphia, 1984), 74–9.

55. J.E.G. Sutton, *A Thousand Years of East Africa* (Nairobi, 1990), 59–60.

56. See A. Pires Prata, *A influência da língua Portuguesa sobre o Suahíli e quatro línguas de Moçambique* (Lisbon, 1983), esp. 29–46, for a list of about 110 words; see also G.S.P. Freeman-Grenville, "The Portuguese of the Swahili Coast: Buildings and Language," *Studia* 49 (1989), 235–54.

57. Ronald B. Inden, *Imagining India* (Oxford, 1990).

58. James Kirkman, "The History of the Coast of East Africa up to 1700," in Merrick Posnansky, ed., *Prelude to East African History* (London, 1966), 106, 110.

59. See the map in James Kirkman, *Gedi*, 8th ed. (Nairobi, 1975); Neville Chittick, "The Coast before the Arrival of the Portuguese," in Martin A. Klein and G. Wesley Johnson, eds., *Perspectives on the African Past* (Boston, 1972), 106; António da Silva, S.J., *Mentalidade missiológica dos Jesuítas em Moçambique antes de 1759*, 2 vols. (Lisbon, 1967), 1: 150, 160; Roland Oliver and Anthony Atmore, *The African Middle Ages, 1400–1800* (Cambridge, 1981), 14; A.H.J. Prins, *The Swahili-Speaking Peoples of Zanzibar and the East African Coast* (London, 1961), 46.

60. J. Spencer Trimingham, *Islam in East Africa* (Oxford, 1964), 71.

61. Quoted in J. F. Mbwiliza, *A History of Commodity Production in Makuani, 1600–1900: Mercantalist Accumulation to Imperialist Domination* (Dar es Salaam, 1991), 136.

62. Quoted in Connah, *African Civilizations*, 210.

63. D. P. Abraham, "Maramuca: An Exercise in the Combined Use of Portuguese Records and Oral Tradition," *JAH* 2, no. 2 (1961), 212.

64. See also Beach, *Shona and Their Neighbours*, 211, n. 5.

65. See, for example, Alexandre Lobato, *A Expansão Portuguesa em Moçambique de 1498 a 1530*, 3 vols. (Lisbon, 1954–60); Eric Axelson, *Portuguese in Southeast Africa, 1488–1600* (Johannesburg, 1973); Axelson, *Portuguese in Southeast Africa, 1600–1700* (Johannesburg, 1960); Neville Chittick, "The East Coast, Madagascar, and the Indian Ocean," in Roland Oliver, ed., *Cambridge History of Africa*, vol. 3, *c. 1050–c. 1600* (Cambridge, 1977), 227–31; for a corrective, see chap. 5 in this book.

66. For a modern and much better account, an attempt to write an indigenous history of Mozambique, see M.D.D. Newitt, *A History of Mozambique* (London, 1994); and for the plateau, D. N. Beach's various publications, especially his overview in *Shona and Their Neighbours*.

67. I was exposed to this sort of thing when I gave a seminar at the University of Delhi in late 1991; see also R. R. Ramchandani, "Indian Emigration to East African Countries from Ancient to Early Colonial Times," in C. Mehaud, ed., *Mouvements de Populations dans l'Ocean Indian* (Paris, 1979), 309–29; and Prithvish Nag, "The Indian Ocean, India, and Africa: Historical and Geographical Perspectives," in Satish Chandra, ed., *The Indian Ocean: Explorations in History, Commerce, and Politics* (New Delhi, 1987), 151–73.

68. R. B. Serjeant, *The Portuguese off the South Arabian Coast* (Oxford, 1963), 3, 9–11.

69. Cyril A. Hromnik, "Goa and Mozambique: The Participation of Goans in Portuguese Enterprise in the Rios de Cuama, 1501–1752" (Ph.D. diss., Syracuse University, 1977), 18, 30, 32, 41–2, 78.

70. Cyril A. Hromnik, "Background and Content of the Historical Archives of Goa," *History in Africa* 5 (1978), 371–6; Hromnik, "Canarins in the Rios de Cuama, 1501–76," *Journal of African Studies* 6, no. 1 (1979), 27–37.

71. Cyril A. Hromnik, *Indo-Africa: Toward a New Understanding of the History of Sub-Saharan Africa* (Cape Town, 1981). See Martin Hall and C. H. Borland, "The Indian Connection: An Assessment of Hromnik's 'Indo-Africa,'" *South African Archaeological Bulletin* 37 (1982), 75–80; and Hromnik's response, "African History and Africanist Orthodoxy: A Response to Hall and Borland," *South African Archaeological Bulletin* 38 (1983), 36–9. See also reviews by C. Ehret, *IJAHS* 15, no. 3 (1982), 549–50; and C. P. Ownby, *JAH* 22 (1982), 415–6.

72. Hromnik, *Indo-Africa*, 81.

73. Judith Aldrick, "The Nineteenth Century Carved Wooden Doors of the East African Coast," *Azania* 25 (1990), 1–19.

74. J.W.T. Allen, ed., *The Customs of the Swahili People* (Berkeley, 1981), 175, and generally 169–77.

75. Prins, *Swahili-Speaking Peoples*, 11.

76. J. de V. Allen, "The Swahili World of Mtoro bin Mwinyi Bakari," an appendix in J.W.T. Allen, *Customs of the Swahili People*, 211–24.

77. Alamin M. Mazrui and I. N. Shariff, *The Swahili: Idiom and Identity of an African People* (Trenton, 1994), 39, and see 36–40 for an excellent discussion of the Swahili and how British policy, which was not constant, affected them and their position in Kenya.

78. J. de V. Allen, "Swahili Culture Reconsidered: Some Historical Implications of the Material Culture of the Northern Kenya Coast in the Eighteenth and Nineteenth Centuries," *Azania* 9 (1974), 105–6; cf. Chittick, "East Coast, Madagascar, and the Indian Ocean," 3: 187.

79. E. A. Alpers, *Ivory and Slaves: Changing Patterns of International Trade in East Central Africa to the Later Nineteenth Century* (London, 1975), 8; Middleton, *World of the Swahili*, 228; Randall L. Pouwels, "The Battle of Shela: The Climax of an Era and a Point of Departure in the Modern History of the Kenya Coast," *Cahiers d'Etudes Africaines* 31 (1991), 382; Aziz Esmail, "Towards a History of Islam in East Africa," *Kenya Historical Review* 3, no. 1 (1975), 152; J. de V. Allen, "Swahili Culture and the Nature of East Coast Settlement," *African Historical Studies* 14 (1981), 316.

80. Randall L. Pouwels, *Horn and Crescent: Cultural Change and Traditional Islam on the East African Coast, 800–1900* (Cambridge, 1987), 29–30.

81. Jan Knappert, *Myths and Legends of the Swahili* (Nairobi, 1986), 90.

82. Usam Ghaidan, *Lamu: A Study of the Swahili Town* (Nairobi, 1975), 63.

83. In J.W.T. Allen, *Customs of the Swahili People*, 212.

84. Ibid., 120, 161–2.

85. For a short sketch of the precarious and threatened situation of the Swahili since independence, see Middleton, *World of the Swahili*, 49–53 and passim, for an elegy to the Swahili past.

86. C. Makokha Kusimba, "Report on Activities, On-Going and Completed Research," *Mvita* 5 (November 1993), 7–8.

87. See the excellent discussion in Mazrui and Shariff, *Swahili*, 131–63, quoting, among others, Ali Mazrui and Shiva Naipaul.

88. For references, see M. N. Pearson, "Brokers in Western Indian Port Cities: Their Role in Servicing Foreign Merchants," *Modern Asian Studies* 22, no. 3 (1988), 461; Irfan Habib, "Merchant Communities in Precolonial India," in James D. Tracy, ed., *The Rise of Merchant Empires* (New York, 1990), nn. 70, 87. Regrettably, I must note that those stressing lack of interaction are all from Hindu backgrounds, while Habib and Qaisar are from Muslim stock.

89. S. Gopal, ed., *Anatomy of a Confrontation: Ayodhya and the Rise of Communal Politics in India* (Delhi, 1991; London, 1994) is a fine example.

Chapter 2. The Swahili Coast in the Afrasian Sea

1. "Introduction" to Frank Broeze, ed., *Brides of the Sea: Port Cities of Asia from the 16th–20th Centuries* (Sydney, 1989), 3, 21; for bibliography on the Indian Ocean, see S. Arasaratnam, "Recent Trends in the Historiography of the Indian Ocean, 1500 to 1800," *Journal of World History* 1, no. 2 (1990), 225–48.

2. I understand from colleagues that linguists have also been playing around with terminology. Apparently, "Afroasiatic" is now being replaced by "Afrasian," this marking then a quite fortuitous conjunction between their creation of neologisms and my independent attempt.

3. On the history of the Indian Ocean, see M. N. Pearson, "Introduction 1: The Subject," in Ashin Das Gupta and M. N. Pearson, eds., *India and the Indian Ocean, 1500–1800* (Calcutta, 1987), 1–24.

4. Randall L. Pouwels, *Horn and Crescent: Cultural Change and Traditional Islam on the East African Coast, 800–1900* (Cambridge, 1987), 31. It should be noted that the actual word *Swahili* has probably been in use for only about two hundred years.

5. Neville Chittick, "East Africa and the Orient: Ports and Trade before the Arrival of the Portuguese," in C. Mehaud, ed., *Historical Relations across the Indian Ocean* (Paris, 1980), 13–22.

6. Thomas Spear and D. Nurse, *The Swahili: Reconstructing the History and Language of an African Society, A.D. 500–1500* (Philadelphia, 1984), 67.

7. J. de V. Allen, "A Proposal for Indian Ocean Studies," in C. Mehaud, ed., *Historical Relations across the Indian Ocean* (Paris, 1980), 137–51.

8. Ashin Das Gupta, *Indian Merchants and the Decline of Surat, c. 1700–1750* (Wiesbaden, 1979), 2.

9. John Middleton, *The World of the Swahili: An African Mercantile Civilization* (New Haven, 1992), 9.

10. J. C. Heesterman, "Littoral et Intérieur de l'Inde," *Itinerario* 1 (1980), 89.

11. M. N. Pearson, "Littoral Society: The Case for the Coast," *Great Circle* 7, no. 1 (1985), 1–8.

12. Fernand Braudel, *The Mediterranean and the Mediterranean World in the Age of Philip II*, 2 vols. (London, 1972), 17.

13. E. Le Roy Ladurie, *The Territory of the Historian* (Chicago, 1979), 142–5.

14. Fernand Braudel, "The Expansion of Europe and the 'Longue Durée,'" in H. L. Wesseling, ed., *Expansion and Reaction: Essays on European Expansion and Reactions in Asia and Africa* (Leiden, 1978), 22.

15. Philip D. Curtin, *Cross-Cultural Trade in World History* (Cambridge, 1984), 26.

16. K. N. Chaudhuri, *Trade and Civilisation in the Indian Ocean: An Economic History from the Rise of Islam to 1750* (Cambridge, 1985), 175, 181.

17. M. N. Pearson, *Pilgrimage to Mecca: The Indian Experience* (Princeton, 1996).

18. On *banjaras*, see Irfan Habib, "Merchant Communities in Precolonial India," in James D. Tracy, ed., *The Rise of Merchant Empires* (New York, 1990).

19. Chittick, "East Africa and the Orient," 13.

20. Ralph Austen, *African Economic History: Internal Development and External Dependency* (London, 1987), 58.

21. M.D.D. Newitt, *A History of Mozambique* (London, 1994), 12, 31, 141 et seq.

22. For "inland port cities," see C. A. Bayly, "Inland Port Cities in North India: Calcutta and the Gangetic Plains, 1780–1900," in Dilip K. Basu, ed., *The Rise and Growth of the Colonial Port Cities in Asia* (Santa Cruz, 1979), 11–15. For "fluvial port cities," see A.J.R. Russell-Wood, "Ports of Colonial Brazil," in Franklin W. Knight and Peggy K. Liss, eds., *Atlantic Port Cities: Economy, Culture, and Society in the Atlantic World, 1650–1850* (Knoxville, 1991), 197.

23. António Bocarro, *Década 13 da história da India* (Lisbon, 1876), 534–5.

24. Summary of letters from António de Saldanha, Sofala, 1511, in *DM*, 3: 15.

25. The Portuguese sources use the terms *kaffir* or *cafre*; I have chosen to translate this as "African," unless it is possible from the context to be more specific and write "Swahili" or "Shona-speaking."

26. Afonso Albuquerque, *The Commentaries of the Great Afonso Dalbuquerque*, ed. W. Birch, 4 vols. (London, 1875–84), 1: 44.

27. Santos, I, i, 20.

28. *DM*, 8: 369; 1 league is roughly 5 kilometers.

29. Tomé Pires, *The Suma Oriental of Tomé Pires*, ed. A. Cortesão, 2 vols. (London, 1944), 1: 46, 2: 268.

30. Musa H. I. Galaal, "Historical Relations between the Horn of Africa and the Persian Gulf and the Indian Ocean Islands through Islam," in C. Mehaud, ed., *Historical Relations across the Indian Ocean* (Paris, 1980), 25.

31. The classic study is E. B. Martin and C.M.P. Martin, *Cargoes of the East: The Ports, Trade, and Cultures of the Arabian Sea and Western Indian Ocean* (London, 1978).

32. Duarte Barbosa, *Livro*, 2 vols. (London, 1918–21), 1: 27.

33. Santos, I, iii, 19.

34. King of Portugal to king of Castile, Italian copy, printed in Rome 23 October 1505, in *DM*, 1: 47.

35. Vasco da Gama, *A Journal of the First Voyage of Vasco da Gama* (London, 1898), 26.

36. See Monclaro's account of the Barreto expedition, in *DM*, 8: 351; MS. "Valentim Fernandes," in *DM*, 1: 525, 531.

37. See Richard Wilding, *The Shorefolk: Aspects of the Early Development of Swahili Communities* (Fort Jesus, 1987).

38. See Graham Connah, *African Civilizations: Precolonial Cities and States in Tropical Africa, An Archaeological Perspective* (Cambridge, 1987), 160–7.

39. See M. N. Pearson, "Indian Seafarers in the Sixteenth Century," in *Coastal Western India* (New Delhi, 1981), 116–47.

40. Barros, I, iv, 6; see also da Gama, *Voyage*, 44–5.

41. Castanheda, 1: 12.

42. James B. McKenna, *A Spaniard in the Portuguese Indies: The Narrative of Martín Fernández de Figueroa* (Cambridge, Mass., 1967), 73. *Brahmans* is certainly a mistake for *banians*.

43. For *banians* in Iran, Central Asia, and Russia, see Dale's excellent book: Stephen Frederic Dale, *Indian Merchants and Eurasian Trade, 1600–1750* (Cambridge, 1994).

44. Castanheda, 1: 10.

45. Da Gama, *Voyage*, 39.

46. See J.E.G. Sutton, *A Thousand Years of East Africa* (Nairobi, 1990), 69–81.

47. Robert G. Gregory, *India and East Africa* (London, 1971), 16; Neville Chittick, "Indian Relations with East Africa before the Arrival of the Portuguese," *Journal of the Royal Asiatic Society* (1980), 119, 125; Wilding, *Shorefolk*, 81–3.

48. Wilding, *Shorefolk*, 112.

49. J.E.G. Sutton, "Kilwa," *Indian Ocean Review* 7, no. 4 (1995), 10–1; see also Sutton, *Thousand Years*, 63.

50. J. M. Gray, "A Portuguese Inscription and the Uroa Coin Hoard: Some Discoveries in Zanzibar," *Azania* 10 (1975), 123–31; Neville Chittick, *Kilwa: An Islamic Trading City on the East African Coast*, 2 vols. (Nairobi, 1974); Helen W. Brown, "Three Kilwa Gold Coins," *Azania* 26 (1991), 1–4.

51. Account of Almeida's voyage, in *DM*, 1: 525, 535, 537.

52. Diogo de Alcaçova to king, 20 November 1506, in *DM*, 1: 397.

53. Neville Chittick, "A New Look at the History of Pate," *JAH* 10, no. 3 (1969), 375–91.

54. Basil Davidson, *The Search for Africa: A History in the Making* (London, 1994), 12, quoting Robin Horton.

55. Barros, I, x, 3.

56. Wilding, *Shorefolk*, 92.

57. Personal observation. There is a photo and caption of this dish in the Lamu Museum.

58. M. C. Horton and T. R. Blurton, "'Indian' Metalwork in East Africa: The Bronze Lion Statuette from Shanga," *Antiquity* 62 (1988), 21–2.

59. E. B. Martin, *The History of Malindi* (Nairobi, 1973), 10. On the difficulties, and

advantages, of Chinese sources, see John Shen, "New Thoughts on the Use of Chinese Documents in the Reconstruction of Early Swahili History," *History in Africa* 22 (1995), 349–58.

60. J. Devisse and S. Labib, "Africa in Intercontinental Relations," in *General History of Africa*, vol. 4, *Africa from the Twelfth to the Sixteenth Century* (Paris, 1984), 658; Martin, *Malindi*, 12–3.

61. João de Sepúlveda to king, Mozambique, 10 August 1542, in *DM*, 7: 131.

62. Couto, X, ii, 8.

63. See the king's instructions, king to viceroy, 12 January 1591, in Cunha Rivara, 3: 272–3. For Mir Ali Bey's expeditions, see the contemporary detailed descriptions in Couto, X, ii, 8, and XI, 5–8; and two modern overviews in C. R. Boxer and Carlos de Azevedo, *Fort Jesus and the Portuguese in Mombasa, 1593–1729* (London, 1960); and A. I. Salim, "East Africa: The Coast," in *General History of Africa*, vol. 5, *Africa from the Sixteenth to the Eighteenth Century* (Paris, 1992), 761–4.

64. Barbosa, *Livro*, 1: 20, 28.

65. Account of Almeida's voyage to India, 22 May 1506, in *DM*, 1: 533.

66. Barbosa, *Livro*, 1: 22–3.

67. Santos, I, i, 13.

68. Correa, 1: 58, 166.

69. J. H. van Linschoten, *The Voyage of John Huyghen van Linschoten to the East Indies*, 2 vols. (London, 1885), 1: 25.

70. For the modern trade, see Philip D. Curtin, "African Enterprise in the Mangrove Trade: The Case of Lamu," *African Economic History* 10 (1981), 23–33.

71. William Foster, ed., *The Voyages of Sir James Lancaster* (London, 1940), 5–6, 23.

72. P. F. Thorbahn, "The Precolonial Ivory Trade of East Africa: Reconstruction of a Human-Elephant Ecosystem" (Ph.D. diss., University of Massachusetts, 1979), 87.

73. Clements Markham, *Colloquies on the Simples and Drugs of India by Garcia da Orta* (London, 1913), chap. 21.

74. Eric Axelson, *Portuguese in Southeast Africa, 1600–1700* (Johannesburg, 1960), 76, n.

75. Account of Almeida's voyage to India, 22 May 1506, in *DM*, 1: 531–3.

76. Pires, *Suma Oriental*, 1: 42.

77. E. A. Alpers, "Gujarat and the Trade of East Africa, c. 1500–1800," *IJAHS* 9 (1976), 39; a more up-to-date estimation would be helpful.

78. Ricardo Teixeira Duarte, *Northern Mozambique in the Swahili World* (Stockholm, 1993), 43.

79. J. Devisse and S. Labib, "Africa in Intercontinental Relations," in *General History of Africa*, vol. 4, *Africa from the Twelfth to the Sixteenth Century* (Paris, 1984), 655.

80. Diogo de Alcáçova to king, 20 November 1506, in *DM*, 1: 395.

81. Vitorino Magalhães Godinho, *Os descobrimentos e a economia mundial*, 2d ed., 4 vols. (Lisbon, 1981–83), 1: 204–7.

82. Manuel Lobato, "Relações comerciais entre a India e a costa Africana nos séculos XVI and XVII: o papel do Guzerate no Comércio de Moçambique," in *Portuguese India and Its Northern Province: Proceedings of the 7th International Seminar on Indo-Portuguese History* (Lisbon, 1995), 169.

83. Treasury Council, Lisbon, to king, 4 April 1614, in *DM*, 9: 381.

84. S.I.G. Mudenge, *A Political History of Munhumutapa, c. 1400–1902* (Harare, 1988), 174.

85. Neville Chittick, "The East Coast, Madagascar, and the Indian Ocean," in Roland Oliver, ed., *Cambridge History of Africa*, vol. 3, *c. 1050–c. 1600* (Cambridge, 1977), 215–7.

86. C. R. Boxer, "A Portuguese El Dorado: Monomotapa and Mozambique,"

Geographical Magazine 33, no. 3 (1960), 284.

87. Summary of letter to king, 20 December 1510, in *DM*, 2: 513.

88. Bashir Ahmed Datoo, *Port Development in East Africa* (Nairobi, 1975), 82–3, 89–90. On "smuggling" see also Godinho, *Descobrimentos*, 1: 196.

89. Sutton, "Kilwa," 10–1.

90. Newitt, *History of Mozambique*, 176–7.

91. Godinho, *Descobrimentos*, 1: 207.

92. Godinho, *Descobrimentos*, 1: 248; Pierre Vilar, *A History of Gold and Money, 1450–1920* (London, 1976), 94.

93. Vilar, *History of Gold and Money*, 56.

94. Harry E. Cross, "South American Bullion Production and Export, 1550–1750," in J. F. Richards, ed., *Precious Metals in the Later Medieval and Early Modern Worlds* (Durham, N.C., 1983), 417.

95. Vilar, *History of Gold and Money*, 104.

96. Kristof Glamman, *Dutch-Asiatic Trade, 1620–1740* (Copenhagen, 1958), 58, 63.

97. A. Kobata, "The Production and Uses of Gold and Silver in Sixteenth- and Seventeenth-Century Japan," *Economic History Review* 18 (1965), 247.

98. Abdul Sheriff, *Slaves, Spices, and Ivory in Zanzibar: Integration of an East African Commercial Empire into the World Economy, 1770–1873* (London, 1987), 10–1; Datoo, *Port Development*, 3–8, 70–7.

99. Bocarro, *Década 13*, 566–7; for other examples, see Linschoten, *Voyage*, 1: 33; certificate of Gomes de Figueiredo, 1509, in *As Gavetas da Torre do Tombo*, 12 vols. (Lisbon, 1960–75), 5: 290–1, 294–5; Foster, *Lancaster Voyage*, 9.

100. For Portuguese mishaps with the monsoons, see C. R. Boxer, ed. and trans., *Tragic History of the Sea*, 2 vols. (London, 1959–68); for Arab accounts, see G. R. Tibbetts, *Arab Navigation in the Indian Ocean before the Coming of the Portuguese* (London, 1971); and Ibrahim Khoury, *As-Sufaliyya, "The Poem of Sofala," by Ahmed ibn Magid translated and explained* (Coímbra, 1983).

101. Duarte interview, 20 December 1993.

102. François Pyrard de Laval, *Voyage of Pyrard of Laval*, 2 vols. (London, 1887), vol. 2, pt. 1: 224.

103. See, for example, king to viceroy, 21 March 1617, in Bulhão Pato, 4: 154; or king to viceroy, 15 March 1617, in Bulhão Pato, 4: 82.

104. M. C. Horton, "Early Muslim Trading Settlements on the East African Coast: New Evidence from Shanga," *Antiquities Journal* 67 (1987), 292; and also a caption in the Fort Jesus Museum, Mombasa.

105. Sheriff, *Slaves, Spices, and Ivory*, 10.

106. See M. N. Pearson, "Conversions in Southeast Asia: Evidence from the Portuguese Records," *Portuguese Studies* 6 (1990), 53–70, and the works cited there.

107. Paul Sinclair, "Archeology in East Africa: An Overview of Current Chronological Issues," *JAH* 32 (1991), 181; Duarte interview, 20 December 1993.

108. Horton's work is described in Sinclair, "Archeology in East Africa," 185.

109. *Independent* (London), 16 March 1992.

110. Buzurg ibn Shahriyar, *The Book of the Wonders of India* (Kitab al Ajaid al Hind), trans. and ed. G.S.P. Freeman-Grenville (London, 1981), 10, 31–6, 38, 102, 105.

111. Al-Biruni, *Alberuni's India*, trans. and ed. Edward Sachau, 2 vols. (Delhi, 1964), 1: 270.

112. John Middleton, *The World of the Swahili: An African Mercantile Civilization* (New Haven, 1992), for example, 37.

113. Sutton, *Thousand Years*, 67–8.

114. H. T. Wright, "Trade and Politics on the Eastern Littoral of Africa, A.D. 800–1300,"

in Thurstan Shaw et al., eds., *The Archeology of Africa: Food, Metals, and Towns* (London, 1993), 669–71.

115. John Obert Voll, "Islam as a Special World-System," *Journal of World History* 5, no. 2 (1994), 213–26, esp. 219–20.

116. Spear and Nurse, *Swahili*, 94–5.

117. Ibn Battuta, *The Travels of Ibn Battuta*, trans. H.A.R. Gibb, 3 vols. (Cambridge, 1962), 2: 380.

118. Eric Axelson, *Portuguese in Southeast Africa, 1488–1600* (Johannesburg, 1973), 68.

119. *Encyclopedia of Islam*, 2d ed., s.v. "Kenya." Scholars have often claimed that the version of Islam dominant in Oman, that is, *Ibadi* Islam, was quite different from the more orthodox *Shafi'i* Islam of the Swahili. Risso, however, claims that while there were theological differences, in most matters there is a large degree of commonality between Ibadi Islam and the various sunni schools. Patricia Risso, *Oman and Muscat: An Early Modern History* (New York, 1986), 22–3.

120. B. G. Martin, "Arab Migration to East Africa in Medieval Times," *IJAHS* 7, no. 3 (1975), 367–90.

121. *DM*, 8: 355. For the term *caciz*, see M. N. Pearson, *Pious Passengers: The Hajj in Earlier Times* (Delhi, 1994), 71–2.

122. Da Gama, *Voyage*, 29, 31, 41.

123. Foster, *Lancaster Voyage*, 7.

124. Samuel Purchas, *Hakluytus Posthumus or Purchas his Pilgrimes*, 20 vols. (Glasgow, 1905), 6: 507.

125. A.H.J. Prins, *The Swahili-Speaking Peoples of Zanzibar and the East African Coast* (London, 1961), 44.

126. Randall L. Pouwels, "Reflections on Historiography and Pre-Nineteenth-Century History from the Pate 'Chronicles,'" *History in Africa* 20 (1993), 283.

127. M. C. Horton, "Asiatic Colonisation of the East African Coastline: The Manda Evidence," *Journal of the Royal Asiatic Society* (1986), 211.

128. Monclaro's account of the Barreto expedition, in *DM*, 8: 349–51, 393–5.

129. Correa, 1: 32–3.

130. Castanheda, 1: 10.

131. Da Gama, *Voyage*, 23.

132. Barros, I, iv, 4.

133. Luís Vaz de Camoens, *The Lusiads*, trans. William C. Atkinson (Harmondsworth, 1952), 47.

134. Correa, 1: 36–7.

135. Barbosa, *Livro*, 1: 8; and similarly in Angoche, Barbosa, *Livro*, 15. On Sofala, see also Alexandre Lobato, *A Expansão Portuguesa em Moçambique de 1498 a 1530*, 3 vols. (Lisbon, 1954–60), 3: 25. For another version of Barbosa, see an anonymous account of c. 1518, in *DM*, 5: 367.

136. Castanheda, 1: 32.

137. Linschoten, *Voyage*, 1: 27–8.

138. Monclaro's account of the Barreto expedition, in *DM*, 8: 345, 351–3.

139. Duarte de Lemos to king, Mozambique, 30 September 1508, in *DM*, 2: 297.

140. See MS. "Valentim Fernandes" account of Almeida voyage, in *DM*, 1: 539.

141. Monclaro's account of the Barreto expedition, in *DM*, 8: 345, 351–3.

142. Linschoten, *Voyage*, 1: 271.

143. Brother Luís Fróis, Goa, 14 November 1559, in António da Silva Rego, ed., *Documentação para a história das Missões do padroado Português do Oriente: India*, 12 vols. (Lisbon, 1947–58), 7: 363.

144. For a good study of inland conversions in northern Mozambique, see J. F. Mbwiliza, *A History of Commodity Production in Makuani, 1600–1900: Mercantalist*

Accumulation to Imperialist Domination (Dar es Salaam, 1991), 65–74.

145. J. Spencer Trimingham, *Islam in East Africa* (Oxford, 1964), 54, 66, 68, 71; for a good critique, see Aziz Esmail, "Towards a History of Islam in East Africa," *Kenya Historical Review* 3, no. 1 (1975), 147–58.

146. Da Gama, *Voyage*, 29.

147. Letter of Fr. Francisco Rodrigues to Portugal, Goa, 2 November 1556, in *DM*, 7: 377; also printed in J. Wicki et al., eds., *Documenta Indica*, 20 vols. to date (Rome, 1948–), 3: 498–500.

148. Santos, I, iii, 19.

149. Sebastian Gonçalves, *Primeira Parte da História dos Religiosas da Companhia de Jesus*, ed. J. Wicki, 3 vols. (Coímbra, 1957–62), 1: 72.

150. Santos, I, i, 19; for the importance of spirits, associated with various sacred sites including tombs and ruined mosques, within coastal Kenyan Islam, see George H. O. Abungu, "Islam on the Kenyan Coast: An Overview of Kenyan Coastal Sacred Sites," in David Carmichael et al., eds., *Sacred Sites, Sacred Places* (London, 1994), 152–62.

151. Monclaro's account of the Barreto expedition, in *DM*, 8: 393–5.

Chapter 3. The Swahili Coast and the Interior

1. For Gujarat, see Ashin Das Gupta, *Indian Merchants and the Decline of Surat, c. 1700–1750* (Wiesbaden, 1979); for Malabar, see Ashin Das Gupta, *Malabar in Asian Trade, 1740–1800* (Cambridge, 1967); for Coromandel, see Tapan Raychaudhuri, *Jan Company in Coromandel* (The Hague, 1962); and Sinnappah Arasaratnam, *Merchants, Companies, and Commerce on the Coromandel Coast, 1650–1740* (Delhi, 1986).

2. A. Jan Qaisar, "The Role of Brokers in Medieval India," *Indian Historical Review* 1, no. 2 (1974), 220, 240.

3. Das Gupta, *Indian Merchants and the Decline of Surat*, 84, and generally 74–88; and also M. N. Pearson, "Brokers in Western Indian Port Cities: Their Role in Servicing Foreign Merchants," *Modern Asian Studies* 22, no. 3 (1988), 455–72.

4. John Middleton, *The World of the Swahili: An African Mercantile Civilization* (New Haven, 1992), 18.

5. See Irfan Habib's standard account: Irfan Habib, "The Monetary System and Prices," in T. Raychaudhuri and Irfan Habib eds., *The Cambridge Economic History of India*, vol. 1, *c. 1200–c. 1750* (Cambridge, 1982), 360–81.

6. J. C. Heesterman, "Littoral et Intérieur de l'Inde," *Itinerario* 1 (1980), 89.

7. For port cities, see Dilip K. Basu, ed., *The Rise and Growth of the Colonial Port Cities in Asia* (Santa Cruz, 1979); and M. N. Pearson, "Merchants and States," in James D. Tracy, ed., *The Political Economy of Merchant Empires* (New York, 1991), 70–7, and other works cited below in note 12. For connections between land empires and their littorals, see also Patricia Risso, *Merchants and Faith: Muslim Commerce and Culture in the Indian Ocean* (Boulder, 1995), a fairly standard and unproblematized discussion.

8. Fernand Braudel, *The Mediterranean and the Mediterranean World in the Age of Philip II*, 2 vols. (London, 1972), 170.

9. S. Arasaratnam, "Recent Trends in the Historiography of the Indian Ocean, 1500 to 1800," *Journal of World History* 1, no. 2 (1990), 235.

10. Audrey N. Clark, *Longman Dictionary of Geography* (Essex, 1985), s.v. "umland."

11. A. J. Sargent, *Seaports and Hinterlands* (London, 1938), 1–17.

12. Perhaps the best discussion is Frank Broeze, "The External Dynamic of Port City Morphology: Bombay, 1815–1914," in Indu Banga, ed., *Ports and Their Hinterlands in India, 1700–1950* (New Delhi, 1992), 245–52, though his attempt to find a maritime hinterland seems to me to be merely confusing. See also B. S. Hoyle, "Maritime Perspectives on Ports and Port Systems: The Case of East Africa," in Frank Broeze, ed., *Brides of the Sea: Port Cities of Asia from the 16th–20th Centuries* (Sydney, 1989), 188–93. These two collections

contain numerous other important studies. See also Frank Broeze, ed., *Gateways of Asia: Port Cities of Asia from the 13th to 20th Centuries* (London, 1997); K. N. Chaudhuri, *Trade and Civilisation in the Indian Ocean: An Economic History from the Rise of Islam to 1750* (Cambridge, 1985), 98–118, 160–81; and Sinnappah Arasaratnam and Aniruddha Ray, *Masulipatnam and Cambay: Two Ports in the Indian Ocean, 1600–1800* (Delhi, 1994). For a brilliant example of the relativity of historical knowledge of one port city, see Richard M. Eaton, "Multiple Lenses: Differing Perspectives of Fifteenth-Century Calicut," in Laurie Sears, ed., *Autonomous Histories, Particular Truths* (Madison, 1993).

13. Justin Willis, *Mombasa, the Swahili, and the Making of the Mijikenda* (Oxford, 1993), 2, 8.

14. A.J.R. Russell-Wood, "Ports of Colonial Brazil," in Franklin W. Knight and Peggy K. Liss, eds., *Atlantic Port Cities: Economy, Culture, and Society in the Atlantic World, 1650–1850* (Knoxville, 1991), 197.

15. Ibid., 207–10.

16. M.D.D. Newitt, "East Africa and the Indian Ocean Trade, 1500–1800," in Ashin Das Gupta and M. N. Pearson, eds., *India and the Indian Ocean, 1500–1800* (Calcutta, 1987), 201–7.

17. See Alamin M. Mazrui, and I. N. Shariff, *The Swahili: Idiom and Identity of an African People* (Trenton, 1994).

18. It should be noted that this *nyika* has various meanings according to region. The Swahili meaning is quite different from the Shona meaning used in Zimbabwe, where it means a chiefdom, and also a kingdom or even empire. It is also the name of a group of tribes who came from the north.

19. Abdul Sheriff, *Slaves, Spices, and Ivory in Zanzibar: Integration of an East African Commercial Empire into the World Economy, 1770–1873* (London, 1987), 8–10, and see the map on p. 9 that shows the *nyika*.

20. Merrick Posnansky, "Connections between the Lacustrine Peoples and the Coast," in Neville Chittick and Robert I. Rotbert, eds., *East Africa and the Orient* (New York, 1975), 217.

21. Neville Chittick, "East Africa and the Orient: Ports and Trade before the Arrival of the Portuguese," in C. Mehaud, ed., *Historical Relations across the Indian Ocean* (Paris, 1980), 13; Chittick, "The Coast before the Arrival of the Portuguese," in B. A. Ogot, ed. *Zamani: A Survey of East African History*, 2d ed. (Nairobi, 1974), 112–3; and Chittick, "The East Coast, Madagascar, and the Indian Ocean," in Roland Oliver, ed., *Cambridge History of Africa*, vol. 3, *c. 1050–c. 1600*, (Cambridge, 1977), 219; also see R. C. Bridges, "Africa, Africans, and the Sea," in J. C. Stone, ed., *Africa and the Sea: Proceedings of a Colloquium at the University of Aberdeen, March, 1984* (Aberdeen, 1985), 20; Norman R. Bennett, *Africa and Europe*, 2d ed. (New York, 1984), 10; Bashir Ahmed Datoo, *Port Development in East Africa* (Nairobi, 1975), 3–8; E. Alpers and C. Ehret, "Eastern Africa," in Richard Gray, ed., *Cambridge History of Africa*, vol. 4, *c. 1600–c. 1790* (Cambridge, 1975), 527–8.

22. James Kirkman, "The History of the Coast of East Africa up to 1700," in Merrick Posnansky, ed., *Prelude to East African History* (London, 1966), 106, 110.

23. Sheriff, *Slaves, Spices, and Ivory*, 10.

24. Graham Connah, *African Civilizations: Precolonial Cities and States in Tropical Africa, An Archaeological Perspective* (Cambridge, 1987), 152–3, 157, 176.

25. Couto, XI, 5–8.

26. Couto, XI, 11; XI, 18–20; F. J. Berg, "The Coast from the Portuguese Invasion to the Rise of the Zanzibar Sultanate," in B. A. Ogot, ed., *Zamani: A Survey of East African History*, 2d ed. (Nairobi, 1974), 122–3.

27. *DM*, 8: 351.

28. Couto, XI, 21.

29. Berg, "Coast from the Portuguese Invasion," 122–3; see also James Kirkman's additions in Justus Strandes, *The Portuguese Period in East Africa* (Nairobi, 1961), 304, 305–6.

30. S.I.G. Mudenge, *A Political History of Munhumutapa, c. 1400–1902* (Harare, 1988), 224–5. For other discussions, see D. N.

Beach, *The Shona and Their Neighbours* (Oxford, 1994), 110, 128, 198; M.D.D. Newitt, *A History of Mozambique* (London, 1994), 66–72; and three important earlier articles: M.D.D. Newitt, "The Early History of the Maravi," *JAH* 23 (1982), 145–62; Matther Schoffeleers, "The Zimba and the Lundu State in the Late Sixteenth and Early Seventeenth Centuries," *JAH* 27 (1987), 337–55; and Christopher Wrigley, "The River-God and the Historians: Myth in the Shire Valley and Elsewhere," *JAH* 29 (1988), 367–83.

31. Hamo Sassoon, "Excavations at the Site of Early Mombasa," *Azania* 15 (1980), 9.

32. J. M. Gray, "Rezende's Description of East Africa in 1634," in *Tanganyika Notes and Records* 23 (1947), 7–12. Parts of this translation are not to be relied on.

33. A. I. Salim, "East Africa: The Coast," in *General History of Africa*, vol. 5, *Africa from the Sixteenth to the Eighteenth Century* (Paris, 1992), 768.

34. David Sperling, "The Growth of Islam among the Mijikenda of the Kenya Coast, 1826–1933" (Ph.D. diss., School of Oriental and African Studies, University of London, 1988); Henry Mutoro, "An Archeological Study of the Mijikenda *Kaya* Settlements on Hinterland Kenya Coast" (Ph.D. diss., University of California–Los Angeles, 1987); W. Howard Brown, "History of Siyu: The Development and Decline of a Swahili Town on the Northern Kenya Coast" (Ph.D. diss., Indiana University, 1985).

35. Willis, *Mombasa*, 6–7, 19 et seq.; see Thomas Spear's review in *IJAHS* 28 (1995), 630–4; and Mutoro, "Archeological Study."

36. Sperling, "Growth of Islam," 12, 20–2, 26–7; see the map in Henry Mutoro, "The Mijikenda *Kaya* as a Sacred Site," in David Carmichael et al., eds., *Sacred Sites, Sacred Places* (London, 1994), 135; Mutoro, "Archeological Study," 45–53.

37. C. R. Boxer and Carlos de Azevedo, *Fort Jesus and the Portuguese in Mombasa, 1593–1729* (London, 1960), 37, 38, 43, 63, 66, 78, 127.

38. Sperling, "Growth of Islam," 34–8.

39. Ibid., 34, table.

40. Thomas Spear, *Kenya's Past: An Introduction to Historical Method in Africa* (London, 1981), 95, and also 85–8. For the comparable situation of the Vumba, around the mouth of the Umba River, and their relations with the Segeju and Digo see ibid., 95–6.

41. Ibid., 93.

42. Eric Axelson, *Portuguese in Southeast Africa, 1488–1600* (Johannesburg, 1973), 56–9; Barros, I, x, 6.

43. Richard Wilding, *The Shorefolk: Aspects of the Early Development of Swahili Communities* (Fort Jesus, 1987), 99–107.

44. See T. H. Wilson, "Settlement Patterns of the Coast of Southern Somalia and Kenya" (paper presented at the First International Congress of Somali Studies, Mogadishu, July 1980).

45. Usam Ghaidan, *Lamu: A Study of the Swahili Town* (Nairobi, 1975), 80; James Kirkman, *Gedi*, 8th ed. (Nairobi, 1975), 3.

46. Brown, "History of Siyu," 100–2; for a directly contrary position, possibly reflective of majority opinion, see Wilding, *Shorefolk*, 57.

47. Wilding, *Shorefolk*, 57; yet Wilding's main thrust is to see the Swahili as coastal, sea-oriented.

48. Brown, "History of Siyu," 43–4.

49. E. A. Alpers, *Ivory and Slaves: Changing Patterns of International Trade in East Central Africa to the Later Nineteenth Century* (London, 1975), 59–64.

50. E. A. Alpers, "Trade, State, and Society among the Yao in the Nineteenth Century," *JAH* 10 (1969), 407, 418–20.

51. Randall L. Pouwels, "The Battle of Shela: The Climax of an Era and a Point of Departure in the Modern History of the Kenya Coast," *Cahiers d'Etudes Africaines* 31 (1991), 382.

52. Duarte Barbosa, *Livro*, 2 vols. (London, 1918–21), 1: 29.

53. Brown, "History of Siyu," 43–4, 100–2, 148–51.

54. George H. O. Abungu, "The Mid to Lower Tana," *Mvita* 6 (October 1995), 3–6.

55. Spear, *Kenya's Past*, 93. Patricia W. Romero's new book, released too late for me to use its findings here, will undoubtedly increase our knowledge of Lamu. See Patricia W. Romero, *Lamu: History, Society, and Family in an East African Port City* (Princeton, 1996).

56. Ghaidan, *Lamu*, 80.

57. Barbosa, *Livro*, 1: 20–1.

58. Thomas Spear, "The *Kaya* Complex: A History of the Mijikenda Peoples of the Kenya Coast to 1900" (Ph.D. diss., University of Wisconsin, 1974), 132. This thesis was published under the same title in Nairobi (1978). I have used the dissertation.

59. Mutoro, "Archeological Study," 67; also Spear, *Kenya's Past*, 94–5; there is, however, some dispute as to when the Mijikenda first became involved in this sort of exchange. Compare Sperling, "Growth of Islam," 34–8; and W. R. Ochieng', "The Interior of East Africa: The Peoples of Kenya and Tanzania, 1500–1800," in *General History of Africa*, vol. 5, *Africa from the Sixteenth to the Eighteenth Century* (Paris, 1992), 839–40.

60. Willis, *Mombasa*, 22–3.

61. Wilding, *Shorefolk*, 47.

62. Alpers, *Ivory and Slaves*, 40–1.

63. Barros, I, iv, 3.

64. Marina Tolmacheva, *The Pate Chronicle* (East Lansing, 1993), 62, 175.

65. Diogo de Alcaçova to king, 20 November 1506, in *DM*, 1: 397–9.

66. See Hamo Sassoon, *The Siwas of Lamu* (Lamu, n.d.).

67. Kerridge, Surat, to East India Company, 9 and 15 February 1619, in William Foster, ed., *The English Factories in India, 1618–1669*, 13 vols. (Oxford, 1906–27), 1618–21: 57–8.

68. For example, Philip D. Curtin, *Cross-Cultural Trade in World History* (Cambridge, 1984), 26–7; Wilding, *Shorefolk*, 47; Spear, *Kenya's Past*, 94–5 ; Spear, "*Kaya* Complex," 118–24; Brown, "History of Siyu," 43–4, 148–51.

69. Wilding, *Shorefolk*, 101.

70. Ochieng', "Interior of East Africa," 828–9, 840, 848. For coverage of interior tribes see good, somewhat dense, chapters in *General History of Africa*, vol. 5, *Africa from the Sixteenth to the Eighteenth Century*, chaps. 21, 22, and 27.

71. J.W.T. Allen, ed., *The Customs of the Swahili People* (Berkeley, 1981), 120, 167.

72. Spear, *Kenya's Past*, 94–5.

73. Middleton, *World of the Swahili*, 18–19; Spear, "*Kaya* Complex," 118–24.

74. Mutoro, "Archeological Study," 90–1, and see also 269–71.

75. Brown, "History of Siyu," 43–4, 148–51.

76. Marguerite Ylvisaker, "The Ivory Trade of the Lamu Area, 1600–1870," in J. de V. Allen and T. Wilson, eds., *From Zinj to Zanzibar: Studies in History, Trade, and Society on the Eastern Coast of Africa [in honour of James Kirkman]* (Wiesbaden, 1982), 222–3.

77. Ochieng', "Interior of East Africa," 831.

78. George H. O. Abungu and Henry Mutoro, "Coast-Interior Settlements and Social Relations in the Kenya Coastal Hinterland," in Thurstan Shaw et al., eds., *The Archeology of Africa: Food, Metals, and Towns* (London, 1993), 695.

79. Ibid., 695–703.

80. Abungu, "Mid to Lower Tana," 3.

81. P. F. Thorbahn, "The Precolonial Ivory Trade of East Africa: Reconstruction of a Human-Elephant Ecosystem" (Ph.D. diss., University of Massachusetts, 1979), 1–2, 34, 39, 101, 129–30, 149–55.

82. Curtin, *Cross-Cultural Trade*, 26–7.

83. See John Ford, *The Role of the Trypanosomiases in African History* (Oxford, 1971); for later discussion, see James Giblin, "Trypanosomiasis Control in African History: An Evaded Issue?" *JAH* 31 (1990), 59–80; and Richard D. Waller, "Tsetse Fly in Western Narok, Kenya," *JAH* 31 (1990), 81–101.

84. Sheriff, *Slaves, Spices, and Ivory*, 78–82.

85. Newitt, "East Africa and the Indian Ocean Trade," 209.

86. António de Silveira to king, post July 1518, in *DM*, 5: 565.

87. Alexandre Lobato, *A Expansão Portuguesa em Moçambique de 1498 a 1530*, 3 vols. (Lisbon, 1954–60), 3: 361.

88. J. F. Mbwiliza, *A History of Commodity Production in Makuani, 1600–1900: Mercantalist Accumulation to Imperialist Domination* (Dar es Salaam, 1991), xiv.

89. Gaudens P. Mpangala, *Major Issues in Tanzanian Economic History*, pt. 1, "Pre-Colonial Economy and Social Formations" (Dar es Salaam, 1992), 12–5; Connah, *African Civilisations*, 210–2; Ochieng', "Interior of East Africa," 837–9; Alpers, "Trade, State, and Society among the Yao," 405–7; Alpers, *Ivory and Slaves*, 17.

90. Wilding, *Shorefolk*, 124.

91. Santos, I, ii, 13; I, iii, 13–5; Fr. André Fernández in Tonge [inland from Inhambane] to Br. Luís Fróis, 25 August 1560, in *DM*, 7: 483; Br. Baltazar to Fr. Marcos in Goa, Tonge, 16 November 1560, in *DM*, 7: 515–7.

92. Lobato, *Expansão*, 3: 185–6.

93. Captain of Kilwa to king, summary, 31 August 1506, in *DM*, 1: 621.

94. Barbosa, *Livro*, 1: 16.

95. Ludovico di Varthema, *The Itinerary of Ludovico di Varthema of Bologna from 1502–1508*, ed. Sir Richard Carnac Temple (London, 1928), 110; Couto, X, vi, 14.

96. F. P. Mendes da Luz, "Livro das Cidades . . . 1582," *Studia* 6 (1960), ff. 37v-38.

97. Monclaro's account of the Barreto expedition, in *DM*, 8: 375; see also Newitt, *History of Mozambique*, 183–4; Barreto letter in Theal, 3: 481, referring to 1567.

98. See generally Alpers, *Ivory and Slaves*, and Alpers, "Trade, State, and Society among the Yao"; see also Sheriff, *Slaves, Spices, and Ivory*, 79, 160–3; Newitt, *History of Mozambique*, 183–4.

99. D. N. Beach, "The Zimbabwe Plateau and Its Peoples," in David Birmingham and Phyllis Martin, eds., *History of Central Africa*, 2 vols. (London, 1983), 1: 246–7.

100. D. N. Beach, *Zimbabwe before 1900* (Gweru, 1984), 19.

101. D. N. Beach, *The Shona and Zimbabwe, 900–1850* (London, 1980), 106–7; Beach, "Documents and African Society on the Zimbabwean Plateau before 1890," in Beatrix Heintze and Adam Jones, eds., *European Sources for Sub-Saharan Africa before 1900: Use and Abuse* (Stuttgart, 1987), 132.

102. Beach, *Shona and Their Neighbours*, 105.

103. Ibid., 160–1; Beach, *Shona and Zimbabwe*, 108; Martin Hall, *The Changing Past: Farmers, Kings, and Traders in Southern Africa* (Cape Town, 1987), 122–4, agrees the Portuguese estimate is exaggerated.

104. Beach, "Zimbabwe Plateau," 1: 260–1.

105. Fr. André Fernández in Tonge [inland from Inhambane] to Br. Luís Fróis, 25 August 1560, in *DM*, 7: 493; and Silveira to Jesuits in Goa, Mozambique, 9 August 1560, in *DM*, 7: 503.

106. Pero Vaz Soares, factor of Sofala, to king, 30 June 1513, in *DM*, 3: 463.

107. Ibid., 461.

108. Newitt, *History of Mozambique*, 53.

109. For example, captain of Kilwa to king, summary, 31 August 1506, in *DM*, 1: 621.

110. Order of captain of Sofala, 24 January 1506, in *DM*, 1: 383.

111. Couto, IX, 20, 21; Santos, I, ii, 10.

112. Barros, I, viii, 4.

113. *Encyclopedia of Islam*, 2d ed., s.v. "Kenya."

114. Cyril A. Hromnik, "Goa and Mozambique: The Participation of Goans in Portuguese Enterprise in the Rios de Cuama, 1501–1752" (Ph.D. diss., Syracuse University, 1977), 14–6.

115. Vitorino Magalhães Godinho, *Os descobrimentos e a economia mundial*, 2d ed., 4 vols. (Lisbon, 1981–83), 1: 188; H.H.K. Bhila, "Southern Zambezia," in *General History of Africa*, vol. 5, *Africa from the Sixteenth to the Eighteenth Century* (Paris, 1992), 674–7.

116. Barros, I, x, 1.

117. Notes by Gaspar Veloso, Mozambique, of the description by António Fernandes of his journey inland, in *DM*, 3: 183, 185 ; see also summary of letters from António de Saldanha, Sofala, 1511, in *DM*, 3: 15.

118. Diogo de Alcáçova to king, 20 November 1506, in *DM*, 1: 391.

119. Monclaro's account of the Barreto expedition, in *DM*, 8: 375, 394–5.

120. Lopo de Almeida to king, Sofala, 27 August 1527, in *DM*, 6: 277–80.

121. Couto, IX, 20; note that Santos, I, ii, 10, has the same story, but he calls them *kaffir* merchants.

122. Pero Vaz Soares, factor of Sofala, to king, 30 June 1513, in *DM*, 3: 461.

123. For modern accounts, see Mudenge, *Political History*, 59–69; or Mudenge, *Christian Education at the Mutapa Court* (Harare, 1986), 3–12, from an "African" viewpoint. For a Portuguese version, see Bertha Leite, *D. Gonçalo da Silveira* (Lisbon, 1946). For contemporary documents, see *DM*, vols. 7 and 8; and J. Wicki et al., eds., *Documenta Indica*, 20 vols. to date (Rome, 1948–), vol. 5.

124. António Caido to a friend, 1561, in *DM*, 8: 5.

125. Letter of Luís Fróis, S.J., Goa, 15 December 1561, in *DM*, 8: 49; for "cacis," see M. N. Pearson, *Pious Passengers: the Hajj in Earlier Times* (Delhi, 1994), 71–2.

126. Sebastian Gonçalves, *Primeira Parte da História dos Religiosas da Companhia de Jesus*, ed. J. Wicki, 3 vols. (Coímbra, 1957–62), 2: 407.

127. João Vaz de Almada, captain of Sofala, to king, 26 June 1516, in *DM*, 4: 277–93; cf. Lobato, *Expansão*, 3: 29, 213–4.

128. Barros, I, x, 1; see also Couto, IX, 22; Santos, passim.

129. Jerónimo de Alcantara Guerreiro, "A acção missionária e a sua organização canónica em Moçambique, no período filipino, 1581–1640," Congresso Internacional de história dos descobrimentos, *Actas*, vol. 5, pt. 2 (Lisbon, 1961), 191.

130. Silveira to Jesuits in Goa, Mozambique, 9 August 1560, in *DM*, 7: 505; Fr. D. Gonçalo [Silveira] to Portugal, Goa, November 1559, in *DM*, 7: 423.

131. Summary of letters from António de Saldanha, Sofala, 1511, in *DM*, 3: 17.

132. Mudenge, *Political History*, 43–4.

133. See a copy made in Tete on 28 June 1629 of the agreement, in "Livros das Monções," Historical Archives of Goa, vol. 13B: ff. 458–9.

134. King to viceroy, 21 March 1608, in *DM*, 9: 119.

135. Jesuit account of their work in Monomotapa, 1607–1608, in *DM*, 9: 169; for a modern acceptance of this claim, see Manuel Lobato, "Relações comerciais entre a India e a costa Africana nos séculos XVI and XVII: o papel do Guzerate no Comércio de Moçambique," in *Portuguese India and Its Northern Province: Proceedings of the 7th International Seminar on Indo-Portuguese History* (Lisbon, 1995), 164.

136. J. M. Gray, "A Journey by Land from Tete to Kilwa in 1616," *Tanganyika Notes and Records* 25 (1948), 39.

137. António Bocarro, "Livro das plantas das fortalezas da India," in Bragança Pereira, IV, ii, 31.

138. Fr. Agustinho d'Azevedo to king, c. 1630s, *Documentação Ultramarina Portuguesa*, 5 vols. (Lisbon, 1960–67), 1: 6.

139. Beach, *Shona and Zimbabwe*, 108; António Bocarro, *Década 13 da história da India* (Lisbon, 1876), 534–5.

140. J. H. Bannerman, "Bvumba—estado pré-colonial Shona em Manica, no fronteira entre Moçambique e o Zimbabwe," *Arquivo* [Maputo] 13 (April 1993), 85–9.

141. See an account by "Pe Frey Phelipe de Assumpção por andar nas ditas terras quatorze annos" in the Ajuda Library, and printed in Maria Manuela Sobral Blanco, "O Estado Português da India: da rendição de Ormuz à perda de Cochim, 1622–1663" (Ph.D. diss., University of Lisbon, 1992, 3 vols.), 2: 763–4.

142. For *prazos*, see M.D.D. Newitt, *Portuguese Settlement on the Zambezi: Exploration, Land Tenure, and Colonial Rule in Eastern Africa* (London, 1973); Allen Isaacman, *Mozambique: The Africanization of a European Institution* (Madison, 1972).

143. Pero Vaz Soares, factor of Sofala, to king, 30 June 1513, in *DM*, 3: 461–3.

144. Barbosa, *Livro*, 1: 12.

145. Captain of Sofala, order of 19 May 1506, in *DM*, 1: 507.

146. For example, Jean-Baptiste Tavernier, *Travels in India*, trans. V. Ball, ed. W. Crooke, 2 vols. (New Delhi, 1977), 1: 153, 2: 124–6; Beach, *Shona and Zimbabwe*, 109–11.

147. Santos, I, iii, 19; J. H. van Linschoten, *The Voyage of John Huyghen van Linschoten to the East Indies*, 2 vols. (London, 1885), 1: 33, 275–6. See also an accumulation of data in Vitorino Magalhães Godinho, *Mito e mercadoria, utopia e prática de navegar, séculos XIII–XVIII* (Lisbon, 1990), 387–95.

148. Shireen Moosvi, "The Gujarat Ports and Their Hinterland," in Indu Banga, ed., *Ports and Their Hinterlands in India, 1700–1950* (New Delhi, 1992), 123, 125.

149. Ricardo Teixeira Duarte, *Northern Mozambique in the Swahili World* (Stockholm, 1993), 61–8.

150. Mbwiliza, *History of Commodity Production*, 21.

151. Beach, *Shona and Zimbabwe*, 25, 33–5.

152. Linschoten, *Voyage*, 1: 25, 28–9; William Foster, ed., *The Voyages of Sir James Lancaster* (London, 1940), 23.

153. Couto, X, vi, 14.

154. Newitt, *History of Mozambique*, 136, 138.

155. Generally see Axelson, *Portuguese in Southeast Africa, 1488–1600*, 88–104; Newitt, *History of Mozambique*, 94–5.

156. Barros, I, x, 3; James B. McKenna, *A Spaniard in the Portuguese Indies: The Narrative of Martín Fernández de Figueroa* (Cambridge, Mass., 1967), 59–61.

157. Francisco de Brito to king, 8 August 1519, in *DM*, 6: 11–3; D. Lopo de Almeida to king, 27 August 1527, in *DM*, 6: 277; António de Silveira to king, post July 1518, in *DM*, 5: 569. For the agreement of 1571 between Barreto and the Kiteve, see Santos, I, i, 18; and generally Lobato, *Expansão*, 2: 81–4, 3: 26.

158. Statement of 15 April 1512, in *DM*, 3: 239–49; Lobato, *Expansão*, 2: 18–20.

159. Couto, IX, 24; for a slightly different version, see Santos, I, i, 17.

160. João de Sepúlveda to king, Mozambique, 10 August 1542, in *DM*, 7: 137–9.

161. Captain of Sofala, order of 19 May 1506, in *DM*, 1: 507.

162. Accounts of Sofala, 1515, in *DM*, 4: 171.

163. Order of captain of Sofala, 7 January 1506, in *DM*, 1: 367.

164. Santos, I, i, 18.

165. M.D.D. Newitt, "Early History of the Sultanate of Angoche," *JAH* 13, no. 3 (1972), 397–406.

166. João Vaz de Almada, captain of Sofala, to king, 26 June 1516, in *DM*, 4: 277–93.

167. Pero Vaz Soares, factor of Sofala, to king, 30 June 1513, in *DM*, 3: 461–5.

168. João de Sepúlveda to king, Mozambique, 10 August 1542, in *DM*, 7: 139.

169. See Mbwiliza, *History of Commodity Production.*

170. Santos, I, iii, 2; Mbwiliza, *History of Commodity Production*, 9, 25; Alpers, *Ivory and Slaves*, 46–56, 82–5.

171. For Beach's most recent summary, see *Shona and Their Neighbours*, 108–11; earlier versions appear in Beach, *Zimbabwe before 1900*, 31–4; Beach, *Shona and Zimbabwe*, 109–43; Mudenge, *Political History.*

172. Newitt, *History of Mozambique*, 40–3.

Chapter 4. East Africa in the World-Economy

1. I posted a synopsis of this chapter on both the world-systems and African history Internet lists in May and June 1996. The responses helped me to firm up the argument.

2. What follows is based on a mass of secondary literature and some original research. See, for example, *Cambridge Economic History of India*, vol. 1, *c. 1200–c. 1750* (Cambridge, 1982); Ashin Das Gupta, *Indian Merchants and the Decline of Surat, c. 1700–1750* (Wiesbaden, 1979); Irfan Habib, *The Agrarian System of Mughal India, 1556–1707* (Bombay, 1963); A. Jan Qaisar, "The Role of Brokers in Medieval India," *Indian Historical Review* 1, no. 2 (1974), 220–46.

3. For overviews and critiques, see, among others, Jan Vansina, *Living with Africa* (Madison, 1994), esp. 197–9, 204, and 289; Ralph A. Austen, "African Commerce without Europeans: The Development Impact of International Trade in the Pre-Modern Era," *Kenya Historical Review* 6 (1978), 1–5; Frederick Cooper, "Africa and the World Economy," in Frederick Cooper, Allen F. Isaacman, Florencia E. Mallon, William Roseberry, and Steve J. Stern, *Confronting Historical Paradigms: Peasants, Labor, and the Capitalist World System in Africa and Latin America* (Madison, 1993).

4. Walter Rodney, *How Europe Underdeveloped Africa* (Washington, D.C., 1982; first published in 1972), vii–viii, 138. See 27–8 for his basic statement.

5. Abdul Sheriff, "Trade and Underdevelopment: The Role of International Trade in the Economic History of the East African Coast before the 16th Century," in B. A. Ogot, ed., *Hadith 5. Economic and Social History of East Africa* (Nairobi, 1976), 1–23.

6. Abdul Sheriff, *Slaves, Spices, and Ivory in Zanzibar: Integration of an East African Commercial Empire into the World Economy, 1770–1873* (London, 1987), 1–33, 247.

7. See J. F. Mbwiliza, *A History of Commodity Production in Makuani, 1600–1900: Mercantalist Accumulation to Imperialist Domination* (Dar es Salaam, 1991), xiv.

8. A. G. Hopkins in C. Fyfe, ed., *African Studies since 1945* (London, 1976), 34–6.

9. E. A. Alpers, "Re-thinking African Economic History," *Kenya Historical Review* 2, no. 2 (1973), 163–88, and esp. 174.

10. E. A. Alpers, *Ivory and Slaves: Changing Patterns of International Trade in East Central Africa to the Later Nineteenth Century* (London, 1975), xvi, xvii, and again on 264–7.

11. Catherine Coquery-Vidrovitch, "Recherches sur un mode de production africain," *La Pensée* 144 (1969), 61–78; and English version "Research on an African Mode of Production," in Martin A. Klein and G. Wesley Johnson, eds., *Perspectives on the African Past* (Boston, 1972), 33–51. The quotation is from the English version, 36.

12. Catherine Coquery-Vidrovitch, "The Political Economy of the African Peasantry and Modes of Production," in Peter C. W. Gutkind and Immanuel Wallerstein, eds., *The Political Economy of Contemporary Africa* (Beverly Hills, 1976), 90–111.

13. See M. N. Pearson, "Land, Noble, and Ruler in Mughal India," in Sir Edmund Leach, S. N. Mukherjee, and John O. Ward, eds., *Feudalism: Comparative Studies* (Sydney, 1985), 175–96; and Pearson, "Merchants and States," in James D. Tracy, ed., *The Political Economy of Merchant Empires* (New York, 1991), 41–116. Marx's Asiatic mode has been abandoned by Indian Marxists.

14. Robin Law, "In Search of a Marxist Perspective on Pre-Colonial Tropical Africa," *JAH* 19, no. 3 (1978), 441–52.

15. See Donald Crummey and C. C. Stewart, eds., *Modes of Production in Africa: The Precolonial Era* (Beverly Hills, 1981). See also B. Jewsiewicki and J. Létourneau, eds., "Mode of Production: The Challenge of Africa," *Canadian Journal of African Studies* 19, no. 1 (1985), 1–174.

16. See Immanuel Wallerstein, *The Modern World-System*, 3 vols. (New York, 1974–89), or, for a synoptic view, Terence K. Hopkins and Immanuel Wallerstein, "Patterns of Development of the Modern World-System," *Review* 1, no. 2 (1977), 111–45. For other summaries, see Thomas Richard Shannon, *An Introduction to the World-System Perspective* (Boulder, 1989); and M. N. Pearson, *Before Colonialism: Theories on Asian-European Relations, 1500–1750* (Delhi, 1988), chap. 1.

17. It is noticeable, on the one hand, that vol. 3 of Wallerstein's *Modern World-System* has received very few reviews, and yet, on the other, the "world-systems" bulletin board on the Internet is active and vigorous.

18. Wallerstein, *Modern World-System*, 1: 348.

19. Quoted in John Obert Voll, "Islam as a Special World-System," *Journal of World History* 5, no. 2 (1994), 219.

20. Immanuel Wallerstein, "Africa in a Capitalist World," *Issue: A Quarterly Journal of Africanist Opinion* 3, no. 3 (1973), 10.

21. In Wallerstein's model of the capitalist world-system, the *core* uses unequal exchange to extract resources from the *periphery*. The *semiperiphery* mediates between the two. Ravi Arvind Palat and Immanuel Wallerstein, "Of What World-System was Pre-1500 'India' a Part?" in S. Chaudhuri and M. Morineau, eds., *Merchants, Companies, and Trade* (forthcoming). Thanks to Ravi Palat for sending me a typescript.

22. Janet Abu-Lughod, *Before European Hegemony: The World System A.D. 1250–1350* (Oxford, 1989); and for shorter versions, see Abu-Lughod, "Restructuring the Premodern World-System," *Review* 13, no. 2 (1990), 273–86; Abu-Lughod, "The World System in the Thirteenth Century: Dead-End or Precursor?" in Michael Adas, ed., *Islamic and European Expansion: The Forging of a Global Order* (Philadelphia, 1993), 75–102; and a more reflective overview in Abu-Lughod, "The World-System Perspective in the Construction of Economic History," *History and Theory* 34 (1995), 86–98.

23. Abu-Lughod, *Before European Hegemony*, 5–6, 364 et seq., and generally 8–40 for her main ideas.

24. André Gunder Frank, "A Theoretical Introduction to 5,000 Years of World System History," *Review* 13, no. 2 (1990), 155–248; and André Gunder Frank and Barry K. Gills, eds., *The World System: Five Hundred Years or Five Thousand?* (London, 1993). Throughout 1996, Frank used the Internet "world-systems" list to prefigure a new study to be called "The Asian-based World Economy, 1400–1800: A Horizontally Integrative Macrohistory." Some of his themes are encapsulated in André Gunder Frank, "The World Economic System in Asia before European Hegemony," *Historian* 55, no. 2 (1994), 259–76. The quotation is from 271. This attack on Braudel and Wallerstein is extended in André Gunder Frank, "The Modern World System Revisited: Rereading Braudel and Wallerstein," in Stephen K. Sanderson, ed., *Civilizations and World Systems: Studying World-Historical Change* (Walnut Creek, Calif., 1995), 163–94.

25. Christopher Chase-Dunn and Thomas D. Hall, eds, *Core/Periphery Relations in Precapitalist Worlds* (Boulder, 1991), 5–44.

See also Eric R. Wolf, *Europe and the People without History* (Berkeley, 1982).

26. Voll, "Islam as a Special World-System."

27. Immanuel Wallerstein, "Africa in a Capitalist World," 10.

28. "Introduction," in Peter C. W. Gutkind and Immanuel Wallerstein, eds., *The Political Economy of Contemporary Africa* (Beverly Hills, 1976), 7.

29. Immanuel Wallerstein, "The Three Stages of African Involvement in the World-Economy," in Peter C. W. Gutkind and Immanuel Wallerstein, eds., *The Political Economy of Contemporary Africa* (Beverly Hills, 1976), 32.

30. N. Buckeridge, *Journal and Letter Book of Nicholas Buckeridge, 1651–1654*, ed. J. R. Jenson (Minneapolis, 1973), 54, 66.

31. Eric Axelson, *Portuguese in Southeast Africa, 1488–1600* (Johannesburg, 1973), 102.

32. António Bocarro, "Livro das plantas das fortalezas da India," in Bragança Pereira, IV, ii, 227.

33. Alexandre Lobato, *A Expansão Portuguesa em Moçambique de 1498 a 1530*, 3 vols. (Lisbon, 1954–60), 3: 320, 362–3, 365; Manuel Lobato, "Relações comerciais entre a India e a costa Africana nos séculos XVI and XVII: o papel do Guzerate no Comércio de Moçambique," in *Portuguese India and Its Northern Province: Proceedings of the 7th International Seminar on Indo-Portuguese History* (Lisbon, 1995), 170.

34. Eric Axelson, *Portuguese in Southeast Africa, 1600–1700* (Johannesburg, 1960), 76, n. 1.

35. Monclaro's account of the Barreto expedition, in *DM*, 8: 391–3.

36. Ashin Das Gupta, "Indian Merchants and the Trade of the Indian Ocean," *Cambridge Economic History of India*, vol. 1, *c. 1200–c. 1750* (Cambridge, 1982), 418.

37. John Irwin and P. R. Schwartz, *Studies in Indo-European Textile History* (Ahmedabad, 1966), 16.

38. S.I.G. Mudenge, *A Political History of Munhumutapa, c. 1400–1902* (Harare, 1988), 162, quoting Bocarro; and see also Santos, I, ii, 13, for a good account, and one much used by others, on gold production. For the best modern overview, see Vitorino Magalhães Godinho, *Os descobrimentos e a economia mundial*, 2d ed., 4 vols. (Lisbon, 1981–83), 1: 184–209.

39. For Portuguese comments on this, see Notes by Gaspar Veloso, Mozambique, on the description by António Fernandes of his journey inland, in *DM*, 3: 183; king to viceroy, 19 March 1610, in *DM*, 9: 215.

40. Santos, I, ii, 8; cf. *DM*, 1: 529.

41. J. M. Gray, "A Portuguese Inscription and the Uroa Coin Hoard: Some Discoveries in Zanzibar," *Azania* 10 (1975), 123–31; Helen W. Brown, "Three Kilwa Gold Coins," *Azania* 26 (1991), 1–4; Monclaro's account of the Barreto expedition, in *DM*, 8: 349–51.

42. Santos, I, ii, 10.

43. Barreto's letter in Theal, 3: 489–92.

44. *DM*, 8: 391.

45. Couto, IX, 24.

46. D. N. Beach, *The Shona and Zimbabwe, 900–1850* (London, 1980), 109.

47. Martin Hall, *The Changing Past: Farmers, Kings, and Traders in Southern Africa* (Cape Town, 1987), 102.

48. Jean-Baptiste Tavernier, *Travels in India*, trans. V. Ball, ed. W. Crooke, 2 vols. (New Delhi, 1977), 1: 221; a similar claim from 1667 is quoted in António da Silva, S.J., *Mentalidade missiológica dos Jesuítas em Moçambique antes de 1759*, 2 vols. (Lisbon, 1967), 1: 164–5.

49. Santos, I, iii, 13–5.

50. J. H. van Linschoten, *The Voyage of John Huyghen van Linschoten to the East Indies*, 2 vols. (London, 1885), 1: 30.

51. Fr. André Fernández in Tonge [inland from Inhambane] to Br. Luís Fróis, 25 August 1560, in *DM*, 7: 483.

52. Alpers, *Ivory and Slaves*.

53. Ibid., 203.

54. Pero Vaz Soares, factor of Sofala, to king, 30 June 1513, in *DM*, 3: 461.

55. Couto, IX, 22.

56. Barros, I, x, 1.

57. Barreto's letter in Theal, 3: 493.

58. Santos, I, iii, 2.

59. Fr. André Fernández in Tonge [30 leagues inland from Inhambane] to Br. Luís Froís, 25 August 1560, in *DM*, 7: 483.

60. D. N. Beach, *The Shona and Their Neighbours* (Oxford, 1994), 58, 66; M.D.D. Newitt, *A History of Mozambique* (London, 1994), 51; Mudenge, *Political History*, 10–1.

61. Wolf, *Europe and the People without History*.

62. Beach, *Shona and Their Neighbours*, 103–5.

63. Mudenge, *Political History*, 167 and generally 161–94 for an excellent discussion; and Beach, *Shona and Their Neighbours*, 97–111.

64. King to viceroy, 21 March 1608, in *DM*, 9: 127.

65. Paul Sinclair et al., "Urban Trajectories on the Zimbabwean Plateau," in Thurstan Shaw et al., eds., *The Archeology of Africa: Food, Metals, and Towns* (London, 1993), 718.

66. Lobato, *Expansão*, 3: 97–9, 122–4, 130–3, 251–2.

67. Account of Almeida voyage, in *DM*, 1: 533; for prices, see among others, king to viceroy, 19 March 1610, in *DM*, 9: 215; king to viceroy, 7 November 1612, in *DM*, 9: 265–7.

68. Account of Almeida voyage, in *DM*, 1: 527.

69. Account of Fernandes journey, 1512, in *DM*, 3: 185.

70. Monclaro's account of the Barreto expedition, in *DM*, 8: 381.

71. Duarte Barbosa, *Livro*, 2 vols. (London, 1918–21), 1: 9; for a variant translation, see *DM*, 5: 359; Godinho, *Descobrimentos*, 1: 204.

72. Monclaro's account of the Barreto expedition, in *DM*, 8: 393, 421.

73. Eric Axelson, ed., "Viagem que fez o Padre António Gomes . . . ao Imperio de Manomotapa . . . " *Studia* 3 (1959), 209.

74. D. N. Beach, *Zimbabwe before 1900* (Gweru, 1984), 37–8, 43.

75. Beach, *Shona and Zimbabwe*, 30–2.

76. Ibn Battuta, *The Travels of Ibn Battuta*, trans. H.A.R. Gibb, 3 vols. (Cambridge, 1962), 2: 374.

77. W. Howard Brown, "History of Siyu: The Development and Decline of a Swahili Town on the Northern Kenya Coast" (Ph.D. diss., Indiana University, 1985), 72–3, 164–71; also Thomas Spear, *Kenya's Past: An Introduction to Historical Method in Africa* (London, 1981), 133.

78. Monclaro's account of the Barreto expedition, in *DM*, 8: 355.

79. Santos, I, v, 1.

80. King to viceroy, 7 November 1612, in *DM*, 9: 263; king's decree of 20 March 1614, in *DM*, 9: 353.

81. Barros, I, x, 1.

82. Beach, *Shona and Their Neighbours*, 107–8; *DM*, 5: 359.

83. Peter Garlake, *Life at Great Zimbabwe* (Gweru, 1982).

84. Silva, *Mentalidade missiológica dos Jesuítas*, 1: 151, 153, 182, 205–6, and see 197–8 for varieties of cloth.

85. Alpers, *Ivory and Slaves*, 21–2.

86. Hall, *Changing Past*, 125.

87. John Thornton, "Precolonial African Industry and the Atlantic Trade, 1500–1800," *African Economic History* 19 (1990), 1–19; and responses to this by Austen, 21–4, Manning, 25–30, Hogendom and Gemery, 31–5, McDougal, 37–43, and reply by Thornton, 45–54.

88. Hall, *Changing Past*, 102.

89. John Middleton, *The World of the Swahili: An African Mercantile Civilization* (New Haven, 1992), 18.

90. Ralph Austen, *African Economic History: Internal Development and External Dependency* (London, 1987), 74.

91. M.D.D. Newitt, "East Africa and the Indian Ocean Trade, 1500–1800," in Ashin Das Gupta and M. N. Pearson, eds., *India and the Indian Ocean, 1500–1800* (Calcutta, 1987), 207–8.

92. For the modern trade, see Philip D. Curtin, "African Enterprise in the Mangrove Trade: The Case of Lamu," *African Economic History* 10 (1981), 23–33.

93. I. Wallerstein, "The Ottoman Empire and the Capitalist World-Economy: Some Questions for Research," *Review* 2, no. 3 (1979), 390–1.

94. Stephen Frederic Dale, *Indian Merchants and Eurasian Trade, 1600–1750* (Cambridge, 1994).

95. James D. Tracy, ed., *The Rise of Merchant Empires* (New York, 1990), the quotation is from p. vii of the preface; and Tracy, ed., *The Political Economy of Merchant Empires* (New York, 1991).

Chapter 5. The Portuguese on the Coast

1. Alexandre Lobato, *A Expansão Portuguesa em Moçambique de 1498 a 1530*, 3 vols. (Lisbon, 1954–60).

2. Eric Axelson, *Portuguese in Southeast Africa, 1488–1600* (Johannesburg, 1973); Axelson, *Portuguese in Southeast Africa, 1600–1700* (Johannesburg, 1960); Axelson, *South East Africa, 1488–1530* (London, 1940).

3. M.D.D. Newitt, *A History of Mozambique* (London, 1994), vi.

4. S.I.G. Mudenge, *A Political History of Munhumutapa, c. 1400–1902* (Harare, 1988).

5. D. N. Beach, *A Zimbabwean Past* (Gweru, 1994); Beach, "The Zimbabwe Plateau and Its Peoples," in David Birmingham and Phyllis Martin, eds., *History of Central Africa*, 2 vols. (London, 1983), 1: 245–77; Beach, *Zimbabwe before 1900* (Gweru, 1984); Beach, *The Shona and Their Neighbours* (Oxford, 1994); Beach, *The Shona and Zimbabwe, 900–1850* (London, 1980).

6. History Department, Universidade Eduardo Mondlane, *História de Moçambique*, vol. 1, *Primeiras sociedades sendantarias e impacto dos mercadores (200/300–1886)*, 2d ed. (Maputo, 1988).

7. A.J.R. Russell-Wood, "The *Estado da India* and the *Estado do Brasil*: Opportunities for Research in Portuguese Overseas History," *Itinerario* 18, no. 2 (1994), 116–29; Sanjay Subrahmanyam, *The Portuguese Empire in Asia, 1500–1700: A Political and Economic History* (London, 1993). What he has on east Africa is sometimes inaccurate, and in any case is based very largely on Mudenge, but he does try to locate the Portuguese in east Africa in a wider imperial context. Richard Hall's *Empires of the Monsoon: A History of the Indian Ocean and Its Invaders* (London, 1996), an excellent "popular" history, pays much attention to events on the Swahili coast, though he is inclined to overemphasize Portuguese activities.

8. Om Prakash, *Asia and the Pre-Modern World Economy* (Leiden, 1995); see also a collection of his many articles published as *Precious Metals and Commerce: The Dutch East India Company in the Indian Ocean Trade* (Aldershot, 1994); and *The Dutch East India Company and the Economy of Bengal* (Princeton, 1985).

9. See S.I.G. Mudenge, "Afro-Indian Relations before 1900: A South-east African Perspective," in Shanti Sadiq Ali and R. R. Ramchandani, eds., *India and the Western Indian Ocean States* (New Delhi, 1981), 39–62.

10. Pero Ferreira Fogaça to king, Kilwa, 22 December 1506, in *DM*, 1: 757.

11. Carta de ley of king, 1595, in Cunha Rivara, 3: 540–2.

12. N. Buckeridge, *Journal and Letter Book of Nicholas Buckeridge, 1651–1654*, ed. J. R. Jenson (Minneapolis, 1973), 45.

13. Gaspar de S. Bernadino, 1606, published in G.S.P. Freeman-Grenville, *The East African Coast: Select Documents from the First to the Earlier Nineteenth Century* (London, 1962), 162.

14. Afonso Albuquerque, *The Commentaries of the Great Afonso Dalbuquerque*, ed. W. Birch, 4 vols. (London, 1875–84), 1: 34–6, 39.

15. This is not to say that this was some sort of pre-European Golden Age, for the Swahili city-states did compete and combat vigorously. They did not, however, attempt anything like the all-encompassing control system that the Portuguese did. Patricia Risso, *Merchants and Faith: Muslim Commerce and Culture in the Indian Ocean* (Boulder, 1995), 52–3, presents a picture of Indian Ocean trade where force was widely used, but her evidence relates mostly to piracy, which certainly was a problem, and to Melaka; one cannot generalize from this to the whole ocean.

16. In a more general context, see M. N. Pearson, *The Portuguese in India* (Cambridge, 1987), chaps. 2 and 3.

17. Petition of Nuno Velho Pereira to king, 7 January 1589, in *DM*, 8: 541.

18. Bragança Pereira, IV, ii, 227.

19. Vitorino Magalhães Godinho, *Os descobrimentos e a economia mundial*, 2d ed., 4 vols. (Lisbon, 1981–83), 1: 204–7.

20. P. F. Thorbahn, "The Precolonial Ivory Trade of East Africa: Reconstruction of a Human-Elephant Ecosystem" (Ph.D. diss., University of Massachusetts, 1979), 87; Clements Markham, *Colloquies on the Simples and Drugs of India by Garcia da Orta* (London, 1913), chap. 21.

21. Viceroy's alvará of 17 January 1614, in Cunha Rivara, 6: 1007–8.

22. King to viceroy, 25 January 1614, in Bulhão Pato, 3: 13–4. For the fort, see C. R. Boxer and Carlos de Azevedo, *Fort Jesus and the Portuguese in Mombasa, 1593–1729* (London, 1960).

23. "Livros das Fazenda," Historical Archives of Goa, 9: 21, meeting of 11 November 1653.

24. King to viceroy, 15 March 1617, in Bulhão Pato, 4: 64–5.

25. As examples, see the account in Correa, 3: 315–6, of a disastrous Portuguese effort off Mombasa in 1528; and for the way a Portuguese attack was beaten off in 1541, see João de Sepulveda to king, Mozambique, 10 August 1542, in *DM*, 7: 135; and for another fiasco, inland from Mozambique, see Santos, I, iii, 2.

26. Alvará of 18 March 1604, in Cunha Rivara, 6: 762.

27. Pero da Fonseca, Mozambique, to king, 9 February 1514, in *DM*, 3: 533.

28. Summary of letter of king of Malindi, Ali, to king of Portugal, n.d., c. 1520, in *DM*, 6: 47.

29. See king to viceroy, 22 February 1617, and 10 March 1617, in Bulhão Pato, 4: 19, 40.

30. "Livros das Fazenda," Historical Archives of Goa, 4: 178–9, meeting of 24 October 1635.

31. King to viceroy, 10 March 1617, in Bulhão Pato, 4: 51; alvará of king, 23 March 1619, in "Alvarás et provisões de sua magestade," Historical Archives of Goa, 1: 160-v, printed in Cunha Rivara, 4: 1189–90.

32. Summary of letter to king of 20 December 1510, in *DM*, 2: 513.

33. King to viceroy, 23 January 1610, in Bulhão Pato, 1: 289.

34. Viceroy to king, January 1616, and 29 December 1616, "Livros das Monções," Historical Archives of Goa, 12, 228–9, 299v-300v; António Bocarro, *Década 13 da história da India* (Lisbon, 1876), 665–8.

35. King to viceroy, 10 March 1618, and viceroy's alvará of 29 July 1619, in Cunha Rivara, 4: 1166–7, 1181.

36. M.D.D. Newitt, "Plunder and the Rewards of Office in the Portuguese Empire," in M. Duffy, ed., *The Military Revolution and the State, 1500–1800* (Exeter, 1980), 26. See also the following complaints: viceroy de Noronha to king, Cochin, 27 January 1552, in *DM*, 7: 257; João Velho, former factor in Sofala, to king, Goa, 4 November 1548, in *DM*, 7: 185–9.

37. King to viceroy, 27 March 1591, in Cunha Rivara, 3: 318–9.

38. Pde Manuel Fernandes, Mozambique, 6 August 1555, in António da Silva Rego, ed., *Documentação para a história das Missões do padroado Português do Oriente: India*, 12 vols. (Lisbon, 1947–58), 6: 17.

39. Royal letter of 1 April 1615 about the Dominicans, in Bragança Pereira, IV, ii, 209.

40. See, for example, king to viceroy, 22 February 1585, in Cunha Rivara, 3: 46.

41. T. Mbuia-João, "The Revolt of Dom Jeronimo Chingulia of Mombasa, 1590–1637 (An African Episode in the Portuguese Century of Decline)" (Ph.D. diss., Catholic University, 1990), a strongly "nationalist" effort that stresses African resistance to European colonialism.

42. See, for example, captain of Mozambique and Sofala to king, Mozambique, 20 September 1517, in *DM*, 5: 203; and generally M.D.D. Newitt, "Early History of the Sultanate of Angoche," *JAH* 13, no. 3 (1972), 397–406.

43. See, for example, Jordão de Freitas to king, Goa, 17 September 1530, in *DM*, 6: 425–7.

44. Duarte Barbosa, *Livro*, 2 vols. (London, 1918–21), 1: 9–10; Godinho, *Descobrimentos*, 1: 204.

45. Santos, I, i, 17. Indeed, as early as 1515, António Fernandes expressed doubt about how easy it would be to get access to the gold.

46. Treasury Council, Lisbon, to king, 4 April 1614, in *DM*, 9: 367.

47. Correa, 1: 785. See also C. R. Boxer, *From Lisbon to Goa, 1500–1750: Studies in Portuguese Maritime Enterprise* (London, 1984), especially "The Principal Ports of Call in the 'Carreira da India'" and "Moçambique Island and the 'Carreira da India,'" for copious detail on the Portuguese in Mozambique, their forts, and their illnesses.

48. Castanheda, 7: 87–8.

49. Monclaro letter, Mozambique, 1 August 1570, J. Wicki et al., eds., *Documenta Indica*, 20 vols. to date (Rome, 1948–), 8: 278.

50. Marina Tolmacheva, *The Pate Chronicle* (East Lansing, 1993), 62, 175.

51. Barros, I, iv, 3.

52. Correa, 1: 273.

53. See, respectively, M. N. Pearson, *Coastal Western India* (New Delhi, 1981), 27; and B. Schrieke, *Indonesian Sociological Studies*, 2 vols. (The Hague, 1955–57), 1: 26, 70.

54. Godinho, *Descobrimentos*, 1: 192–4.

55. Correa, 1: 537–4.

56. Gaspar da Gama to king, n.d. [1505], in Bragança Pereira, IV, i, 86.

57. On plunder see Newitt, "Plunder and the Rewards of Office," esp. 22.

58. For the treaty of 1629, see a copy made in Tete, 28 June 1629, of the agreement signed by Manuza, emperor of Monomotapa, 24 May 1629, in "Livros das Monções," Historical Archives of Goa, 13B: 458–9.

59. D. N. Beach, "The Zimbabwe Plateau and Its Peoples," in David Birmingham and Phyllis Martin, eds., *History of Central Africa*, 2 vols. (London, 1983), 1: 259.

60. Lobato, *Expansão*, 3: 362–3.

61. See works by Axelson cited in note 2 above; and Newitt, *History of Mozambique*; for the period to 1530, see Lobato, *Expansão*. Also see Vitorino Magalhães Godinho, *Les finances de l'état portugais des Indes Orientales, 1517–1635* (Paris, 1982), 41–4; and especially Luís Frederico Dias Antunes, "The

Trade Activities of the *Banyans* in Mozambique: Private Indian Dynamics in the Portuguese State Economy, 1686–1777," in K. S. Mathew, ed., *Mariners, Merchants, and Oceans: Studies in Maritime History* (New Delhi, 1995), 301–31, notably 324, where he usefully identifies the various trading regimes between 1686 and 1786.

62. For details on this farce, an example of the wealth of information available, see king to viceroy, 31 March 1593, and 7 March 1595, in *DM*, 9: 23–5; 35–7; see also king to viceroy, 31 March 1591, "Livros das Monções," Historical Archives of Goa, IIA, f. 118-v; provisão of 31 March 1593, in ibid., I, ff. 30–3; and further discussion in ibid., IIA, ff. 82–.

63. For a typical contract with a new governor, see king's alvará of 20 March 1614, in Cunha Rivara, 6: 1046–7.

64. See for examples: P.S.S. Pissurlencar, ed., *Regimentos das Fortalezas da India* (Bastorá, 1951), 527–30; Luís de Figueiredo Falcão, *Livro em que se contém toda a fazenda* (Lisbon, 1859), 125–6; Simão Botelho, "Tombo," in R. J. de Lima Felner, ed., *Subsídios para a história da India Portuguesa* (Lisbon, 1868), 8–246; "Livro da Feitoria," Historical Archives of Goa, ff. 16–30; and a useful compilation of the official accounts of the revenues of the Estado, all translated to *reis* for comparative purposes, for the years 1574, 1581, 1588, 1607, 1610, 1620, 1630, and 1635, in Maria Manuela Sobral Blanco, "O Estado Português da India: da rendição de Ormuz à perda de Cochim, 1622–1663" (Ph.D. diss., University of Lisbon, 1992, 3 vols.), 1: facing p. 300.

65. The classic account is still C. R. Boxer, *Race Relations in the Portuguese Colonial Empire, 1415–1825* (Oxford, 1963).

66. Fr. António da Conceição, "Tratado dos Rio de Cuama, 1696," *O Chronista de Tissuary* 2 (1867), 86.

67. Moçambique, *Documentário Trimestral* 72–79 (1952–53), 75: 177–8.

68. C. R. Boxer, *The Church Militant and Iberian Expansion* (Baltimore, 1978), 46.

69. Freeman-Grenville, *East African Coast*, 47.

70. Axelson, *Portuguese in Southeast Africa, 1600–1700*, 84, quoting an Arab history of Mombasa.

71. John Middleton, *The World of the Swahili: An African Mercantile Civilization* (New Haven, 1992), 47. *Manoel* is used to refer to Portuguese in general.

72. Buckeridge, *Journal*, 21.

73. For the ideological background, see A.J.R. Russell-Wood, "Iberian Expansion and the Issue of Black Slavery: Changing Portuguese Attitudes, 1440–1770," *American Historical Review* 83, no. 1 (1978), 23–9.

74. Orders for Almeida's fleet, 5 March 1505, in *DM*, 1: 181.

75. Conclusions of men of learning, 23 January 1569, in *DM*, 8: 163–71.

76. Couto, IX, 24.

77. For example, Treasury Council, Lisbon, to king, 4 April 1614, in *DM*, 9: 361–85.

78. Couto, IX, 22.

79. King to viceroy, 21 March 1608, in *DM*, 9: 119–21.

80. An otherwise unattributed "Report" of 1614–15, in *DM*, 9: 459–67.

81. Axelson, *Portuguese in Southeast Africa, 1600–1700*, 101.

82. See Mudenge, *Political History*, 201–21; 253–79; History Department, *História de Moçambique*, 1: 79–89.

83. For a detailed report, so far little used, of the situation in 1693, see the account by "Pe Frey Phelipe de Assumpção por andar nas ditas terras quatorze annos" from the Ajuda Library, in Blanco, "O Estado Português da India," 2: 762–9.

84. King to Fogaça, captain of Kilwa, 1507, in *DM*, 2: 27–9.

85. Santos, I, i, 2; I, ii, 8; I, iii, 4.

86. Bocarro, *Década 13*, 534–5.

87. Census of 24 January 1722, in Bragança Pereira, IV, ii, 88–9.

88. King to viceroy, 24 February 1635, in Bragança Pereira, IV, ii, 179–80.

89. Axelson, *Portuguese in Southeast Africa, 1600–1700*, 99–114.

90. Eric Axelson, ed., "Viagem que fez o Padre António Gomes . . . ao Imperio de Manomotapa . . . " *Studia* 3 (1959), 240–1.

91. For example, viceroy to king, 24 January 1683, and king to viceroy, 20 March 1690, in P.S.S. Pissurlencar, ed., *Assentos do Conselho do Estado*, 5 vols. (Bastorá, 1953–57), 4: 441–2, 569–70.

92. Axelson, *Portuguese in Southeast Africa, 1600–1700*, 151.

93. Viceroy to king, 20 January 1678, in Pissurlencar, *Assentos*, 4: 276.

94. "Livros das Monções," Historical Archives of Goa, v. 45, ff. 137–8v.

95. See Axelson, *Portuguese in Southeast Africa, 1600–1700*, 154, for some slightly different figures, and for the total Portuguese population in 1680.

96. Conceição, "Tratado dos Rio de Cuama, 1696," 87.

97. Viceroy to king, 30 December 1700, in Bragança Pereira, III, i, 127.

98. See, for example, Lobato, *Expansão*, 2: 18–20; and numerous examples printed in *DM*: for example, order from captain of Sofala, 28 October 1505, in *DM*, 1: 301–3.

99. Orders from captain of Sofala to factor of Kilwa, in *DM*, 2: 37–9, 65.

100. Pero da Fonseca, Mozambique, to king, 9 February 1514, in *DM*, 3: 533.

101. Viceroy to king, 20 December 1561, in *DM*, 8: 63–5.

102. Monclaro, quoted in Freeman-Grenville, *East African Coast*, 140.

103. Monclaro's account, in Wicki, *Documenta Indica*, 8: 721.

104. Couto, IX, 23.

105. Certificate of Gomes de Figueiredo, 1509, *As Gavetas da Torre do Tombo*, 12 vols. (Lisbon, 1960–75), 5: 297–8.

106. See viceroy to king, 29 December 1616, "Livros das Monções," Historical Archives of Goa, v. 12, 304v; and Bocarro, *Década 13*, 632–7, for this incident.

107. Bocarro, *Década 13*, 223.

108. Conceição, "Tratado dos Rio de Cuama, 1696," 85–6.

109. William Foster, ed., *The English Factories in India, 1618–1669*, 13 vols. (Oxford, 1906–27), 1618–21: 272.

110. King to viceroy, 21 March 1608, in *DM*, 9: 127.

111. See Newitt, *History of Mozambique*; Newitt, *Portuguese Settlement on the Zambezi: Exploration, Land Tenure, and Colonial Rule in Eastern Africa* (London, 1973); Allen Isaacman, *Mozambique: The Africanization of a European Institution* (Madison, 1972).

112. Allen Isaacman and Barbara Isaacman, "The Prazeros as Transfrontiersmen: A Study in Social and Cultural Change," *International Journal of African Historical Studies* 8 (1975), 1–39. The term was first coined by Philip D. Curtin.

113. Barreto's letter, 11 December 1667, in Theal, 3: 468.

114. See the splendid dissertation of Timothy Joel Coates, "Exiles and Orphans: Forced and State-Sponsored Colonizers in the Portuguese Empire, 1550–1720" (Ph.D. diss., University of Minnesota, 1993).

115. Couto, XI, 8; king to viceroy, 25 January 1601, February 1603, 23 March 1604, in *DM*, 9: 59, 77, 79–81.

116. King to viceroy, 25 January 1614, in Bulhão Pato, 3: 13–4.

117. Boxer, *Church Militant*, 108–10.

118. Eric Axelson, ed., "Viagem que fez o Padre António Gomes," 181; for St. Paul's see C. R. Boxer, *The Portuguese Seaborne Empire* (London, 1969), 250.

119. Gaspar de S. Bernadino, 1606, quoted in Freeman-Grenville, *East African Coast*, 161–2.

120. Personal observation. There is a photograph with caption of this dish in the Lamu Museum.

121. See Maria Augusta Lima Cruz, "Exiles and Renegades in Early Sixteenth Century Portuguese India," *Indian Economic and Social History Review* 23 (1986), 3; C. R. Boxer, *Francisco Vieira de Figueiredo: A Portuguese Merchant-Adventurer in South East Asia, 1624–1667* (The Hague, 1967).

122. Newitt, "Plunder and the Rewards of Office," 23.

123. Lobato, *Expansão*, 2: 83.

124. King to Fogaça, captain of Kilwa, 1507, in *DM*, 2: 27–9.

125. Correa, 1: 161.

126. Certificate of Gomes de Figueiredo, *Gavetas da Torre do Tombo*, 5: 297–8.

127. Correa, 3: 314.

128. Axelson, *Portuguese in Southeast Africa, 1600–1700*, 14; Boxer and Azevedo, *Fort Jesus and the Portuguese in Mombasa*, 42, but on p. 84 he reduces this to 100.

129. For António Fernandes, see A.J.R. Russell-Wood, *A World on the Move: The Portuguese in Africa, Asia, and America, 1415–1808* (New York, 1992), 11–2; Hugh Tracey, *António Fernandes: Descobridor do Monomotapa, 1514–1515* (Lourenço Marques, 1940); W. A. Godlonton, "The Journeys of António Fernandes—The First Known European to Find the Monomotapa and to Enter Southern Rhodesia," *Transactions of the Rhodesia Scientific Association* 40 (April 1945), 71–103.

130. Santos, I, i, 2; I, ii, 8; I, iii, 4.

131. Santos, I, v, 2–3; Couto, XI, 8.

132. Couto, X, ii, 8.

133. Monclaro, quoted in Freeman-Grenville, *East African Coast*, 140.

134. Fr. Francisco Cabral Annual Letter, Goa, 15 November 1593, in Wicki, *Documenta Indica*, 16: 305.

135. Gaspar de S. Bernadino, 1606, in Freeman-Grenville, *East African Coast*, 157. The name presumably derives from *rapaz*, "a young fellow." An alternative reading of *rapozeira* would give the meaning "foxhole."

136. Jerónimo Lobo, *The Itinerário of Jerónimo Lobo* (London, 1984), 52, 54, 69; Buckeridge, *Journal*, 75–6.

137. Vasco da Gama, *A Journal of the First Voyage of Vasco da Gama* (London, 1898), 35, 36, 44–5; the English editor, reflecting all too well his own feeling of superiority not only to Indians but also to Portuguese, footnoted that of course the Indians "looked upon these Romish images and pictures as outlandish representations of their own gods or idols." See also the version in Luís de Albuquerque, *Crónica do descobrimento e conquista da India pelos Portugueses* (Coímbra, 1974), 8.

138. See M. N. Pearson, "The Search for the Similar: Early Contacts between Portuguese and Indians," in Jens Christian V. Johansen, Erling Ladewig Petersen, and Henrik Stevnsborg, eds., *Clashes of Cultures: Essays in Honour of Niels Steensgaard* (Odense, 1992), 144–59.

139. Barros, I, iv, 6; for a retrospective version, see Castanheda, 1: 29. Portugal's national poet, Camoens, presents the Mombasa misidentification as being a trick by Bacchus to fool the Portuguese: Luís Vaz de Camoens, *The Lusiads*, trans. William C. Atkinson (Harmondsworth, 1952), 58–9.

Chapter 6. Conclusion

1. Richard H. Grove, *Green Imperialism: Colonial Expansion, Tropical Island Edens, and the Origins of Environmentalism, 1600–1860* (Cambridge, 1995), would be fundamental as one began such a study.

2. James Warren, *The Sulu Zone, 1768–1898: The Dynamics of External Trade, Slavery, and Ethnicity in the Transformation of a Southeast Asian Maritime State* (Singapore, 1981).

3. Luís Frederico Dias Antunes, "A crise no Estado da India no Final do Século XVII e a Criação das Companhias de Comércio das Indias Orientais e dos Baneanes de Diu," in *Portuguese India and its Northern Province, Proceedings of the 7th International Seminar on Indo-Portuguese History* (Lisbon, 1995), 19–29; Antunes, "The Trade Activities of the *Banyans* in Mozambique: Private Indian Dynamics in the Portuguese State Economy, 1686–1777," in K. S. Mathew, ed., *Mariners, Merchants, and Oceans: Studies in Maritime History* (New Delhi, 1995), 301–31.

4. The National Library in Lisbon holds a reputedly excellent "History of Mombasa," and publication is promised. My thanks to Rene Barendse for this and other information on sources. His book on the "Arabian Seas" is due out from Leiden very soon.

5. Richard Burton, *Goa and the Blue Mountains* (London, 1851), 88, 97.

6. See C. A. Bayly, *Indian Society and the Making of the British Empire* (Cambridge, 1987).

7. Quoted in Colin Simmons, "'De-industrialisation,' Industrialisation, and the Indian Economy, c. 1850–1947," *Modern Asian Studies* 19, no. 3 (1985), 600.

8. For Oman from 1750 to 1800, see Patricia Risso, *Oman and Muscat: An Early Modern History* (New York, 1986).

9. Simon Digby, "The Maritime Trade of India," *Cambridge Economic History of India*, vol. 1, *c. 1200 o c. 1750* (Cambridge, 1982), 149–50.

10. M.D.D. Newitt, *A History of Mozambique* (London, 1994), 187–203. For discussion of how slaves were acquired, see, among others, Santos, I, iii, 19; Surendranath Sen, ed., *Indian Travels of Thevenot and Careri* (New Delhi, 1949), 188–9.

11. See Jeanette Pinto, *Slavery in Portuguese India* (Bombay, 1992); Ann Pescatello, "African Presence in Portuguese India," *Journal of Asian History* 9, no. 1 (1977), 26–48; and an accumulation of data in Vitorino Magalhães Godinho, *Mito e mercadoria, utopia e prática de navegar, séculos XIII–XVIII* (Lisbon, 1990), 387–95.

12. N. Buckeridge, *Journal and Letter Book of Nicholas Buckeridge, 1651–1654*, ed. J. R. Jenson (Minneapolis, 1973), 31.

13. Ralph Austen, *African Economic History: Internal Development and External Dependency* (London, 1987), 59. For a counterargument, see Abdul Sheriff, *Slaves, Spices, and Ivory in Zanzibar: Integration of an East African Commercial Empire into the World Economy, 1770–1873* (London, 1987), 13 and n. 4, 31, 33–4. For the nineteenth century trade, see a valuable collection: Gervase Clarence-Smith, ed., *The Economics of the Indian Ocean Slave Trade in the Nineteenth Century* (London, 1989).

14. See Gwyn Campbell, "Madagascar and Mozambique in the Slave Trade of the Western Indian Ocean, 1800–1861," in Gervase Clarence-Smith, ed., *The Economics of the Indian Ocean Slave Trade in the Nineteenth Century* (London, 1989); and the conclusion of the argument in "The East African Slave Trade, 1861–1895: The 'Southern Complex,'" *IJAHS* 22, no. 1 (1989), 1–26.

15. For an argument along rather similar lines, see Sheriff, *Slaves, Spices, and Ivory*.

16. John Ford, *The Role of the Trypanosomiases in African History* (Oxford, 1971).

17. See a report from the Economic Commission for Africa, circulated on the H-NET list for African history (on the Internet) on 11 June 1996.

Index

Library of Congress Cataloging-in-Publication Data

Pearson, M. N. (Michael Naylor), 1941–

Port cities and intruders : the Swahili Coast, India, and Portugal in the early modern era / Michael N. Pearson.

p. cm. — (Johns Hopkins symposia in comparative history : 23rd)

Includes bibliographical references and index.

ISBN 0-8018-5692-2 (alk. paper)

1. Africa, East—History—To 1886. 2. East Indians—Africa, East—History. 3. Portuguese—Africa, East—History. 4. Swahili-speaking peoples—History. 5. Portugal—Relations—Africa, East. 6. Africa, East—Relations—Portugal. I. Title. II. Series.

DT432.P43 1998

967.6′01—dc21 97-20627

CIP

CPSIA information can be obtained at www.ICGtesting.com
Printed in the USA
243810LV00004B/182/A